AN INTRODUCTION
to the
NEW TESTAMENT

Volume 1

THE GOSPELS AND ACTS

By

D. EDMOND HIEBERT

MOODY PRESS

CHICAGO

© 1975 by
THE MOODY BIBLE INSTITUTE
OF CHICAGO

All scripture quotations in this book are from the American Standard Version (1901), except where indicated otherwise.

The use of selected references from various versions of the Bible in this publication does not necessarily imply publisher endorsement of the versions in their entirety.

ISBN: 0-8024-4137-8

Second Printing, 1979

Printed in the United States of America

CONTENTS

PREFACE

THE FOUR GOSPELS AND THE ACTS are foundational to the Christian faith. There can be no adequate understanding of the origin, life, and message of the Church of Jesus Christ apart from the story told in these five historical books of the New Testament. They constitute the first major division of the New Testament canon and account for about fifty-eight percent of its entire contents. The initial position and the comparative length of these invaluable documents witness to their fundamental importance for Christianity. They demand serious study and yield rich rewards to efforts expended by the persevering Bible student.

This volume is intended to be a guide to the systematic study of the gospels and Acts. It is not a commentary on these books, neither is it intended to replace any commentary. Its aim is to offer sufficient background information concerning these writings, to promote effective study, and to direct the student's efforts to master their contents through a suggested study procedure and fairly detailed outlines charting their accounts. The student's study of the biblical text itself is indispensable and this volume is not a substitute for such study.

The initial survey presents an overview of the entire New Testament and aims at setting this study in its larger context. Part 1 is devoted to the four gospels, while Part 2 deals with the book of Acts.

Part 1 opens with a general introduction to the four gospels and deals with them as a distinctive group of writings. The suggested study procedure advocates the book method as a basic approach to the study of the gospels, to be followed by a comparative study.

The material under each gospel falls into three parts: an introduction, an outline, and a book list for detailed study. The usual introductory matters, such as authorship, purpose, place and date of writing, and characteristics of the gospel, are dealt with in the introduc-

7

tions. A critical study of the gospels reveals numerous difficult and perplexing problems. The beginning student will find it desirable to gain considerable personal familiarity with the contents of the gospels themselves before seeking to delve into these critical problems.

The outlines aim at offering the student guidance in tracing the varied contents of these books. They are suggestive and not presented with any thought of finality. The gospels are difficult to outline and the independent student will arrive at different divisions in numerous places. The outlines are intended to chart the contents of the gospels. The student should feel free to modify them according to his own discoveries as he works his way through these books.

A wealth of commentary material is available on each gospel, as indicated in the annotated booklists. The books listed represent a wide range as to level of treatment, thoroughness, and theological perspective. It is hoped that in their diversity the booklists will offer something to meet the needs of each individual student. A favorable comment does not imply endorsement of the entire contents of a volume. Commentaries represent aids to a fuller unfolding of the riches of the gospels. They should not be substituted for study of the gospels themselves.

A survey of the synoptic problem appears after the material on the first three gospels. This survey aims at presenting information concerning this much discussed problem and makes no pretense at solving the enigma.

Part 2 deals with the book of Acts. It is arranged similarly to Part 1. Due to its nature and contents, Acts stands alone, but as the sequel to the third gospel, it is intimately related to the story told in the gospels. A study of it logically follows a study of the gospels.

The student who attempts to deal with these five historical books of the New Testament cannot escape the realization that they present numerous problems and perplexing critical difficulties. And he will readily acknowledge his debt to others who have labored in this area. The notes and bibliography indicate something of my own vast obligation to the varied sources that I have drawn upon. These sources have influenced the views concerning the gospels and the Acts which I articulate in this book.

1

SURVEY OF THE NEW TESTAMENT

THANKS TO MODERN PRINTING, we have the entire New Testament in one handy little pocket volume. This convenience may serve, however, to blur our consciousness of the fact that it is not a single book. Impressed with its profound spiritual unity, Christians rightly acclaim this volume as *The Book*; yet its contents declare that it is a library of twenty-seven different books. Each book makes its own distinct contribution to the message of the New Testament.

NAME

The common name for this entire collection of documents is *The New Testament*. It is derived from the Latin *Novum Testamentum* which served to translate the Greek designation *Hē Kainē Diathēkē*, which our English versions render "the new testament" or "the new covenant." The Greek term *diathēkē* was generally used to mean "a last will and testament." In the Hellenistic period the testator normally had the right to stipulate the conditions of the agreement being entered into. The second party could not demand certain conditions but his consent was necessary for ratification. Once the agreement was ratified by mutual acceptance its terms were binding on both parties.

The translators of the Septuagint usually employed *diathēkē* to render the Hebrew term *berith*, commonly translated "covenant." The general New Testament usage of *diathēkē* supports its translation as "covenant." The designation "the new testament" or "the new covenant" first occurs in our New Testament in connection with Jesus' institution of the Lord's Supper on the night before His crucifixion (Lk 22:20; 1 Co 11:25; Mt 26:28; Mk 14:24).[1] The author of

---

1. Critical editions of the Greek New Testament omit the word "new" in Mt 26:28 and Mk 14:24.

Hebrews (8:7-13) relates the new covenant which Jesus established and ratified to the new covenant which Jeremiah had announced as God's plan for the future (Jer 31:31-34). In Jeremiah's announcement the contrast is between the "old" Mosaic covenant and the coming "new" covenant. The fact that the Septuagint uses the Greek term *diathēkē* for both the Mosaic covenant and the new covenant (Jer 38:31-34 LXX) establishes the same basic nature for both. The covenant made at Mount Sinai was not arrived at by mutual consultation; the sovereign Lord proposed it to Israel for their voluntary acceptance, as an expression of His will and purpose for them. Upon their acceptance of the stipulations in the covenant, its terms became binding upon both God and Israel.

Because of their covenantal relationship with Jehovah, the Israelites thought of themselves as God's chosen people. God's covenant promised them blessing and a future inheritance, if they met the conditions of the covenant. But Israel's repeated failures in keeping their covenantal obligations caused God to announce a "new covenant" wherein He would establish a new way of dealing with sinners through Christ Jesus. In the upper room Jesus spoke of the new covenant having its foundation in His shed blood (Lk 22:20). The author of Hebrews stresses that Christ is the mediator of a new and better covenant upon the basis of His atoning work (Heb 8:6-13; 9:15; 12:24). Sealed by the precious blood of Christ, the new covenant certifies the "precious promises" and guarantees the inheritance of the saints. Tenney draws the following contrast between the two covenants:

> The Old Covenant involved a revelation of the holiness of God in a righteous standard of law which those who received it were solemnly enjoined to keep. The New Covenant embodied a revelation of the holiness of God in an utterly righteous Son, who empowered those who received the revelation to become sons of God by making them righteous (John 1:12).[2]

Since the New Testament documents record the establishment and character of God's new way of dealing with men, the term "the new covenant" is appropriately applied to them. These writings are

---

2. Merrill C. Tenney, *The New Testament: An Historical and Analytical Survey*, p. 22.

called "the *new* covenant" in distinction from the Hebrew scriptures, which record the contents and history of the *old* covenant. The theme of God's dealing with sinful men on the basis of this new covenant is basic to the entire New Testament. It is this unified spiritual emphasis that justifies calling "the books of the New Testament" The New Testament.

ORIGIN, FORM AND CONTENT

While all the books of the New Testament proceed from the common foundation of the redemptive revelation of God in Christ Jesus, they reveal a remarkable diversity in origin, form and content. Each of the twenty-seven books originated as an independent document. Each arose out of a definite historical context and was written to meet a specific life need.

In length they vary from a single papyrus sheet to a thirty-two foot scroll. As to their *expressed* authorship, seven of these documents are anonymous, thirteen bear the name of Paul, two each are attributed to Peter and "the elder." James, Jude, and John are each named as the author of one book. Views concerning the authors of the anonymous books have been expressed in the church from early times. Modern critical scholarship has not always agreed with those views. Conservative scholars have generally held that the entire New Testament was written by nine different authors, but modern liberal scholars count a dozen different authors for all the books. Apparently all of the writers, except Luke, had Jewish backgrounds. But the various writers exhibited marked differences as to personality, sphere of activity, and literary achievement.

It is generally accepted that all twenty-seven books of the New Testament were written during a period of little more than one-half century. The very earliest date proposed for any of them is about A.D. 45; the latest is about A.D. 95. But some modern critical scholars would date some of the books as late as the middle of the second century.

LANGUAGE

All of the New Testament was originally written in Greek. Greek was the international language of that age. People continued to speak local languages, but most were bilingual (cf. Ac 14:8-18).

The entire Old Testament was written in Hebrew, with the exception of a few sections in Aramaic, a language related to Hebrew. But the four-hundred-year period which elapsed between the writing of the last book of the Old Testament and the New Testament era had brought great changes. When the Jews returned from the Babylonian Captivity they brought with them the Aramaic language which was the mother tongue of the Palestinian Jews during the time of the New Testament. The scribes maintained Hebrew as the language of religion and worship but most of the common people did not understand it. As a result of the hellenizing efforts of Alexander the Great and his successors, Greek had become the common language of culture and commerce. It was the bond of the civilized world. It was even used in Rome, although Latin was the official language of the Roman Empire. In Palestine, where Aramaic was persistently maintained, knowledge of Greek was an economic necessity. Jews scattered beyond the borders of Palestine were familiar with Greek and commonly adopted it as their mother tongue. The Old Testament was translated into Greek around 250-150 B.C. in Alexandria, Egypt, the center of rabbinical learning and Greek culture. The New Testament writers doubtless knew Greek from boyhood.[3]

The context of the new revelation of God in Christ was the Jewish people, whom God had chosen as His instrument for the communication of His message to the world. It is possible that the New Testament writers, all of whom had close ties with Judaism, recorded the good news about Christ Jesus in Aramaic. But an Aramaic New Testament would have had comparatively few readers outside Palestine. The Greek language naturally offered them the best medium for the world-wide propagation of their message. Thus providentially God "gave to the devout Hebrew heart a Greek tongue in order to make itself intelligible to the world."[4] The New Testament has quite appropriately been described as having "a Greek body, a Hebrew soul, and a Christian spirit that animates them both."[5]

The Greek language was marvelously fitted to be the medium for the communication of God's revelation to the entire world. This is

3. James Hope Moulton, *A Grammar of New Testament Greek*, vol. 1, *Prolegomena*.
4. Everett F. Harrison. *Introduction to the New Testament*, p. 50.
5. As quoted in J. A. M'Clymont, *The New Testament and Its Writers*, p. 2.

true because it was the international language and it was characterized by unrivaled richness, clearness, precision, and flexibility.

The Greek of the New Testament is not the Greek of the great
classical writers but rather the vernacular of daily life. This has been
amply confirmed by contemporary Greek documents recovered from
the sands of Egypt. It is commonly designated as "Koine" Greek,
i.e., "common" Greek, which was spoken daily throughout the Greco-
Roman world. The New Testament writers used the ordinary language of the people to proclaim to them their transforming message.
The books of the New Testament are, however, generally superior
to the average papyri. Harrison remarks that this superiority is
"occasioned in part by the ability of its writers to produce a more
polished result, in part by the more elevated nature of the themes
that engrossed them, and in part by their religious and cultural
heritage."[6]

LITERARY GROUPINGS

The grouping of the books in our New Testament reflects a logical
rather than a chronological order. The arrangement of the books
conforms to the logical order of God's program of action as declared
in the New Testament revelation. Basic to that program is the four-
fold gospel account of the life, death, and resurrection of Christ.
All that follows the gospel account cannot be properly understood
or appreciated apart from it. The book of Acts relates events subsequent to the ascension of Jesus Christ. It recounts the origin and
growth of the early church and the missionary labors of some of its
leaders. This history is followed by a series of letters which, at least
in part, are contemporaneous with the story in Acts. Addressed to
churches or individuals, they deal with varied conditions and needs
of believers in Christ. They discuss the loftiest religious themes
relating to the Christian faith, refute doctrinal and practical perver-
sions of the faith, stress the fitting duties of believers, and abound
in affectionate expressions of mutual love and fellowship in Christ.
The final book, the Revelation, discloses the prophetic consummation
of the entire program of redemption.

On the basis of their literary character, the books of the New Testa-

6. Harrison, p. 54.

ment fall into three major groups: the historical, the epistolary, and the prophetical. The first group consists of the first five books. They are historical in character and narrative in form, and are basic to the entire New Testament. The first four are devoted to the life of Jesus Christ, while the fifth tells of the founding and early history of the Christian church. The story told in the four gospels forms the very heart of the Christian faith. These four histories of Jesus' earthly ministry, standing at the head of the New Testament, eloquently testify that Christianity is not an abstract theological system but a faith firmly rooted in history, centering in God's supreme self-revelation to men in the incarnation. All four gospels are anonymous; the writers withdraw behind their engrossing portrayals of the matchless Christ.

The fifth book in this group, the book of Acts, is also anonymous. It records the beginnings of the superstructure constructed on the foundation laid in the gospels. It describes the spread of the Christian faith during the thirty years following Jesus' death and resurrection and the results produced by the Christians' Spirit-empowered witness.

Twenty-one books constitute the epistolary section. These epistles interpret the Christian faith and apply it to the lives of believers. This large section of epistolary writings is unique to the New Testament. None of the sacred writings of other oriental religions use the epistolary form as a medium of revelation.[7] As they appear in our New Testament these twenty-one books may be divided conveniently into two groups, the Pauline and the non-Pauline epistles.

The thirteen Pauline letters are explicitly ascribed to Paul. Nine are addressed to churches and four to individuals who were more or less closely associated with Paul's missionary activities. Those addressed to churches are first in order, and they are arranged according to length.

The other eight books in the epistolary section are generally referred to as "Hebrews and the General Epistles." For convenience this heterogeneous group may be characterized as "the non-Pauline epistles." Two of these books, Hebrews and 1 John, are anonymous

7. Dwight M. Pratt, "Epistle," in *The International Standard Bible Encyclopaedia,* p. 966.

and lack the characteristic epistolary opening. Of this group only the two brief communications from "the elder" (2 and 3 John), traditionally ascribed to the apostle John, are addressed to individuals. The others, ascribed to James, Peter, and Jude, are addressed to churches or groups of churches in various places. Controversy surrounded the admittance of several of these to the canon, and serious critical problems remain to this day.

The third group is prophetical in character and consists of only one book, the Revelation, which majestically stands as the fitting conclusion to the entire New Testament. While the New Testament contains passages that are prophetic, it includes only one book of prophecy. This book brings the entire redemptive program, centering in the person of Jesus Christ, to its grand climax.

Such a classification of the books of the New Testament according to their literary form is not to be viewed as absolute. There is, of course, doctrinal teaching in the historical books, while the epistles are rooted in history and contain historical material. And both the historical and epistolary books contain important prophetic elements. The classification stresses the literary mold of the New Testament books, and does not imply that one group is more or less authoritative than the others.

Each book of the New Testament has its own characteristic features and message. But amid all the diversity there rings out the basic message summarized in the majestic opening words of the book of Hebrews:

> God, after He spoke long ago to the fathers in the prophets in many portions and in many ways, in these last days has spoken to us in His Son (Heb 1:1-2*a*, NASB).

A CHART OF NEW TESTAMENT LITERATURE

Literary Type	New Testament Book (Canonical Order)	Author	Place of Writing	Date (A.D.)
Historical Literature (5)	Matthew	Matthew	Antioch of Syria (?)	66-68
	Mark	Mark	Rome	64-65
	Luke	Luke	Outside Palestine	66-67
	John	John	Ephesus	80-97
	Acts	Luke	Outside Palestine	67-68
Epistolary Literature (21)	Romans	Paul	Corinth	58
	1 Corinthians	Paul	Ephesus	57
	2 Corinthians	Paul	Macedonia	57-58
	Galatians	Paul	Corinth (?)	52
	Ephesians	Paul	Rome	62
	Philippians	Paul	Rome	63
Pauline Epistles (13)	Colossians	Paul	Rome	62
	1 Thessalonians	Paul	Corinth	50-51
	2 Thessalonians	Paul	Corinth	50-51
	1 Timothy	Paul	Macedonia (?)	63
	2 Timothy	Paul	Rome	66
	Titus	Paul	Corinth (?)	63
	Philemon	Paul	Rome	62
	Hebrews	Unknown	Unknown	64
	James	James	Jerusalem	46
Non-Pauline Epistles (8)	1 Peter	Peter	"Babylon" (Rome)	64
	2 Peter	Peter	Rome	65
	1 John	John	Ephesus	80-97
	2 John	John	Ephesus	80-97
	3 John	John	Ephesus	80-97
	Jude	Jude	Unknown	67-68
Prophetic Literature (1)	Revelation	John	Ephesus or Patmos	80-97

Places of writing and dates are disputed. The suggested places and dates presuppose the discussions in this volume and the author's companion volumes on New Testament introduction.[8]

8. D. Edmond Hiebert, *An Introduction to the Pauline Epistles* and *An Introduction to the Non-Pauline Epistles.*

Part 1

THE GOSPELS

2

A GENERAL INTRODUCTION TO THE FOUR GOSPELS

FOR THE AVERAGE CHRISTIAN the four gospels are probably the most familiar part of the entire New Testament. Their narrative form as well as their vital subject matter make them appealing reading. They seem to speak for themselves and have an enduring power to kindle and quicken faith. As the main source of our knowledge concerning the earthly life of our Lord Jesus, the gospels have always held a place of particular interest for Christians. Their crucial importance to the Christian faith and their profound impact on human history declare their abiding significance.

THE MEANING OF "GOSPEL"

Our modern English word "gospel" is derived from the Anglo-Saxon word *godspell*, from *god* (God) or *gōd* (good) and *spell* (a story). It may thus mean either "God-story" or "good story." Opinion is divided but the latter meaning, "good story" or "good tidings," is in harmony with the meaning of the Greek term *euanggelion* for which it is the common translation. The Greek word *euanggelion* is an adjectival substantive derived from *euanggelos*, "a bringer of good news," and denotes that which is proper for such a messenger. Thus from the standpoint of the messenger himself it denotes the reward for bringing good news. From the standpoint of the one to whom he comes, however, it means the good news itself.[1] In specialized usages it may mean the news of victory, or the utterance of an oracle. In the New Testament it always connotes God's good news to men in Christ. It is the message of salvation which Christianity

---

1. Gerhard Friedrich in *Theological Dictionary of the New Testament*, 2:721-22.

proclaims to sinful men. In the Septuagint the term is sometimes used in the plural, but in the New Testament it is uniformly used in the singular. The "good news" of Christianity is unique.

In the New Testament the word "gospel" always designates the message itself, not a book. The gospel message was usually made known through oral proclamation, but it might also be presented in writing. When this message of good news, bearing witness to Christ and His words and deeds, was embodied in written form, the term naturally came to be applied to these written accounts.

When first these individual written accounts of the good news were spoken of as gospels is not certain. In the middle of the second century Justin Martyr in his *Apology*, written at Rome and addressed to the Roman Senate, spoke of "the memoirs composed by the Apostles, which are called Gospels."[2] His words imply that calling the individual books "gospels" was in vogue at that time. Since the four accounts were versions of the same gospel, the names of the writers with the preposition "according to" (Gr., *kata*) were added in order to distinguish the accounts from each other: "the Gospel according to Matthew," etc. Some critics have maintained that *kata* was not intended to indicate authorship but rather the authority guaranteeing its contents. But if *kata* were intended simply to denote the source of authority, then the second gospel, according to the traditional views concerning it, should have been called "the gospel according to Peter." That the expression can denote authorship is certain from the parallel title "The History of Herodotus" (*hē kath Hērodoton historia*).

THE CENTRALITY OF THE GOSPELS

1. THEIR LENGTH

The four gospels account for nearly one-half (forty-eight percent) of the entire New Testament. They are among the longest books in the New Testament library. Arranged according to length they are: Luke, Matthew, John, Mark. The shortest gospel, Mark, is longer than the book of Revelation, the longest of the other New Testament books.

Our four gospels are notable for their brevity. Their moderate

2. Justin Martyr *Apology* 1.66.

length was not due to limited subject matter (cf. Jn 20:30; 21:25) but rather to the materials with which they were produced. Presumably they were written on papyrus scrolls. A scroll consisted of papyrus sheets, a foot square or less in size, which were glued together. Rollers were usually attached to both ends of the sheet so that it could be rolled together. For convenience in handling, such a scroll was limited to a length of thirty feet. Thus the gospel writers found it necessary to compress their material to meet the space restrictions. This accounts for the fact that Luke's story, the Luke-Acts narrative, although forming one continuous story, was produced in two parts.

2. THEIR POSITION

The gospels were placed at the beginning of the New Testament not because the early church thought that they were written first but because it was clearly recognized that they constitute the very foundation of the Christian faith. They form the roots of Christianity, and all of the other books are the fruitage of those roots. Without the historical facts recorded in the gospels concerning the person and work of Jesus Christ the other books cannot be properly understood. Since the gospels are the main source of its information concerning its Saviour and Lord, the Christian church has always esteemed them as priceless treasures. Wikenhauser observes, "They were the most frequently copied of all the parts of the Sacred Scripture, and copies were often laid out with great artistry."[3]

The gospels stand at the center of the scriptural record of God's redemptive revelation. The Old Testament records the promise of and the preparation for the coming of the Saviour; the gospels depict the historic manifestation of the promised Messiah. Anyone who attentively reads the gospels becomes aware that the story which they relate has its beginnings in the Old Testament. That relationship is evident in each of the gospels. The very first verse of the first gospel proclaims its connection with the Old Testament, "The book of the generation of Jesus Christ, the son of David, the son of Abraham" (Mt 1:1). This statement points back to a connection with the historical books of the Old Testament as well as the Pentateuch. The second gospel roots its story in the Old Testament with a quotation

3. Alfred Wikenhauser, *New Testament Introduction*, p. 151.

from two of the prophetical books (Mk 1:2-3). Luke indicates that
his story has connections with the Old Testament legal system, by
naming "the course of Abijah" and Aaron (Lk 1:1-5). Likewise
the fourth gospel in its magnificent prologue (1:1-18) refers to Moses
(v. 17) and in commencing its historical narrative mentions Elijah
and the coming prophet and records that John the Baptist identified
himself with a quotation from the Old Testament (1:19-23).

The exact number of references to the Old Testament in the gospels is differently estimated.[4] There are various specific quotations,
but many references are less direct. Many Old Testament passages
are combined or summarized. There are also many less obvious allusions. Most of these quotations and allusions relate to the promised
Messiah and are used to confirm that the Old Testament prophecies
were fulfilled in Jesus of Nazareth. These references connect with
all the major phases of the gospel accounts.

The four gospels also bear a definite relationship to the other books
of the New Testament. They "are related to the rest of the New
Testament as furnishing the material without which they could not
be understood, nor indeed could they have been written."[5] The book
of Acts constitutes the logical continuation of the story begun in the
gospels. The opening statement in Acts, concerning "all that Jesus
began both to do and to teach" (Ac 1:1) alludes to the gospel of
Luke and implies that the Acts narrative carries forward the story
connected with the proclamation of the risen and glorified Christ.

The epistles tell of the Holy Spirit's interpreting and applying the
new life operative in the Church, which acknowledges the living
Christ as its head. The grand theological themes treated in the epistles cannot be adequately understood and have no logical foundation
apart from the revelation of the person of Christ set forth in the
gospels. They unfold the nature and purpose of Christ's redemptive
work which is portrayed in the gospels; they depict the outworking
of the new life imparted by the Holy Spirit to believers in fulfillment
of the promises by Christ recorded in the gospels.

The book of Revelation assumes a knowledge of the gospel story.

4. For a study of allusions to the Old Testament contained in the gospels and the
teaching of Jesus, see R. V. G. Tasker, *The Old Testament in the New Testament;*
F. F. Bruce, *New Testament Development of Old Testament Themes;* Ernest
Clapton, *Our Lord's Quotations from the Old Testament;* Robert P. Lightner,
The Saviour and the Scriptures; R. T. France, *Jesus and the Old Testament.*
5. S. Ridout, *The Four Gospels,* p. 15.

There are references to the one who "was dead" and is "alive for evermore" (1:18), "a Lamb standing, as if slain" (5:6, NASB), and the one whose "name is called The Word of God" coming in glory to execute judgment upon the world (19:11-16). These references would lose much of their thrilling significance without the gospels. The book of Revelation carries the story of the self-revelation of God in Christ, begun in the gospels, to its glorious climax.

THE NUMBER OF THE GOSPELS

From the very earliest times the Christian church has accepted four, and only four, separate and independent gospel accounts. Various other "gospels" were produced and circulated,[6] but none were commonly accepted as authoritative or sanctioned as inspired accounts. The writings of the Church Fathers, as well as surviving catalogues of the New Testament books, mention only four authentic gospels. Around A.D. 160 Tatian used our four gospels in producing his *Diatessaron*, a unification of the separate gospels into one continuous narrative. In A.D. 180 Irenaeus, Bishop of Lyons, named our four gospels and remarked, "He who was manifested to men has given us the Gospel under four aspects, but bound together by one Spirit."[7] His comments reveal that the church accepted only four gospels as authentic. The position of Marcion (*c.* 100-165) presented a singular exception. He rejected Matthew, Mark, and John and accepted as the only authentic *euanggelion* his own edited version of Luke. But the church rejected his view as heretical. Bruce observes, "The documents of the anti-Marcionite reaction (e.g. the anti-Marcionite prologues to the Gospels and, later, the Muratorian Canon) do not introduce the four-fold Gospel as something new, but reaffirm its authority in reply to Marcion's criticisms."[8]

The question of why there were four gospels did not escape the consideration of the Church Fathers. Irenaeus expressed the quaint argument that there could be only four gospels as analogous to the four quarters of the world, the four winds, and the four pillars necessary for an edifice.[9] We may feel that his argument is fanciful, but

6. See William L. Lane, "Apocrypha," in *The Encyclopedia of Christianity*, 1: 333-47; J. Hutchison, "Apocryphal Gospels," in *The International Standard Bible Encyclopaedia*, pp. 195-200.
7. Irenaeus *Against the Heresies* 3. 11. 8.
8. F. F. Bruce, "Gospels," in *The New Bible Dictionary*, p. 487.
9. Irenaeus *Against the Heresies* 3. 11. 8.

it is important, since it testifies to the exclusive acceptance of our four gospels in the church. Like other orthodox Christian leaders, Irenaeus was embarrassed by the fact that heretical sects appealed to one or the other of these gospels in support of their views; his response was not to repudiate the gospels but to object to the way the heretics used them, insisting that the truth will be found as they are carefully read.[10] Although the eastern churches made wide use of Tatian's *Diatessaron*, leaders of the churches opposed it because it tended to destroy the apostolic tradition of four separate accounts.

The fact that we have four canonical accounts of the person and work of Christ cannot be without significance. It has received much discussion.[11] The story of Jesus is the only subject in the New Testament to be taken up by four writers.

Harrison remarks that the multiplicity of gospel accounts shows "the sheer fascination of the subject."[12] This is clearly revealed in Luke's prologue to his gospel (1:1-3). The life and teaching of Jesus were so alluring that many men felt themselves challenged to record what they had seen or heard. Our gospels clearly reflect that fascination.

The inclusion of four separate accounts of our Lord's earthly life underlines the importance of that story. No one reading through the Bible can fail to be impressed with the fact that these books deal with the most fundamental issues in the entire Scripture. If these four books were omitted from the Bible, we would be left with only the barest outline of our Lord's life and work. The few references contained in the epistles would remain vague and often enigmatical.

With their distinctive, but not mutually exclusive, individual emphases our four gospels in a unique way "are earth-girdling and race-embracing."[13] They are eminently suited to appeal to the needs of different human types. Each writer, while presenting the same Saviour and Lord, portrays Him in a manner best suited to appeal to the particular readers who apparently were the original recipients.

---

10. Ibid., 3. 11. 7.
11. See Andrew Jukes, *The Differences of the Four Gospels;* S. Ridout, *The Four Gospels;* D. S. Gregory, *Why Four Gospels? or, The Gospel for All the World;* Arthur W. Pink, *Why Four Gospels?;* H. Framer Smith, *Why Four Gospel Accounts?;* Louis Talbot, *Why Four Gospels?;* Wayne G. Rollins, *The Gospels: Portraits of Christ.*
12. Everett F. Harrison, *Introduction to the New Testament,* p. 139.
13. J. Sidlow Baxter, *Explore the Book,* 5:126.

Matthew's gospel is suited to appeal to the Jewish mind. It vividly sets forth the evidence that Jesus of Nazareth, of Davidic descent, is the Messiah promised in the Old Testament, the expected King of the Jews. The first gospel helped to establish the faith of Jewish Christians and conveyed a strong apologetic message to the Jewish people.

The gospels of Mark and Luke were suited to a Gentile audience. Mark's gospel portrays Jesus as the mighty and tireless Servant of the Lord, meeting every man's needs and faithfully proclaiming the truth of God. According to tradition, this gospel was written in Rome and primarily had in view a Roman audience. The gospel presents a portrait of Jesus Christ which would have special appeal to the aggressive, practical Roman mind.

The gospel of Luke may be viewed as portraying Jesus as the perfect Son of Man, the perfect answer to the needs and aspirations of the human race. Written by a Greek doctor, it was especially suited to appeal to the Greek mind. Luke's picture of the perfect Son of Man would be highly challenging to the Greeks who regarded themselves as having the mission of perfecting man. Thus the portrait of Jesus in Luke's gospel may be viewed as the answer to the idealistic Greek, ever in search of the truth. In Jesus Christ God had provided the sinless Saviour of a sinful race which was constantly falling short of perfection.

The fourth gospel is the gospel for the believing heart; it gives an interpretative portrait of Jesus as the incarnate Son of God. It is a portrait that is precious to every believer, whether Jew or Gentile. It is a gospel for the entire human race, since it sets forth the grace of God for all men as revealed in the incarnate Word. It appeals to all men everywhere to receive the gift of eternal life in Christ Jesus.

The fact that each gospel was originally directed to a distinct group of readers does not mean that its message was directed exclusively to them. Christ came to fulfill and transcend the noblest ideals of each class of men. In Him was fused all that was best and highest in them all; He is the answer to the yearnings and needs of each. The ideologies of the Jews, the Romans, and the Greeks represent streams of thought that are operative in our world today, and all stand in need of the grace of Christ. Our four gospels offer a message suited for all groups of humanity.

The four portraits of Jesus Christ presented in the four gospels give a full-orbed picture of His unique person and mission. Each gospel presents Him with its own distinctive emphasis. He is successively pictured as the Messianic King, the Servant of the Lord, the Son of Man, and the Son of God. Together, these four emphases give a full description of the unique person who is the very essence of Christianity: *sovereign* and *humble; human* and *divine.* Baxter summarizes this "quadripartite delineation" as follows:

Matthew	The promised One is here; see His credentials.
Mark	This is how He worked; see His power.
Luke	This is what He was like; see His nature.
John	This is who He really was; see His Godhead.[14]

Various descriptions of the primary thrust of each gospel have been presented.[15] But it is obvious that each gospel makes its own distinctive contribution toward a full portrayal of the person of Christ. "As representations of Jesus, Mark can be called a collection of candid snapshots of Jesus in action; Matthew is a formal photograph from the studio of Scripture; Luke is a moving picture of Jesus as He walked among men; and John is an X-ray photograph of His personality."[16] The composite portrait reveals "a face that the imagination of mortal could not have created. And when that face is seen, the books in which it is sketched are joyfully accepted as a divine revelation."[17]

THE NATURE OF THE GOSPELS

Our four gospels constitute a distinctive form of literature. Klijn asserts that they "cannot be compared to any literary genre of the Hellenistic world."[18]

14. Baxter, p. 312.
15. Wayne G. Rollins, *The Gospels: Portraits of Christ;* Ralph Martin, *Mark: Evangelist and Theologian;* I. Howard Marshall, *Luke: Historian and Theologian;* James Montgomery Boice, *Witness and Revelation in the Gospel of John.*
16. Merrill C. Tenney, *The Genius of the Gospels,* pp. 59-60.
17. Herbert L. Willett and James M. Campbell, *The Teachings of the Books,* p. 12.
18. A. F. J. Klijn, *An Introduction to the New Testament,* p. 7.

Although the gospels recount the story of a historical person, they are not biographies in the modern sense of that term. They do not present a balanced account of the life of Jesus of Nazareth, but concentrate on the events connected with His death and resurrection. Only two gospels relate events connected with His birth (Mt 1:18–2:23; Lk 1:5–2:39), and only one records a specific incident from his boyhood days (Lk 2:41-52). They leave the first thirty years of His life shrouded in obscurity. It is generally held that His public ministry lasted three and one-half years, but the specific events which have been recorded apparently transpired on about fifty different days. Only the last week of His life is told in comparative fullness. Clearly the gospel writers did not intend to relate all the historical facts known concerning Jesus (cf. Jn 20:30; 21:25). It is unwarranted to assume that a writer did not know about a certain event because he did not include it in his account. The gospel accounts give comparatively little attention to the contemporary historical situation beyond Jesus' immediate environment. They provide no description of His physical appearance or His dress. They make no effort to describe His inner thoughts and struggles or depict His character development. They say nothing about the various influences that affected His formative years or His reactions to them. Obviously our gospels cannot be classified as biographies in the modern sense of the term.

Neill, however, protests against the common assertion that the gospels are not biographies. He recognizes that they are not psychological biographies, but insists that they are biographical in nature. He rightly observes, "If it is the aim of biography to give succinctly a living and vivid impression of someone who really lived, it is hard to see into what other category the Gospels are to be placed."[19] This is a needed corrective to recent attempts to minimize the biographical aspects of the gospels. While a full biography cannot be constructed from them, they do present biographical information about the historical Jesus.[20]

Kümmel well observes that our gospels do not belong to "the category of the Hellenistic miracle narratives, in which in more or less fixed style the great deeds of ancient miracle workers were glori-

19. Stephen Neill, *The Interpretation of the New Testament: 1861-1961*, p. 259.
20. See Tenney, chap. 2.

fied."[21] Jesus' miracles are an essential part of the story concerning
Him, but they are not the central concern of the writers. The gospels
were not intended merely to preserve the memory of a miracle
worker. The miracles were included in order to give a true picture
of the person of Jesus Christ.

Justin Martyr spoke of the gospels as the "memoirs" of the apostles.[22] But these memoirs were not intended simply to be treasured
recollections of the words and teachings of Jesus. The gospel writers
recalled and recorded the words and teachings of Jesus of Nazareth
because they had abiding contemporary significance for the church
as aiding in the understanding of the nature of its living Lord.

The gospels arose out of the missionary task of the Christian
church. They were written proclamations of the good news of redemption in Christ Jesus. The controlling concern of the gospel writers was to awaken and strengthen faith in the living Christ whom
they had come to know personally through a transforming experience. They desired to set forth the reality concerning their Saviour
in order that others too might come to know Him. Accounts of His
profound teachings and miraculous deeds were necessary to give a
true portrayal of His character.

Their chief interest, however, was not in His deeds, but in His
identity as the incarnate Son of God. An understanding of His atoning work demanded that the events of His passion and resurrection
be told in considerable detail since they demonstrated who and what
manner of man He was and why He was put to death. It gave significance to their proclamation of Him as the risen Saviour and
Lord. The heart of Christianity lies in a personal relationship with
this living person.

The gospel writers were not consciously attempting to create a
distinctive form of literature. In their effort to set forth the true
story concerning their glorified Lord they made use of biographical
and historical facts, but they were not concerned about conforming
to conventional literary patterns. They were Christ-possessed men
intent upon leading others into a similar experience.

The written gospels obviously served an apologetic function in the
ministry of the church to the non-Christian world. Questions con-

21. Werner Georg Kümmel, *Introduction to the New Testament*, p. 32.
22. Justin Martyr *Apology* 1. 66.

cerning the person and work of Christ Jesus arose in the minds of those who heard the oral proclamation of the gospel. Such questions were answered in these authoritative accounts. Those who read the gospels found in them the answers to their questions and also experienced an awakening of faith in the One set forth therein. This evangelistic function of the four gospels is clearly indicated in John 20:30-31.

It is obvious that the gospels also serve a catechetical function in the work of the church. While they did not eliminate the need for oral instruction of the converts, the church very early used them as authoritative material. These gospels served to broaden the knowledge of the converts concerning their Saviour and also deepened the personal assurance of the catechumens concerning the certainty of the faith which they had accepted. This function is indicated in Luke 1:4.

THE ORIGINAL LANGUAGE OF THE GOSPELS

For centuries it was universally held that the gospels were originally written in Greek. Within modern times this view has been controverted. Many now hold that the gospels were originally written in Aramaic and later translated into Greek. The leading advocate of this view has been C. C. Torrey.[23] Torrey points to the Semitic idioms of thought and expression which are found in the gospels, which are commonly recognized, and to certain passages in our gospels (about 250 in all) which he views as mistranslations and proposes to correct on the basis of the assumed Aramaic original. The views of Torrey have received support from some scholars but have been vigorously assailed by others.

This view is valuable as a reminder that the gospel accounts of the teachings of our Lord root in an Aramaic background. The retention of some Aramaic words and phrases in the records of Jesus' teaching reminds us that He customarily spoke in the Aramaic when addressing Jewish audiences. That Jesus also understood Greek and on occasion used it as the medium of His teaching is very probable. Recent discoveries of ossuary inscriptions in Judea have demonstrated that the inhabitants of first century Palestine were trilingual, speaking Hebrew, Aramaic, and Greek.[24] On the basis of this evi-

23. C. C. Torrey, *The Four Gospels.*
24. See Robert H. Gundry, "The Language Milieu of First-Century Palestine," *Journal of Biblical Literature* 83(1964):405-7 and the literature there cited.

dence Gundry holds it likely "that Jesus the Galilean and the apostles, who were predominantly if not exclusively Galilean, commonly
used Greek in addition to the Semitic tongues."[25]

Since the earliest preaching of the gospel was in Aramaic, an
Aramaic flavor or coloring is to be expected. But Gundry maintains
that it is unwarranted to assume that parts of the gospel tradition
which do not reflect this Aramaic background are unauthentic. Such
a critical assumption would be unjustified in view of the language
milieu of first-century Palestine. Instead of being stamped as unauthentic because they sound too hellenistic, "many of the domin-
ical sayings in the present Greek text of the Gospels may be closer
to the *ipsissima verba* of Jesus than had been supposed."[26]

Research into the Aramaic background of Jesus' message is valuable for a fuller understanding of His teaching. But to recognize
the Aramaic background is not to prove that our gospels were originally written in Aramaic. Torrey's view has not won wide acceptance. Its advocates have not clearly proved their view and scholars
today generally feel that it has been rather positively disproved. Tell-
ing objections have been advanced against the theory.

There is no objective evidence that such Aramaic gospels ever
existed. The claim that they once existed and were later lost or
destroyed is a hypothesis drawn from the Aramaic theory. No such
manuscripts are known. When later gospels in the Aramaic or Syriac
language were required they were translated from our Greek gospels.
In 1933 George M. Lamsa published *The Four Gospels,* in which he
asserts that they were a translation from the original Aramaic gospels.
Lamsa stands alone among students of the New Testament in making such a claim. Filson expresses the prevailing scholarly reaction
that "his assertion is utterly unfounded."[27] He points out that Lamsa
"has translated the Peshitta, a fifth-century revision of the Syriac version of the Gospels" which were earlier translated from the Greek,
and concludes that "Lamsa's attempt to reverse this relationship
between the two is as regrettable as it is futile."[28]

25. Ibid., p. 407.
26. Ibid., pp. 407-8.
27. Floyd V. Filson, *Origins of the Gospels,* p. 57.
28. Ibid.

The case for the Aramaic theory based on "mistranslations" in our Greek gospels is not convincing. The theory is weakened by the fact that the scholars who accept it cannot agree on the passages in which such "mistranslations" occur.[29] Passages that are appealed to as establishing mistranslations do not present any difficulty as they stand or the difficulty can be better explained in some other way. The fact that the Greek may present a difficulty does not prove that the difficulty is due to a mistranslation of an Aramaic original. And as Harrison observes, "Even if the possibility of such mistranslations be conceded, it remains difficult to suppose that they could have passed undetected and uncorrected into the Greek Gospel tradition."[30] This theory is too subjective in its attempts to establish an Aramaic original. Since there are no contemporary Aramaic documents available, there is no objective basis for demonstrating the asserted Aramaic original behind our Greek texts. Advocates of this view must range far and wide into other Semitic languages in order to build up their evidence for the asserted mistranslations.

It is difficult to understand why our four gospels should originally have been produced in Aramaic. There were Greek-speaking Jewish believers in the Jerusalem church from the very beginning (Ac 6:1; 9:29). Hellenistic believers were prominently associated with the church's outreach beyond Palestine (Ac 8:5; 11:19-20), and they would need Greek rather than Aramaic accounts of the gospel. By the time our gospels were written there were many Gentile believers to whom Aramaic was quite unintelligible. The missionary outreach of the church would not have been served by gospels written in Aramaic.

The view that shorter documents in Aramaic lie behind our Greek gospels, or at least certain parts of them, is quite probable. Eusebius quoted Papias as saying that Matthew composed his *logia* in the Hebrew (Aramaic).[31] But the identification of the *logia* with our first gospel is improbable. That our gospels in one way or another reveal traces of the Aramaic origin of their message need not be questioned. While accepting an Aramaic source behind our gospels,

29. D. W. Riddle, "The Logic of the Theory of Translation Greek," *Journal of Biblical Literature* 51(1932): 18.
30. Harrison, p. 165.
31. Eusebius *Ecclesiastical History* 3. 39. 16.

Black remarks, "Whether that source was written or oral, it is not possible from the evidence to decide."[32] But the view of Torrey that our gospels were originally written in Aramaic and later translated into Greek is quite unacceptable.

THE ORDER OF THE GOSPELS

The gospels arose independently as accounts of the gospel message. When they were collected to form a distinct group among the writings accepted by the church as inspired and authoritative, there was no uniform tradition as to the order in which they were arranged. The sequence which has become established in our English Bibles is as old as the *Muratorian Canon*, a list of the New Testament books which apparently represents the views of the Roman church around A.D. 200. The order appears in Irenaeus,[33] Origen,[34] and Eusebius.[35] The order is also attested by the two fourth century Greek uncial manuscripts *Vaticanus* and *Sinaiticus* as well as the overwhelming majority of the later Greek manuscripts and the versions. This order apparently was intended to be chronological.

On the other hand, the Greek uncial manuscripts D and W, and some of the Old Latin manuscripts, have the order Matthew, John, Luke, Mark. This order apparently intends to place first the gospels written by apostles, followed by those written by close associates of the apostles. Occasional variations from either order occur.

Neither order, of course, is to be regarded as determinative in deciding questions of date or authorship.

THE GROUPING OF THE GOSPELS

Each of the four gospels has its own distinctive character. Yet, despite their obvious differences, Matthew, Mark, and Luke have much in common and are properly grouped together as distinguished from the fourth gospel. The contents of the first three gospels run parallel to a large extent. All three employ the same broad historical outline in recounting the story of Jesus Christ. They reveal marked similarities in contents, arrangement, and phraseology. For this reason they are commonly called "the synoptic gospels," meaning

32. Matthew Black, *An Aramaic Approach to the Gospels and Acts*, p. 206.
33. Irenaeus *Against the Heresies* 3. 11. 8.
34. Origin *Commentary on the Gospel of John* 1. 6.
35. Eusebius *Ecclesiastical History* 6. 25. 3-6.

that they "see things together" or present a common view. They have been likened to birds of a feather that flock together.

On the other hand, the fourth gospel has been likened to an eagle that flies alone. After reading the synoptics, an observant reader cannot fail to be impressed by the distinctive approach and contents of the fourth gospel. It is a profoundly individual gospel.

Some of the more obvious differences may be summarized.

1. The *locality* of Christ's ministry. In the synoptics, until Passion Week, the scene of the ministry is in and around Galilee; in John it is chiefly in Judea. The synoptics begin the account of Jesus' ministry with the great Galilean ministry, following the imprisonment of John the Baptist; John reports an earlier ministry in Judea and Samaria. John says very little (chap. 6) of the great Galilean ministry prominent in the synoptics, but records a later ministry in Judea not mentioned in the synoptics.

2. The *duration* of the ministry. The synoptic gospels make no explicit mention of Passover, or other annual Jewish feasts, until Passion Week; they *seem** to crowd the entire ministry into a little more than a year. The fourth gospel, on the other hand, mentions two, probably three Passovers (if the feast mentioned in 5:1 was a Passover as seems probable) before the final Passover, thus making it clear that the ministry extended over several years.

3. The *events* narrated. The fourth gospel includes only two of the events which transpired before Passion Week related in the synoptics (feeding the 5,000 and walking on the water). The fourth gospel has only two events from Passion Week in common with the synoptics (the anointing by Mary in Bethany and the triumphal entry) before the scene in the upper room on Thursday night. The remainder of the material in the fourth gospel is largely unique to it. John characteristically omits events prominent in the synoptics, while he records other events which the synoptics omit.

4. The *messages* of Jesus. The teaching of Jesus recorded in the fourth gospel is remarkably different from that given in the synoptics.

---

*The synoptics do not expressly assert that the ministry was no longer. Mark's gospel seems to require a period of at least two years for the ministry in Galilee: the plucking of the ears of grain in 2:23 (April-June) points to spring, while the green grass during the feeding of the 5,000 in 6:39 points to the end of the rainy season (March-April), thus implying a second spring. The final Passover was during a third spring season.

In the synoptics there are numerous parables, which are presented as characteristic of Jesus' teaching. The fourth gospel contains no comparable parables, but it does include some allegories or extended metaphors, such as the Good Shepherd and the vine and the branches. (The word "parable" in 10:6 means proverb or figurative saying. It is not the word that is translated "parable" in the synoptics.) It is generally recognized that John's narratives have symbolic meaning, but this is no warrant for regarding them as parables like those in the synoptics. John clearly presents his narratives as actual historical events.

In John's gospel the words of Jesus are often occasioned by His signs and serve to interpret and apply their significance. At other times His recorded words are controversial discussions with the Jewish leaders. In the synoptics the teachings of Jesus are eminently ethical and practical; they are public messages directed to the common people of Galilee. In John they are often discussions with the learned Jewish leaders in Jerusalem. In the fourth gospel the didactic messages are revelatory of the person of Christ; His noted "I am" sayings appear only in this gospel.

The differences between the synoptics themselves on the one hand and between the synoptics and John on the other are to be understood as complementary rather than contradictory. While each gospel conveys its own distinctive message, none of them alone could do full justice to the many-sided life and character of Jesus Christ. In presenting his own portrait of Christ each writer selected that which was most congenial and useful for his specific purpose. The portrait presented in each gospel gives an impression of completeness and perfection, yet the various pictures blend together to give a more comprehensive and grander whole. F. W. Farrar remarks:

> The first three evangelists give us diverse aspects of one glorious landscape; St. John pours over the landscape a flood of heavenly sunshine which seems to transform its very character, though every feature of the landscape remains the same.[36]

36. As quoted in J. A. M'Clymont, *The New Testament and Its Writers*, p. 15.

3

A SUGGESTED STUDY PROCEDURE

For the Gospels

Students beginning a study of the New Testament usually find that the gospels seem easiest to understand. Their narrative form and vivid stories suggest that the gospels are simple and uncomplicated accounts whose significance may be readily comprehended. They seem much easier to grasp than the epistles with their involved sentences and closely-knit thought structures or the book of Revelation with its confusing symbolism. But the student who turns to contemporary scholarly deliberations concerning the gospels soon discovers that they are the center of numerous complex and controversial discussions. These discussions relate not only to the problems of interpretation and harmonization but also concern themselves with problems of evaluation, authentication, origination, and motivation.

The beginning student, seeking to grasp the contents of the gospels, soon recognizes that such problems are better left to the advanced student. For the beginner it is the better part of wisdom to concentrate on the text of the gospels. Delving into intricate problems concerning their origin and literary relations properly comes later. In accepting that our gospels were produced under the inspiration of the Holy Spirit, the student must view it as his primary task to seek to understand the gospels as they are. His mastery of the biblical text is the essential thing. He can proceed "on the assumption that it is the Gospels themselves and not their sources or origins which have moulded Christian history, and that the latter must be approached by means of the former."[1] The study procedure here

---

1. Donald Guthrie, *New Testament Introduction*, p. 13.

suggested is intended for the student whose primary concern is to acquire a personal grasp of the rich contents of our four gospels.

The very fact that we have four parallel accounts of the earthly life of Jesus Christ in our Bibles at once invites two different methods of study, namely, the concentrated study of an individual gospel, and a comparative study of the four gospels. Both methods are important, but the former is the proper foundation for a profitable pursuit of the latter.

THE BOOK METHOD OF STUDY

Our four gospels were written and intended to be read as independent works. They are separate and distinct witnesses to the Incarnate Christ. It is most profitable to concentrate on one gospel until its contents are clearly grasped and its aim and emphasis understood and appreciated. The more thoroughly the student acquaints himself with each individual gospel the more profitable will be his later comparative study.

1. REPEATED READING

The concentrated study of a specific gospel logically begins with the repeated reading of the gospel itself. A vital personal mastery of its contents cannot be derived from reading books about it, informative as that may be, but from the repeated, attentive, personal reading of the gospel itself. The student of literature does not presume to master the plays of Shakespeare or *The Divine Comedy* of Dante without personal study of those masterpieces themselves. So a personal mastery of each gospel comes through a repeated reading of the gospel itself.

First of all read through the gospel at one sitting if possible. Seek to follow the unfolding of the thought as you proceed, disregarding the man-made chapter divisions since they do not necessarily indicate the true turning points in the sequence of its contents. Do not stop to puzzle over minor points so that you lose the larger unfolding of the material. In this reading, aim to acquire an overview of the contents and thrust of the gospel.

Reading through an entire gospel at one sitting may appear difficult. It will require self-discipline, but it will prove to be a rewarding experience. Besides, you have probably spent more time in the continuous reading of a popular novel than is required for the reading of even the longest of our four gospels. Endeavor to make the task as easy, natural, and pleasant as possible. The point is not how rapidly but how comprehendingly you read it. If you read only a portion at one time, continue from where you left off upon a brief review of what has preceded.

Read and re-read the entire gospel. Each successive reading will add to your comprehension of the nature and significance of its contents. Try to identify and characterize in a phrase the main divisions. Then outline the sequence of development within each division. Record on paper what you understand to be the major divisions of the gospel with the references for each. Then analyze each successive portion, noting the contents and length of the different subdivisions. Concentrated study for detailed interpretation of individual portions will be most meaningful following an understanding of the general arrangement of the material as a whole. The individual parts are best understood in the light of the whole.

For this repeated reading of the entire gospel it may be helpful to use different versions.[2] The new versions may give freshness to the message and call attention to aspects not previously noticed. For detailed study a reliable standard translation, rather than a popular paraphrase,[3] is essential. For this study use of either the *American Standard Version* (1901) or the *New American Standard Bible* (1971) is strongly recommended. These translations seek to present the precise force of the original Greek. The careful student of the gospels will ever remember that they were originally written in Greek, not English. We rightly demand that our English versions effectively communicate to the modern reader, but we must always be concerned to get back to the original as nearly as possible.

2. INTRODUCTORY INFORMATION

Your repeated reading will make you aware that these gospels

2. Such as J. N. Darby, *The Holy Scriptures: A New Translation from the Original Languages;* H. B. Montgomery, *New Testament in Modern English;* R. F. Weymouth, *New Testament in Modern Speech;* C. B. Williams, *New Testament in the Language of the People; Modern Language Bible (New Berkeley Version in Modern English); New English Bible; New International Version; Revised Standard Version.*
3. Such as *The Living Bible* or *New Testament in Modern English,* translated by J. B. Phillips.

arose out of a specific historical situation. The contents of any document are more fully understood when seen in the light of the historical situation from which it arose. The introduction to each gospel is intended to provide essential information concerning its background. The usual problems of introduction are dealt with, such as authorship, readers, place and date, purpose, and characteristics. Each introduction will also acquaint you with some of the critical problems connected with these gospels. Review your own impressions concerning the gospel in the light of these introductory matters.

3. GENERAL OUTLINE

Your readings of the gospel will give you an awareness of its over-all contents and broad development. First study the appended outline and compare it with your own suggested divisions. The general divisions are not always readily apparent and the divisions you have suggested may well differ from those given in the outline. Go back over the gospel to confirm or modify your impressions of its main divisions. Having satisfied yourself concerning the main divisions, mark them in the margin of your study Bible. Look again at the general contents of each division to aid you in phrasing the appropriate caption for it. With these broad divisions before you, notice the various subdivisions for each and observe how they unfold the section.

The outlines here proposed are based upon an analysis of the contents. They generally conform to the paragraphing in the American Standard Version. They are presented as suggested roadmaps for your study. It is hoped that they will be helpful in charting the road as you make your way through the gospel itself.

4. DETAILED STUDY

Now you begin a concentrated study of the gospel. The logical unit of study is the paragraph. First gain an understanding of the paragraph as a whole and then make a detailed study of its contents. Basic to your independent study is careful observation of what the passage says. Seek to determine the precise meaning of each sentence, analyzing the individual phrases and words in the light of the grammatical construction and the context. Make an honest personal endeavor to understand it for yourself. This may be achieved through persistent application and self-discipline. Making your own discoveries will be of more lasting benefit to you than merely reading what others think, even though such reading will naturally enlarge and modify your original understanding.

But independent Bible study goes hand in hand with instruction received from others. This is clearly illustrated in the Acts account of the examples of the Bereans, of whom we read that "they received the word [spoken by Paul] with all readiness of mind, and searched the scriptures daily, whether those things were so" (Ac 17:11, KJV).

Supplement your own study of the text with the reading of a good commentary. Be prepared to accept and profit from the insights gained by other students. Your open-minded, thoughtful consideration of the views of others will broaden your understanding and allow you to share the blessings which God gives others who faithfully labor in study. Christian teachers are a gift of the living Christ to His Church. We do well to profit from their labors and instruction, not as a substitute for, but as a supplement to our own studies.

The appended lists of commentaries are intended to indicate something of the riches of the material available to the student for further study. They should be used discriminatingly.

For lasting results the student is urged to keep a notebook of his own findings and comments together with valuable insights gained from other writers. Recording your insights will help to clarify them as well as preserve them for your future use.

5. PRAYERFUL APPLICATION

To achieve lasting spiritual benefits from your study, you must faithfully digest and individually apply your findings. Your intellectual achievements must be combined with prayerful meditation and faithful personal application. Bible study may produce little lasting spiritual result if the student fails to assimilate the truths into his daily living. Jeremiah bears testimony to the result when there is a person "eating" of the Word: "Thy words were found and I ate them, And Thy words became for me a joy and the delight of my heart; For I have been called by Thy name, O LORD God of hosts" (Jer 15: 16, NASB). The ultimate aim of Bible study is a transformed personality as well as an informed intellect.

THE COMPARATIVE STUDY OF THE GOSPELS

The fact that we have four accounts of the gospel makes it natural and logical that they be subjected to systematic comparison. Scholars have engaged in such study from earliest times. The early church accepted all four as accounts of the one God-given gospel which, despite their differences, revealed a spiritual unity in their message. This conviction lay behind Tatian's *Diatessaron* which combined the four gospels into one account of the life and work of Jesus. Similar attempts to combine the gospels into one continuous narrative without omission or repetition of their contents continue to be made to the present day.[4] Such a unification has the superficial advantage of presenting the contents of all four in one convenient record without repetition or omission. But such a unification loses more than it gains. It destroys the individual features and emphases which characterize each gospel. Our four gospels were never intended to be harmonized in this way, nor can such a harmonization successfully replace the separate accounts.

Modern harmonies of the gospels proceed on the principle of preserving each gospel as it stands. They seek to harmonize the parallel passages by placing them in parallel columns, thus conveniently showing their agreements and actual variations.[5] They also indicate topics dealt with, time and place, and general order of events. Some of them, e.g., Robertson's *Harmony of the Gospels*, also contain valuable footnotes and appendices.

Such harmonies are very valuable for a comparative study of the

4. See Arthur T. Pierson, *The One Gospel: or The Combination of the Narratives in One Complete Record;* Charles E. Ebersol, *The Four Gospels in One Made Plain;* Edward F. Carey, *The Life of Jesus in the Words of the Four Gospels;* Charles L. Allen, *The Life of Christ;* Johnston M. Cheney, *The Life of Christ in Stereo: The Four Gospels Combined as One.*

5. Modern harmonies fall into two groups, those which deal with only the synoptics, and those which deal with all four gospels. For the former see Ernest DeWitt Burton and Edgar Johnson Goodspeed, *A Harmony of the Synoptic Gospels;* H. F. D. Sparks, *A Synopsis of the Gospels: The Synoptic Gospels with the Johannine Parallels;* Burton H. Throckmorton, *Gospel Parallels: A Synopsis of the First Three Gospels.* For a harmony of the synoptics in Greek, see Albert Huck, *Synopsis of the First Three Gospels.* For harmonies which include all four gospels see W. Arnold Stevens and Ernest DeWitt Burton, *A Harmony of the Gospels for Historical Study;* A. T. Robertson, *A Harmony of the Gospels for Students of the Life of Christ;* Albert C. Wieand, *New Harmony of the Gospels;* John Franklin Carter, *A Layman's Harmony of the Gospels.* For a harmony in the Greek text, see Kurt Aland, *Synopsis Quattuor Evangeliorum.* For a Greek-English edition see Kurt Aland, editor, *Synopsis of the Four Gospels, Greek-English Edition of the Synopsis Quattuor Evangeliorum with the Text of the Revised Standard Version* (1972).

gospels. They enable the student to see where the gospel accounts run parallel and where they are unique. When two or more gospels relate the same occurrence, the account in any one is often supplemented and enriched by a parallel account. A fuller picture of the situation is obtained as the various individual touches in each gospel are brought together. The blank spaces left on the pages are likewise suggestive as indicating what events are omitted in a gospel.

An examination of these different harmonies reveals that they do not fully agree in their individual arrangement of the comparative accounts. The nature of the gospel materials permits different plausible arrangements. A complete harmony of the four gospels in strict chronological order is not possible for the simple reason that the writers, while observing a broad chronological order as to the beginning and end of their narrative, did not necessarily observe a strict chronological sequence in arranging their accounts of the ministry of Jesus. Each arranged his material in a way best suited to his own plan and purpose. It has been remarked that the attempt to bring the four gospels into strict and complete harmony with each other is like trying to make four men agree who had never quarreled.

A few suggestions are offered to help you derive the most benefit from a comparative study of the gospels. When reading a harmony, always observe which gospel or gospels relate the event under consideration. Notice which features are unique to each account and seek to understand how the character of the account reveals the characteristic features and purpose of that gospel. In seeking to harmonize the accounts notice how they complement and supplement each other. You will find that some of the differences are not readily harmonized. But it would be unwarranted to stamp these differences as contradictions. Note carefully what each actually says, and endeavor to understand the presentation in the light of the purpose of the gospel. Often a satisfactory harmonization is obtained through viewing the differences in the light of historical circumstances and precise grammatical interpretation. But there are admittedly some instances in which a fully satisfactory harmonization on the basis of information now available is not apparent. The key to a full harmonization may not be available today. But only those who hold that the gospel writers are often at war with each other will stamp such instances as certain contradictions.

This method is most rewarding when the distinctive features of each gospel are kept in mind. Avoid the tendency to blur the actual differences in the parallel accounts through an effort to lump all of them together. What a certain gospel says and how, as well as what it does not say, may be significant as revealing the distinctive purpose and emphasis of the writer.

Bear in mind as you study that similar occurrences related by two gospels do not necessarily refer to the same historical event. This is a mistaken assumption in some of the harmonies. Similarities do not necessarily prove historical identity, even as differences do not prove that one of the writers has garbled the account. It should be recognized that similar events in the ministry of Jesus occurred at different times and places. The indications of time and place given in the individual gospels should be noted with care.

Compared to the massive biographies about various noted men of the world, our four gospels recounting the story of Jesus Christ are remarkably slender documents. They may be read through attentively in some eight or nine hours, yet the world's massive literature is not to be compared to them in terms of lasting value. These writings are worthy of the most diligent and prolonged study. Many evangelicals read them primarily for devotional purposes and spiritual enrichment. The gospels should be approached with faith and in believing dependence upon the illuminating work of the Holy Spirit. But there is nothing irreverent in approaching the gospels with a questioning attitude, endeavoring to understand them better with the help of all available sources, whether historical, textual, or literary. In the study of them the Christian student must always endeavor to bring all knowledge and "every thought to the obedience of Christ" (2 Co 10:5). Let him approach their study in the spirit of the poet,

> Before Thy mercy-seat, O Lord,
>   Behold, Thy servants stand,
> To ask the knowledge of Thy Word,
>   The guidance of Thy hand.

WILLIAM H. BATHURST

4

THE GOSPEL ACCORDING TO MATTHEW

THE EARLY CHRISTIAN CHURCH almost without exception placed the gospel of Matthew first in the canon of the New Testament. It forms a natural bridge from the Old Testament to the New Testament. Readers who are familiar with the Old Testament find that this gospel with its distinctive message provides the smoothest passage to the New Testament. It "links the New Testament with the Old Testament and at the same time insists that God's central act in Jesus Christ brings the new age."[1]

Matthew was the most widely read gospel in the early church. The patristic writers quoted from it more than from any of the others. It greatly influenced the thinking of early Christians. Its comprehensive record of the discourses of Jesus, especially the Sermon on the Mount, fitted it for public reading in the church. Its apt phraseology made it readily quotable. It has retained its appeal through the centuries. Even today Matthew's form of the Lord's Prayer and the Sermon on the Mount are commonly used.

THE CHARACTERISTICS OF THE GOSPEL

1. MESSIANIC EMPHASIS

A prominent feature of the gospel is its emphasis upon Jesus Christ as the Messianic King promised by the Old Testament prophets. The central thrust of the gospel may be summarized as follows: Jesus is the anticipated Messiah, and in Him the Old Testament promises have their fulfillment. This gospel appeals directly to the Jews' Messianic expectation. No other gospel connects the story of Jesus so

1. Floyd V. Filson, "A Commentary on the Gospel According to St. Matthew," *Harper's New Testament Commentaries*, p. 1.

43

closely with the Old Testament as does Matthew. Harrison well summarizes this emphasis as follows:

> Matthew goes out of his way to provide an Old Testament setting for significant events in Jesus' life, especially in its early stages: his birth (1:23), his birthplace (2:6), the return from the Egyptian sojourn (2:15), the killing of the babes of Bethlehem (2:18), residence in Nazareth (2:23), the work of the forerunner (3:3), the location of his principal labors (4:15-16), his healing ministry (8:17), his demeanor as God's servant (12:18-21), the parabolic cast of his teaching (13:35), the offer of himself to Israel (21:5), and his arrest (26:56). With the exception of the reference in 2:6, which is attributed to the scribes, each one of these is prefaced with a formula indicating the fulfillment of Scripture.[2]

Matthew thus stresses that the historical events related in his account were of epochal significance as the fulfillment of God's ancient promises. His gospel was not merely a record of astonishing, isolated events. Rather, it was the fulfillment of the divine purpose in the promised Messiah. Many of the Old Testament quotations which he cites are from the Septuagint, but others are quoted from the Hebrew Bible.

2. ROYAL GOSPEL

In this gospel "the kingdom," with Jesus Christ as the promised Davidic king, is prominently mentioned. The word "kingdom" occurs about fifty-six times, more often than in any other gospel. The familiar expression "the kingdom of heaven" is employed thirty-two times in Matthew, but it occurs nowhere else in the New Testament; "the kingdom of God" occurs four times. Jesus is called "son of David" nine times in Matthew, three times each in Mark and Luke, but never in John. Only this gospel quotes Jesus' reference to "the throne of his glory" (19:28; 25:31). Only in Matthew is Jerusalem called "the holy city" (4:5) and "the city of the great King" (5:35). Jesus initially announced the Kingdom as "at hand" (4:17), indicated that it was spiritual in nature (12:28), but that it would ultimately be manifested materially (8:11; 13:40-43). But Matthew's portrait of the Messiah goes beyond the political figure expected by the Jews.

2. Everett F. Harrison, *Introduction to the New Testament*, p. 170.

He is presented not only as the King but also as the coming Judge (19:28; 24:29-31; 25:31-46; 26:64) as well as the suffering Servant of the Lord (16:21; 17:22-23; 20:18-19; 26:54-56).

3. JEWISH BACKGROUND

The gospel makes it very clear that the story of Jesus had a Jewish setting. Jesus' genealogy is placed at the very beginning of the book. The Jewish custom of ceremonial washings is mentioned without explanation (cf. Mt 15:2 with Mk 7:2-4). This gospel pictures the Jewish emphasis upon external acts of piety and stresses the Jewish leaders' ostentation in observing those practices (6:1-18), is familiar with Jewish proselytizing activities (23:15), and hints at the existence of the two Jewish schools of thought concerning divorce (19:3). It records numerous conflicts between Christ and the Jewish leaders, especially the Pharisees, on Jewish views and practices. Throughout this gospel there is evident a diametrical contrast between the inadequate or incorrect teachings and messianic expectations of the Pharisees and the teachings and deeds of the true Messiah. Schodde observes,

> Nowhere else do we find such pronounced denunciations of the Pharisees and their system from the lips of Jesus (cf. 9:11ff; 12:1ff; 15:1ff; 16:1ff; and on particular points 5:20ff; 9:13; 23:23). It is from this point of view, as representing the antithesis to the narrow Pharisaic views, that we are to understand the writer's emphasis on the *universality* of the kingdom of Jesus Christ (cf. 3:1-12; 8:10-12; 21:33-44; 28:18-20).[3]

4. GENTILE INTEREST

Matthew is distinctly a book for Jewish readers, but it is likewise a book for the entire world. It declares the gospel of God's grace for Jew and Gentile alike. Matthew recognizes Israel's position of privilege (see Mt 10:5-6 for Jesus' remark that His ministry was to the "lost sheep of the house of Israel"). But he also recognizes the larger scope of the story of the Messiah, as indicated by the coming of the Magi (2:1-12), which is related only in this gospel. Matthew's interest in Gentiles is suggested by his inclusion of the follow-

---

3. G. H. Schodde, "Matthew, The Gospel of," in *International Standard Bible Encyclopaedia*, 3:2009-12.

ing: the names of two non-Jewish women in Jesus' genealogy (1:5),
Jesus' warning that the Jews would be shut out of the kingdom be-
cause of their unbelief while others from all parts of the world would
enter (8:10-12), the prophecy that Messiah would declare judgment
to the Gentiles and that Gentiles would hope in Him (12:18-21).
Only Matthew relates a parable spoken by Jesus during Passion
Week which clearly indicated that the Jews, because of their un-
belief, would be supplanted by others who were faithful (21:33-43).
Consistent with this universalism is the fact that only the gospel of
Matthew mentions the Church (16:18; 18:17).

5. THEMATIC GROUPING

The gospel of Matthew is characterized by the systematic arrangement of its contents. The material in the first four chapters and the
story of Passion Week is arranged chronologically, but the rest of the
gospel is ordered thematically. Similar narratives and the sayings
of Jesus are grouped together.

The narrative events are not recorded in strict chronological order,
and the sequence of events often differs considerably from that found
in Mark. Matthew's narratives are generally more concise than parallel events in Mark. While Matthew keeps his narratives terse, he
gives much space to the words of Jesus, recording six great discourses: the Sermon on the Mount (chaps. 5-7), the commission to
the Twelve (chap. 10), the seven parables of the Kingdom (chap.
13), the discourse on humility, offences, and forgiveness (chap. 18),
the denunciation of the scribes and Pharisees (chap. 23), and the
Olivet Discourse (chaps. 24-25). The gospel contains fifteen parables of Jesus, ten of which are exclusive to it. Matthew presents
Jesus as the King of the Jews and as the great Teacher of a new Law,
thus injecting a strong emphasis on ethics.

The arrangement of the material in clear alternations between
narrative and discourse conveys a full view of the person portrayed.
The reader must know both the teachings and deeds of Jesus in
order to gain a proper understanding of His royal person.

6. UNITY

Matthew's grouping of his material did not result in "a piece of literary patch-work. Its materials are woven together into one harmonious whole. It has unity, continuity, increase, climax."[4] Guthrie comments, "It shows an author with an astonishingly orderly mind."[5] The gospel of Matthew may be likened to a majestic river which increases in volume as it sweeps onward in its irresistible flow.

THE AUTHORSHIP OF THE GOSPEL

Numerous quotations and allusions to the gospel of Matthew in the patristic writers firmly establish that it was known early and unhesitatingly accepted as authentic and authoritative.[6] The first gospel is an anonymous document, yet the early church had a specific and unvarying tradition as to its authorship.

1. SUPERSCRIPTION

The gospel's identifying superscription, "The Gospel According to Matthew," is the oldest known witness concerning its authorship. The earliest form of the title was simply "According to Matthew" (*kata Matthaion**). To this brief, elliptical caption the only word that can be supplied is "gospel." It implies that there were other known accounts of the gospel. This title is not a part of the original document but was early added by a scribe for purposes of identification. The superscription is found on all known manuscripts of this gospel and agrees with the testimony of the Church Fathers. The title must date at least from the time when the gospels were brought together as one collection. The date cannot be fixed with absolute precision since it is bound up with larger questions concerning the text and canon of the New Testament. Ropes,[7] Guthrie,[8] and others accept that these titles may reasonably be dated as early as A.D. 125. But it is obvious that they were not then affixed to the gospels at random. They expressed the views of the church held before A.D. 125. Stonehouse observes:

> Since half of these names are not of apostles, there is confirmation

4. Herbert L. Willett and James M. Campbell, *The Teachings of the Books*, p. 26.
5. Donald Guthrie, *New Testament Introduction*, p. 29.
6. For a summary of citations see Henry Clarence Thiessen, *Introduction to the New Testament*, pp. 130-31.

*The name is spelled Maththaios in the uncials Aleph, B, and D.

7. J. H. Ropes, *The Synoptic Gospels*, p. 103f.
8. Ibid., p. 33.

of the view that in the Church for a considerable time prior to A.D. 125, and perhaps as early as the time of their individual publication, these very persons were associated with the Gospels as their authors.[9]

Plummer points out that the expression "according to" in itself "neither affirms nor denies authorship; it implies *conformity to a type*."[10] Admittedly the expression may simply denote the norm and may mean no more than that the account was drawn up "according to the teaching of." Thus "the gospel according to the Hebrews" or "the gospel according to the Egyptians" does not denote authorship but rather the gospel as accepted by the Hebrews or the Egyptians. But Plummer rightly remarks:

> It is certain that the Christians of the first four centuries who gave these titles to the Gospels meant more than this: they believed, and meant to express, that each Gospel was written by the person whose name it bears.[11]

If the designation "according to" had been intended to denote only the norm or source from which the author drew, then our second gospel should have been called "the gospel according to Peter." According to uniform tradition Mark drew the material for his gospel from Peter, but it is always called "according to Mark" as indicating accepted authorship. Behind our "gospel according to Luke" stand Paul and the sources mentioned in 1:1-3, yet the third gospel is always designated "according to Luke" as denoting authorship. All of the captions to our gospels must have identical meanings. The scribal designation "according to Matthew" can only be taken to mean that it was an account of the gospel as drawn up by Matthew.

2. PATRISTIC WITNESS

The witness of the caption to the first gospel concerning its authorship receives strong and uniform support in the testimony of the early church. The earliest is the testimony of Papias, bishop of Hierapolis, dating to the first half of the second century. It is usually dated as around A.D. 150, but Robert and Feuillet think that the work of Papias

9. Ned B. Stonehouse, *Origins of the Synoptic Gospels*, pp. 17-18.
10. Alfred Plummer, *An Exegetical Commentary on the Gospel According to S. Matthew*, p. vii.
11. Ibid.

should be dated about 120 at the latest.[12] Albright and Mann give the date of Papias as around A.D. 130.[13] Only a fragment of his total testimony has come down to us, preserved by Eusebius:

> Matthew therefore wrote the oracles (*ta logia*) in the Hebrew dialect, and every one interpreted them as he was able.[14]

The next witness is Irenaeus who wrote his famous *Against Heresies* around A.D. 185:

> Matthew, indeed, produced his Gospel among the Hebrews in their own dialect, while Peter and Paul were preaching at Rome and founding the church.[15]

A further witness is that of Origen (*c.* 185-254), as quoted by Eusebius from the first book of Origen's now incomplete *Commentary on the Gospel of Matthew:*

> Among the four Gospels, which are the only indisputable ones in the Church of God throughout the world, I have learned by tradition that the first was written by Matthew, who was once a publican, but afterwards an apostle of Jesus Christ, and it was prepared for the converts from Judaism, and published in the Hebrew language.[16]

Eusebius himself in his *Ecclesiastical History*, published in A.D. 324 or 325, says of our gospels:

> Of all the disciples of our Lord, only Matthew and John have left us written memorials, and they, tradition says, were led to write only under the pressure of necessity. For Matthew, who had at first preached to the Hebrews, when he was about to go to other people, committed his Gospel to writing in his native tongue, and thus compensated those whom he was obliged to leave for the loss of his presence.[17]

This testimony, which reaches back at least to the middle of the second century, presents a uniform tradition ascribing the first gospel to Matthew. No contradictory testimony or doubts concerning its validity are heard. Gundry observes, "False ascription to a relatively

12. A. Robert and A. Feuillet, *Introduction to the New Testament*, pp. 182-83.
13. W. F. Albright and C. S. Mann, "Matthew," in *The Anchor Bible*, p. CLXXIX.
14. Eusebius *Ecclesiastical History* 3. 39. 16.
15. Irenaeus *Against Heresies* 3. 1. 1. Cf. Eusebius *Ecclesiastical History* 5. 8. 2.
16. Eusebius *Ecclesiastical History* 6. 25. 4.
17. Ibid. 3. 24. 6.

obscure apostle such as Matthew seems unlikely until a later date
when all the apostles became canonized in Christian imagination."[18]
But the validity of the whole chain of tradition has been questioned
since it seems clear that the others are simply repeating the view of
Papias. Filson remarks, "No tradition demonstrably independent
of Papias exists."[19] But Albright and Mann assert:

> There is no necessity whatever to suppose that Irenaeus was de-
> pendent on Papias for his information—Irenaeus, on his own show-
> ing, was near enough to the same authorities as those used by Papias
> himself.[20]

That the later witnesses may have been based on Papias does not
necessarily prove the entire tradition to be suspect. Rather, it may
point to the confidence that the later writers had in the validity of the
tradition. Eusebius reported and himself accepted the traditional
statement of Papias. It is clear that he did not do so simply because
of its age or source, since he rejected the millennial views of Papias
with the disparaging comment that he was a man of "very limited
understanding."[21] Eusebius accepted the traditional testimony because it commended itself to him as trustworthy.

3. MEANING OF TRADITION

The bit of Papias' testimony preserved by Eusebius is not clear.
Close examination of his quoted words has resulted in different
interpretations. The differences center around the meaning assigned
to *ta logia* and the verb rendered "interpreted" (*hērmēneuse*) in
connection with the language Matthew reportedly used.

The prevailing modern view is that *logia* refers to a collection of
sayings or discourses by Jesus which Matthew compiled. This view
is furthered by the current solution to the synoptic problem which
postulates the existence of such a collection, commonly called Q
(for the German *Quelle*, "source"), as one of the sources employed
in the production of this gospel. But there is no historical proof that
such a document as Q ever existed. If this meaning of *logia* is

18. Robert H. Gundry, *A Survey of the New Testament*, p. 84.
19. Filson, p. 16.
20. Albright and Mann, p. CLXXIX.
21. Eusebius *Ecclesiastical History* 3. 39. 13.

adopted and the hypothetical existence of *Q* is accepted, the identification is logical.

Another view is that the *logia* consisted of a collection of Messianic proof texts from the Old Testament drawn up by Matthew for the church's use in establishing the claims of Jesus Christ as the Messiah. But Eusebius, who was acquainted with the writings of Papias, clearly understood Papias to refer to a writing by Matthew comparable to the gospel of Mark, not a mere catena of Old Testament quotations. Guthrie further remarks:

> There is no certain evidence of the existence of Christian *testimonia* books as early as this, and even if the identification were conceded, it would be extremely difficult to imagine how Matthew's name was transferred from such a document to a Gospel in which it formed so small a part of the author's sources.[22]

The other documents of the New Testament use a number of such *testimonia* from the Old Testament, but most of those do not appear in Matthew's gospel.

The most probable view is that *logia* was meant to denote a gospel account. Kittel observes that *logia* may be used of individual sayings. He concludes, however, that in the light of its usage in the Septuagint, the New Testament, and the early church there is no justification for limiting the meaning of *logia* to individual sayings. It could also denote the divine action in making known the new covenant revelation.[23] He holds that the title of Papias' work, *Interpretations of the Lord's Logia,* which is now lost, was "obviously not meant to limit the work to a collection of sayings."[24] It could be used to include both the things said and done by Jesus. This is evident from Papias' own use of the term in connection with Mark's gospel; Eusebius quotes him as saying that Mark in his gospel recorded "the things said or done by our Lord" and then a few lines later refers to the same material as "our Lord's logia."[25] Thus it seems most natural to hold that Papias meant a gospel account when he referred to Matthew's *logia.* Robert and Feuillet point out that "the Syriac version of Eusebius' work renders *logia* by 'gospels.' "[26] This

22. Guthrie, p. 37.
23. See Gerhard Kittel, *Theological Dictionary of the New Testament,* 4:137-41.
24. Ibid., p. 140.
25. Eusebius *Ecclesiastical History* 3. 39. 15.
26. Robert and Feuillet, p. 183.

interpretation of the term is in harmony with the ancient superscription for the first gospel. The view is established if it is granted that the testimony of Irenaeus is identical with that of Papias, for Irenaeus specifically referred to Matthew's producing a "gospel." Since Irenaeus was acquainted with the writings of Papias it seems clear that he understood Papias to refer to a gospel account rather than just a collection of the sayings of Jesus. While scholarly views concerning the intended meaning of *logia* in Papias will doubtless continue to differ, the view that he referred to some kind of gospel account seems most probable.

The great difficulty with the traditional view concerning the origin of the first gospel is the uniform testimony that Matthew wrote "in the Hebrew dialect." It is commonly accepted that by "Hebrew" Papias means Aramaic, a language related to Hebrew. That the reference cannot be to our Greek gospel seems obvious. Thus the second difficulty in Papias' statement about the *logia* is what he means by his comment that "every one interpreted them as he was able."

It has indeed been suggested that Papias' reference is to our Greek Matthew, the reference being to the *style*, not the language, in which Matthew wrote. Thus his book was an "interpretation" or "explanation" of the life of Jesus adapted to the Hebrew mind. While such a meaning for "interpreted" is linguistically possible, later writers did not understand it so.

It is generally held that "interpreted" refers to the translation of Matthew's original Aramaic. This opens up the question: Did Papias have oral or written translations in view? On the one hand, he may have been referring to a sort of oral targum, a paraphrastic translation made by the reader in an assembly for the benefit of his hearers. But then the imperfect tense, rather than the aorist tense, of "interpreted" would have been more natural. Or he may have been referring to people who read Matthew's account privately. Not being well versed in the Aramaic, they did their best to get Matthew's meaning. Another possibility is that he was referring to Christian workers who in their efforts to witness about their Lord used the Aramaic Matthew as they were able to interpret his message.

If Papias had written translations in view, the reference is to the fact that honest attempts, more or less successful, were made to put Matthew's work into Greek. But the surviving words of Papias then do not contain any evaluation of those translations. Nor do they explicitly state that our Greek Matthew is an authoritative translation of the Aramaic work. While the patristic witnesses uniformly asserted an Aramaic original for the gospel, they accepted the Greek Matthew as unquestionably authoritative. They offered no explanation, however, concerning the change in language. They apparently regarded the Greek Matthew which they used as an authoritative translation or satisfactory representation of the Hebrew original. Not until the time of Jerome (*c.* 354-430) was it stated that, "who afterwards translated it into Greek is not certainly known."[27] The gap in the tradition concerning the transition from the Hebrew to the Greek creates an element of confusion.

4. PROPOSED SOLUTION

Jerome's explanation that our Greek Matthew is a translation of the Aramaic original is beset with difficulties. The linguistic features of our Matthew indicate that it was originally written in Greek. Hadjiantoniou observes:

> The idiomatic use of Greek, the play of the language (6:16; 21:41; 24:30, etc.), the author's habit of translating the Hebrew terms, and especially the comparison of this Gospel with those of Mark and Luke in passages dealing with the same events, all testify to the fact that it is an original work and not a translation.[28]

As further linguistic evidence Harrison points to the frequent use of the *men . . . de* construction as well as the genitive absolute, which are not characteristic of translation Greek.[29] In a few instances no Greek equivalents are given for Aramaic terms (5:22; 10:25; 27:6). These terms, however, would be readily intelligible to Greek readers, especially Greek-speaking Jews. Westcott notes eleven words and phrases which he feels point to a Hebrew background. He remarks, "The style is not nearly so Hebraizing as that of St. John, nor is the language so rich as that of St Mark. Yet there are words and phrases which mark the Hebrew Evangelist."[30] It must be remembered that the Septuagint influenced the language of Greek-speaking Christians.

27. Jerome *Lives of Illustrious Men* 2. 3.
28. George A. Hadjiantoniou, *New Testament Introduction*, p. 110.
29. Harrison, p. 169.
30. Brooke Foss Westcott, *An Introduction to the Study of the Gospels*, pp. 363-64, footnote.

This influence makes even more difficult the task of determining what is certain evidence that a document is translation Greek. Until the beginning of the nineteenth century it was commonly accepted that our Greek Matthew was a translation from an Aramaic original. The prevailing view today, however, is that our Matthew was originally composed in Greek. A Greek origin of the gospel best accounts for its linguistic features.

How then is the persistent tradition that Matthew wrote in the Aramaic to be understood? One alternative is that Papias was mistaken concerning the language. Thus Kümmel asserts, "We must admit that the report about the Matthew composed by Matthew 'in the Hebrew language' is false."[31] To account for the persistent tradition concerning a Hebrew origin it has been suggested that it was simply an inference drawn from the gospel's character and the fact that it was directed to Palestinian Christians. It would be understandable for Papias to assume that a gospel written for Palestinian Jewish believers would be in Aramaic. There is no evidence that Papias had actually seen or read a Hebrew Matthew. Another suggestion is that the tradition arose out of a mistaken identification of Matthew's gospel with another book, like the *Gospel According to the Hebrews*. This was Jerome's mistake, but he later admitted the confusion. Stonehouse suggests the further possibility that a Semitic translation of the Greek Matthew may have been mistaken by Papias for the original.[32]

But the very fact that later witnesses referred to an Aramaic original is presumptive evidence that Papias was not in error. Because of their knowledge of the Greek Matthew this statement about the language must have raised questions in the minds of Irenaeus and Origen, yet they did not simply conclude that Papias was wrong. Certainly Eusebius was not uncritical of his sources, yet he accepted the testimony of Papias on this point.

The other alternative is that Papias was correct concerning the original language of Matthew, yet he accepted the evidence that our Greek Matthew was originally composed in Greek. The reconciliation lies in the unexpressed assumption of the patristic witnesses that Matthew originally wrote a gospel in Hebrew for Jewish readers

31. Werner Georg Kümmel, *Introduction to the New Testament*, p. 85.
32. Stonehouse, p. 92.

and later wrote our Greek gospel as a satisfactory representative of or replacement for the original work for a broader group of readers. Such a view, that Matthew produced a gospel in two forms, would suit the tradition concerning authorship and language yet account for the character of our Greek Matthew. When Matthew's ministry was extended beyond Palestinian Christian circles he found it necessary to put his account into a new form and language while retaining in essence the message of his other work. This would be consistent with Eusebius' remark that Matthew wrote "under the pressure of necessity" (see p. 49).

The official position of the Roman Catholic Church is that Matthew wrote his original gospel in Aramaic and that our canonical gospel is "substantially identical" with the original Aramaic. Following the lead of Jerome it was long held that the Greek Matthew is a translation of the Aramaic original. But recent Catholic scholars recognize that it is difficult to maintain that our Matthew is simply a translation. Robert and Feuillet conclude, "We incline to give up the idea of a mere translation, while we maintain a 'substantial identity' between Matthew and the Aramaic original; an identity similar to that which exists between the Hebrew text of Jeremias and the Septuagint translation, in spite of the changes in the order of the text, the abridgment of some passages, etc."[33] Likewise Wikenhauser remarks:

> It may be taken as certain that an Aramaic original of the Gospel of St. Matthew can be defended only if we regard Greek Matthew not as a literal translation of the Aramaic, but as a thorough revision made with frequent use of the Gospel of St. Mark. . . . Since there are no remains of Aramaic Matthew, and no one knows what it was like, we cannot make any more accurate or more definite statement about the relationship between the two forms of St. Matthew's Gospel.[34]

The view that Matthew wrote two forms of his gospel has commended itself to a number of Protestant scholars as a feasible position. This view recognizes Matthew as the direct author of our gospel and avoids introducing an unknown translator or a later compiler who drew material from Aramaic Matthew and other sources. This

33. Robert and Feuillet, p. 189.
34. Alfred Wikenhauser, *New Testament Introduction*, p. 195.

view is consistent with the known position and training of Matthew as a former publican. Goodspeed asserts, "Among the disciples, the presence of a man with plenty of writing experience, Greek as well as Aramaic (he would interview the taxpayers in Aramaic, and write up his reports in Greek), is a fact of great importance."[35] His bilingual abilities would equip him to produce a gospel in both languages. It may be assumed that when Matthew later wrote his gospel in Greek for a larger circle of readers he retained the essential thrust of his earlier work but felt free to modify and enlarge it as judged desirable. It is known that Josephus, who was bilingual, wrote his *Wars of the Jews* in Aramaic and then secured the assistance of Greek writers in freely reproducing and improving it in the Greek language.

5. OBJECTIONS TO MATTHEAN AUTHORSHIP

Modern scholars are not adverse to accepting the tradition of Papias that Matthew wrote the *logia* in Aramaic, whatever its actual nature may have been. But many of them find it difficult to accept him as the real author of our canonical Matthew. They are willing to accept his connection with this gospel only insofar as his *logia* was one of the sources of the Greek Matthew. Thus Allen, while rejecting Matthean authorship for this gospel, suggests that it was ascribed to Matthew due to its known use of the Matthean *logia* because of "an irresistible tendency to find for it Apostolic sanction."[36] But Goodspeed counters that this claim "shatters completely upon the fact that no such sanction was found for any other Gospel— Mark, Luke, or John." He points out that under Allen's "theory of nomenclature, Mark should have been called Peter, under the irresistible tendency to find for it an apostolic sanction, a thing Mark shows no trace of! This irresponsible disposition to broad and alluring generalizations on Gospel authorship can be shown to be simply without foundation, in Greek Christian usage."[37]

The Matthean authorship is rejected on the ground that the character of the gospel itself speaks against apostolic authorship. The view that it is non-apostolic is supported by the observation that the

35. Edgar J. Goodspeed, *Matthew: Apostle and Evangelist*, p. 112.
36. Willoughby C. Allen, "A Critical and Exegetical Commentary on the Gospel According to S. Matthew," in *International Critical Commentary*, p. lxxxi.
37. Goodspeed, pp. 25-26.

gospel lacks the vivid, lifelike touches which we would expect from an eyewitness of the events narrated. Whenever the same event is recorded in both Matthew and Mark the former commonly is more condensed and devoid of the details which would indicate personal observation. Admittedly the vivid touches of an eyewitness, occurring in Mark as derived from Peter, are not characteristic of Matthew. But they are not totally absent. Lenski suggests that this "may well be due to the type and the character of the man. His eye and his ear did not catch so many of the little details that we love to see retained. To the present day eyewitnesses differ very markedly in this respect."[38] Since Matthew's plan for his gospel called for the inclusion of much of Jesus' teaching, considerations of space would force him to condense his material by giving only the main facts and omitting details.

Kümmel advances as an argument against the traditional authorship "the systematic (and that means nonbiographic) manner of Matthew's outline."[39] But it is difficult to see how the systematic arrangement of the material disproves Matthean authorship. At most it proves that the author was not seeking to write a biography of Jesus. It may be held that this systematic arrangement rather points to Matthew the former tax collector; his former occupation must have instilled in him habits of system and order.

The claim of Kümmel that the Matthean authorship is discredited by "the late-apostolic theological attitude" reflected in the gospel is a subjective evaluation influenced by presuppositions.[40] The view that the "editorial tendencies" of the gospel point to a later time than Matthew's is based on the assumption that the later church developed the tradition ascribed to Jesus in this gospel. Guthrie replies, "It is equally possible to maintain that Matthew's editorial tendencies reflect a genuine early tradition, provided a more comprehensive picture of the teaching of Jesus is maintained."[41]

The strongest objection to apostolic authorship is that this gospel is held to incorporate almost *in toto* the work of Mark, a non-apostolic author. Thus Taylor asserts, "It is improbable in the extreme that an Apostle would have used as a source the work of one who was not

38. R. C. H. Lenski, *The Interpretation of St. Matthew's Gospel*, p. 22.
39. Kümmel, p. 85.
40. Ibid.
41. Guthrie, p. 42.

an eyewitness of the ministry of Jesus."[42] (This objection lacks force for those who reject the currently assumed priority of Mark as providing the basis for a solution to the synoptic problem.) But does acceptance of Marcan priority necessarily rule out apostolic authorship? Guthrie points out that this argument is based upon "a particular view of apostolicity, which considers that it would have detracted from Matthew's apostolic dignity if he had quoted a non-apostolic author."[43] Why should it be beneath the dignity of an apostle to use a non-apostolic source when his own apostolic experience would enable him to recognize the authenticity of the material being used for his own purpose? Goodspeed testifies:

> I have seen writers who had been eyewitnesses of an educational drama, even active participants in it, seeking additional evidence of the larger picture from what might well be called "secondary authorities," whose memories and impressions they were not above consulting and even adopting, to give their work breadth and fulness. And if with modest and conscientious men in the twentieth century, why not in the first?[44]

Harrison further suggests that in using Mark's material Matthew "was not deferring to Mark so much as to Peter, the acknowledged leader of the apostles, whom tradition makes responsible for the material in Mark."[45] An examination of the material allegedly copied from Mark reveals that this writer did not simply incorporate Mark unaltered into his own work. He used Mark's material critically and for his own purpose. Goodspeed asserts:

> While he used virtually all of it, he transposes to such an extent that he may well be called the despair of the harmonist! Nor does Matthew precisely "base" his work upon Mark; he transposes Mark's sections mercilessly, using them where they fit his purpose. His view of Jesus is less the Man of Action, as Mark pictured him, than the Teacher, and for his great sermons he uses Mark's vivid narratives for frames![46]

We conclude that the objections to apostolic authorship for the

42. Vincent Taylor, *The Gospels: A Short Introduction*, p. 95f.
43. Guthrie, p. 41.
44. Goodspeed, p. 28.
45. Harrison, p. 177.
46. Goodspeed, p. 28.

first gospel do not succeed in overthrowing the traditional testimony concerning Matthean authorship.

6. SUPPORTING EVIDENCE

The traditional Matthean authorship finds some support in the gospel itself. The evidence admittedly is meager but it is consistent with the tradition. In the four lists of the Twelve in the New Testament (Mt 10:2-4; Mk 3:16-19; Lk 6:14-16; Ac 1:13) Matthew is always named in either seventh (Mk and Lk) or eighth place (Mt and Ac), but only in Matthew is he described as "the publican" (10:3). This seems to be a conscious personal touch by the writer to bear witness to the grace of Christ to him personally. Some critics would stamp the insertion of the identification as a device of pseudonymity, but surely in a gospel writing it is more natural to expect a personal, though very modest, testimony to grace than a subtle attempt to establish a false identity.

Matthew 9:9 briefly records Jesus calling a man named Matthew from the place of toll to be His follower; Mark 2:14 and Luke 5:27-28 in almost identical language record the call of a man named Levi, but they do not mention the call of a man named Matthew. Since the name Levi, however, is never mentioned in the lists of the Twelve, it seems clear that it refers to Matthew, although some of the ancient writers did distinguish between Levi and Matthew. Objection to the identification has been made on the ground that a Jew would not have two Jewish names. Admittedly this would be somewhat unusual, since the second name of a Jew was usually Greek or Latin. But instances of Semitic second names do occur: Simon called Cephas (Jn 1:42), Joseph called Barnabas (Ac 4:36), Joseph called Caiaphas.[47] The simplest hypothesis is that his original name was Levi and that the second name Matthew, which means "gift of God," was either self-assumed or given to him by Jesus after his call. The second name superseded his original name and commemorated the grace shown him in his call. Following his call, this disciple made a feast for Jesus about which both Mark (2:15) and Luke (5:29) state that Levi entertained Jesus "in his house." The possessive pronoun "his," however, is omitted in Matthew (9:10).

47. Josephus *Antiquities of the Jews* 18. 2. 2.

As further evidence in support of the traditional authorship Guthrie points to "the agreement between the attention to detail essential to the tax-collector's profession and the methodical arrangement of this Gospel."[48] Certain details seem to reflect the precise terminology of the tax collector. All of the synoptics relate the dispute concerning the payment of tribute to Caesar (Mt 22:15-22; Mk 12:13-17; Lk 20:20-26), but only Matthew uses the more precise term "tribute money" (*nomisma*) rather than the common term *denarius* employed by Mark and Luke. Only the first gospel records that Peter was questioned by the collectors of the annual half-shekel temple tax (*to didrachmon*) as to whether Jesus paid the tax (17:24-27). Goodspeed feels that the large figures in the story of the unforgiving debtor, recorded only in Matthew (18:23-25), reveal that "here we are pretty clearly in the tax collector's vocabulary. This is high finance in the writer's world."[49] He is also impressed with the numerical interests reflected in this gospel as evidence that the writer was a tax collector and holds that the author of this gospel was clearly "a man of figures—arithmetic was the lifeblood of the tax collector."[50] Albright and Mann also nominate Matthew as the most likely author, holding that the view has the advantage of "taking Papias and those who cite him seriously, and of accepting historical and archaeological evidence of chaotic conditions in Palestine between A.D. 60 and 75."[51]

The question of the authorship of the first gospel is admittedly a thorny problem. Liberal scholars generally rest in the negative conclusion that the identity of the real author is entirely unknown. Even conservative scholars are often hesitant to declare themselves. But Guthrie summarizes his discussion of authorship with the remark, "It may be said that there is no conclusive reason for rejecting the strong external testimony regarding the authorship of Matthew." He recognizes, however, that modern synoptic source hypotheses do create some difficulties.[52] We accept Matthean authorship as the most probable solution to this difficult problem. Both external and internal evidence are agreeable to it.

48. Guthrie, p. 44.
49. Goodspeed, p. 3.
50. Ibid., p. 36.
51. Albright and Mann, p. CLXXXIV.
52. Guthrie, p. 44.

THE AUTHOR OF THE FIRST GOSPEL

The gospels record only a few historical details concerning the apostle Matthew. He was the son of a man named Alphaeus (Mk 2:14). Another disciple, James, was also identified as the son of Alphaeus (Mk 3:18; Lk 6:15), but there is no indication that these two disciples were brothers. Matthew was an employee at the toll house in Capernaum. He was either employed directly by Herod Antipas, the ruler of Galilee, or he worked under a person who had the taxes of the district in tenure. Matthew's immediate positive response to the call of Jesus makes it obvious that he had been among the multitudes attending the preaching of Jesus and had been deeply impressed. After Jesus called him, Levi (Matthew) gave "a great feast in his house" (Lk 5:29) in honor of his new Master to which he invited many other publicans. This may hint that he was a man of considerable means and owned a large house.

He is named among the "twelve apostles" chosen by Jesus (Mk 3:13-19; Lk 6:12-16). The lists of the Twelve divide into three groups of four men each, and the name of Matthew always stands third or fourth in the second group. His name is not connected with any incident other than his call. The last time his name appears in the New Testament is in the list of the Twelve in the upper room after the ascension of Jesus (Ac 1:13).

Little reliable information concerning the life of Matthew is available. There is an early tradition that he, with the other apostles, remained at Jerusalem twelve years before going out to preach in other lands. Trustworthy sources concerning the scenes of his missionary labors are lacking, but various foreign lands are mentioned. The tradition concerning Matthew is garbled because of confusion between Matthew and Matthias (cf. Ac 1:26). Barclay remarks that the later legends concerning Matthew "are so fantastic that they can have no solid basis in fact."[53] Apocryphal claims ascribe martyrdom to Matthew but he probably died a natural death.

THE INTENDED READERS OF THE GOSPEL

According to the testimony of Irenaeus, Origen, and Eusebius (see

---

53. William Barclay, *The Master's Men*, p. 65. See pp. 64-68 for a summary of the traditional material concerning Matthew. See also William Stewart McBirnie, *The Search for the Twelve Apostles*, p. 46.

p. 49), Matthew wrote his gospel for Jewish believers in Palestine. This is self-evident in the case of his Aramaic *logia,* whatever its precise contents may have been. If there is "substantial identity" between the *logia* and our Greek Matthew, this testimony would also apply to our canonical gospel. The Jewish coloring in the gospel and its Hebraic outlook and appeal are consistent with this view. While its appeal is especially adapted to the Jewish mind, its message of the revelation of God in Jesus the promised Messiah has relevance for all men everywhere. It seems most probable that our Greek Matthew was primarily intended for Greek-speaking Christian communities the majority of whose members were of Jewish extraction. But these Jewish believers had regular contacts with the Jews among whom they lived and whom they sought to win to their faith in Jesus who fulfilled the prophetic promises.

THE PLACE AND DATE OF THE GOSPEL

1. PLACE

It is obvious that the material in this gospel has a Palestinian origin and that it was written by someone familiar with Jewish views and practices. But the place of its composition cannot be definitely determined. Lenski asserts, "The place of writing is unknown, and not even a guess can be hazarded."[54] But others are not so hesitant. The two places of origin commonly suggested are Palestine and somewhere in Syria, perhaps Antioch.

The traditional testimony connects the place of writing with the Aramaic language. The comment of Irenaeus that Matthew "produced his Gospel among the Hebrews" implies a Palestinian origin since the place is contrasted to Rome, where Peter and Paul worked. The assertion of Eusebius that Matthew first preached to the Hebrews and committed his preaching to writing for them when he was about to go to other nations likewise demands a Palestinian origin. That the *logia* was written in Palestine is certain. But the traditional testimony does not touch the question of the place of origin of our Greek Matthew.

Since in New Testament times Aramaic was the language of the Jews in Palestine,[55] the fact that our gospel according to Matthew

54. Lenski, p. 19.
55. Charles F. Pfeiffer, "Aramaic Language," in *The Encyclopedia of Christianity,* 1:387-88.

was written in Greek speaks against a Palestinian origin. It suggests rather a place outside Palestine where Greek-speaking Jews predominated. Syria seems the most probable place since there were large numbers of Jewish Christians in those areas (Ac 11:19, 27). Support for a Syrian origin has been drawn from Matthew 4:24, in which the writer seems to assume that the readers are acquainted with the geography of Syria. Mark 3:8, however, explains that the people came from around Tyre and Sidon. Williams points out that "the many explanations of Aramaic words is against the theory that the readers were Palestinian Jews. They would know the meaning of Aramaic words, while foreign Jews, who learned from infancy to speak Greek, would not know Aramaic words."[56]

Many scholars suggest Antioch as the place of origin. Gundry holds that "the remarkable concern for Gentiles may tip the scale in favor of Antioch, the city with the church that sent Paul on his Gentile missions."[57] Harrison thinks that the prominence of Antioch as a Christian center makes this the likely place of origin "since the other Gospels are associated with prominent centers."[58] Antioch seems to be favored by the fact that Ignatius, bishop of the church in Antioch, in his writings from the first quarter of the second century reveals knowledge of our gospel.[59] But the strength of this suggestion depends largely on the date accepted for the gospel. If we can accept that our gospels really reflect the interests and development of the churches from which they came, our Greek Matthew may well have been written in Antioch of Syria.

2. DATE

The dating of our gospel is complicated by problems raised by the traditional testimony. If the *logia* of Matthew was simply a collection of sayings by Jesus, significant only as a minor source, its precise date of composition is quite immaterial to the date of our Greek Matthew. But those who hold that Matthew wrote a gospel in Aramaic and later wrote our Greek gospel are naturally interested in the comparative dating of the two works.

According to the report of Eusebius (p. 49) Matthew wrote his

56. Charles B. Williams, *An Introduction to New Testament Literature*, p. 46.
57. Gundry, p. 88.
58. Harrison, p. 174.
59. Ignatius *Epistle to the Smyrnaeans*, chap. 1; *Epistle to Polycarp*, chap. 2.

Aramaic gospel before he left Palestine to preach in foreign lands. He also quotes a tradition that the separation of the apostles, according to the command of Christ, came after twelve years.[60] According to Thiessen, this traditional date may not be very far wrong. He suggests that the Aramaic Matthew may be dated roughly A.D. 45.[61] But Wikenhauser holds that a date in the mid-fifties is more probable. Since he accepts "the substantial identity of Aramaic and Greek Matthew," he feels that the internal evidence points to a time when mission work to the Gentiles was already in full operation. He points out that Acts 15 and Galatians 2:1-10 show that the apostles were still in Jerusalem around the year 49. He holds that according to Galatians 2:7-9, the Twelve had not as yet undertaken any specific missionary work outside Palestine. Hence his date for the *logia* is in the mid-fifties.[62]

The comment of Irenaeus that Matthew wrote his gospel while Peter and Paul were preaching at Rome and founding the church contains an obvious error concerning the date of the Roman church's origin. Paul's letter to the Romans proves that it was in existence some years before he arrived there. The actual time of Peter's and Paul's preaching at Rome would require a date around A.D. 60-64. This seems entirely too late for the Aramaic work of Matthew. A date between A.D. 50 and 55 seems the best guess for the *logia*.

Suggested dates for our Greek Matthew have ranged widely, all the way from A.D. 40 to 140.[63] This wide range in proposed dates proves that the whole problem lies largely in the realm of subjective evaluation and depends upon the interpretation given to the features of the gospel and the environment which they are held to reflect. Any dating of the gospel is also influenced by the relationship between Matthew and Mark as accepted in a proposed solution to the synoptic problem. The currently accepted solution to the synoptic problem requires that Matthew was written some time after Mark.

Some slight hints concerning a date are contained in the gospel. The two occurrences of the expression "unto this day" (27:8; 28:15) point to a considerable lapse of time between the events recorded

60. Eusebius, *Ecclesiastical History* 5. 18. 14.
61. Thiessen, p. 137.
62. Wikenhauser, pp. 196-97.
63. See the table of authors and dates in James Moffatt, *An Introduction to the Literature of the New Testament*, p. 213.

and the time of writing. But the exact number of years is not evident. However, the statement in 27:8, "Wherefore that field was called, The field of blood, unto this day," naturally points to a date before A.D. 70. After the destruction of Jerusalem the field would no longer be thus identified or used as a place for the burial of strangers. It may also be held that such expressions as "the holy city," "the holy place," and "the city of the great King" suggest that Jerusalem was still standing. Williams sees a strong argument for a date before A.D. 70 in the caution expressed by the writer in 24:15-17. He says, "It would have been preposterous for the writer to have inserted this caution as to how they might escape when they saw the Roman armies in the holy place, if he was writing after the Romans had taken the city."[64] It has also been urged that if Jerusalem had already been destroyed a clearer distinction would have been made between the fall of Jerusalem and the final coming of Christ in chapter 24. Dods holds that "the warning, 'whoso readeth, let him understand', interjected by the Evangelist into the Lord's discourse (xxiv. 15), is proof that the outbreak of the war, though imminent, was not yet present."[65]

Others have drawn arguments from the gospel for a date after A.D. 70. Thus Klijn accepts a date after A.D. 70 as "most plausible, for in 22, 7 it is said that the king will 'set their town on fire'," thus assuming that it is a backward glance at the fate of Jerusalem.[66] Harnack placed the writing of the gospel around A.D. 75 because he felt that "the catastrophe of Jerusalem vibrates in this Gospel as in no other."[67] The statement reflects Harnack's subjective reading of the situation. Johnson holds that the eschatological discourse in Matthew 24 is obviously a rewriting of Mark 13 which was adapted to the situation some time after the destruction of Jerusalem.[68] But such a view questions the reliability of the gospel writers in presenting the teachings of Jesus whether they wrote before or after that event. Arguments for a late date drawn from the eschatological discourse seem suspicious of our Lord's ability to predict the future. The internal evidence is best taken as pointing to a date before A.D. 70.

64. Williams, p. 45.
65. Marcus Dods, *An Introduction to the New Testament*, p. 20.
66. A. F. J. Klijn, *An Introduction to the New Testament*, p. 34.
67. Adolf Harnak, *Chronologie*, 1:654, as quoted in Harrison, p. 175.
68. Sherman E. Johnson and George A. Buttrick, "The Gospel According to St. Matthew," in *The Interpreter's Bible*, 7:240-41.

If our gospel according to Matthew drew material from Mark, then it must be dated some time after A.D. 65, the generally accepted date for Mark. The length of the interval between Mark and Matthew can only be conjectured. Our suggested date for the Gospel of Matthew is between A.D. 66 and 68, the earlier date being the more probable.

THE PURPOSE OF THE GOSPEL

Unlike the fourth gospel (20:30-31), Matthew contains no statement of purpose. But clearly this gospel, like the others, generally aims to set forth the facts concerning Jesus Christ in order to awaken and establish faith in Him and the gospel.

According to the testimony of Origen, Matthew's gospel was written for "converts from Judaism," while Eusebius commented that it was written for Aramaic readers as a substitute for Matthew's personal instructions when he was on the point of going to foreign lands. This clearly implies an instructional aim for the gospel. Matthew intended it to confirm and encourage persecuted Jewish believers in their faith. They needed to be grounded in their views concerning the nature and mission of Christ. A faithful account of His teaching and deeds would show that He was truly the fulfillment of their messianic hopes. It would give them answers for the calumnations being leveled against their Lord by unbelievers. Believers also needed guidance concerning the nature of the life expected of them as members of the messianic community. The ethical teachings of Jesus recorded in this gospel provide instructive and valued guidance. This instructional function is reflected in the closing statement of the Great Commission (28:19-20).

This gospel also provided its Jewish readers with a valuable evangelistic tool. Having been grounded in their own faith through it, they would naturally use it to win others to the same faith. They would be challenged by its references to the Old Testament, which they accepted as authoritative, to show that Jesus of Nazareth was indeed the promised Messiah.

The very contents of this gospel assured that its value would not be limited to Jewish Christians. It proved to be highly popular among Gentile believers. This is confirmed by the widespread use of it by Christian writers in the second century. The universalism of the gospel message proclaimed in Matthew appeals to all believing hearts. Tasker thus summarizes its functional value for the church:

> It provided the Church with an indispensable tool in its threefold task of defending its beliefs against attacks from Jewish opponents, of instructing converts from paganism in the ethical implications of their newly-accepted religion, and of helping its own members to live a disciplined life of fellowship based on the record of the deeds and words of their Lord and Master, which they heard read week by week in the orderly and systematic form provided by this evangelist.[69]

An Outline of Matthew

The contents of Matthew, while revealing careful arrangement, are not readily arranged in a systematic outline. The arrangement of the material is largely topical and the central portion of the gospel revolves around five discourses by Jesus. This is indicated by the fivefold use of the phrase "when Jesus had finished" (7:28; 11:1; 13:53; 19:1; 26:1). But efforts to outline the gospel around these discourses are not fully satisfactory. They tend to regard the opening and concluding portions of the gospel as mere prologue and epilogue. More satisfactory is a chronological division indicated by the two occurrences of the phrase "from that time Jesus began to" (4:17; 16:21). The expression indicates that Matthew intended to divide his story of Jesus into distinct periods. The first occurrence of the words marks the beginning of Jesus' public ministry, thus underlining the transition from His private life to the commencement of His public work. The second occurrence marks the specific introduction of the cross as the central emphasis until His resurrection in triumph.

The theme of the gospel is "Jesus Christ the Messianic King."

I. Coming of the Messianic King, 1:1—4:16
   A. Ancestry of the King, 1:1-17
      1. Title to the genealogy, v. 1
      2. Names of the genealogy, vv. 2-16
      3. Summary of the genealogy, v. 17

69. R. V. G. Tasker, "The Gospel According to St. Matthew," in *Tyndale New Testament Commentaries*, pp. 17-18.

B. Birth of the King, 1:18—2:23
1. Mystery of His nature, 1:18-25
2. Events during His infancy, 2:1-23
    a) Coming of the Magi, vv. 1-12
    b) Flight into Egypt for safety, vv. 13-15
    c) Slaughter of the babes at Bethlehem, vv. 16-18
    d) Return and residence in Nazareth, vv. 19-23
C. Inauguration of the King, 3:1-17
1. Preparatory ministry of John the Baptist, vv. 1-12
2. Baptism of Jesus by John, vv. 13-17
D. Testing of the King, 4:1-11
E. Transition to the King's work, 4:12-16

II. Proclamation of the Messianic Kingdom, 4:17—16:20
A. Beginning of the King's work, 4:17-25
1. Announcement of the impending kingdom, v. 17
2. Enlistment of individual subjects, vv. 18-22
3. Campaign throughout Galilee, vv. 23-25
B. Manifesto of the Kingdom, 5:1—7:29
1. Setting for the manifesto, 5:1-2
2. Citizens of the Kingdom, 5:3-20
    a) Character of the citizens, vv. 3-12
    b) Influence of the citizens, vv. 13-16
    c) Observance of law in the kingdom, vv. 17-20
3. Laws of the Kingdom, 5:21—7:12
    a) Social requirements of the Kingdom, 5:21-48
        (1) Sacredness of life, vv. 21-26
        (2) Sanctity of marriage, vv. 27-32
        (3) Requirement of truth, vv. 33-37
        (4) Reaction to evil, vv. 38-42
        (5) Practice of love, vv. 43-48
    b) The spiritual requirements in the Kingdom, 6:1-34
        (1) Basic principle of action, v. 1
        (2) Practices of the religious life, vv. 2-18
            (*a*) Requirement in giving alms, vv. 2-4
            (*b*) Requirement in prayer, vv. 5-15
            (*c*) Requirement in fasting, vv. 16-18
        (3) The attitude toward material things, vv. 19-34

        (*a*) Attitude toward wealth, vv. 19-24

        (*b*) Attitude toward necessities, vv. 25-34

     c) The summary of the principles of action, 7:1-12

       (1) Social relations of the citizens, vv. 1-6

        (*a*) Exclusion of censoriousness, vv. 1-5

        (*b*) Practice of discrimination, v. 6

       (2) Provision of needs through prayer, vv. 7-11

       (3) Golden rule for action, v. 12

  4. Tests of the Kingdom, 7:13-27

     a) Test of personal entry, vv. 13-14

     b) Test of professed leaders, vv. 15-20

     c) Test of personal obedience, vv. 21-27

       (1) Statement of the test, vv. 21-23

       (2) Illustration of the test, vv. 24-27

  5. Reaction to the manifesto, 7:28-29

C. Manifestations of messianic authority, 8:1–9:34

  1. First series of manifestations, 8:1-22

     a) Narration of the manifestations, vv. 1-17

       (1) Cleansing of a leper, vv. 1-4

       (2) Healing of a palsied servant, vv. 5-13

       (3) Restoration of Peter's mother-in-law, vv. 14-15

       (4) Ministry of deliverance to the multitude, vv. 16-17

     b) Reactions to the manifestations, vv. 18-22

  2. The second series of manifestations, 8:23–9:17

     a) Narration of the manifestations, 8:23–9:10

       (1) Stilling of the storm at sea, 8:23-27

       (2) Deliverance of two demoniacs, 8:28-34

       (3) Forgiveness and healing of a paralytic, 9:1-8

       (4) Call and response of Matthew, 9:9-10

     b) Responses to the manifestations, 9:11-17

       (1) Criticism of the Pharisees, vv. 11-13

       (2) Inquiry about fasting by John's disciples, vv. 14-17

  3. Further series of manifestations, 9:18-34

     a) Narration of the manifestations, vv. 18-33*a*

       (1) Woman healed and the dead girl raised, vv. 18-26

       (2) Healing of two blind men, vv. 27-31

       (3) Deliverance of a demon-possessed man, vv. 32-33*a*

     b) Reactions to the manifestations, vv. 33*b*-34

D. Promulgation of the messianic message, 9:35—11:1
   1. Masses needing the message, 9:35-36
   2. Preparation of the messengers, 9:37—10:4
      a) Lesson in prayer for laborers, 9:37-38
      b) Bestowal of power for service, 10:1
      c) Names of the messengers, 10:2-4
   3. Commission to the Twelve, 10:5-42
      a) Limited assignment in Galilee, vv. 5-15
      b) Coming service amid persecution, vv. 16-23
      c) Experiences of the persecuted messengers, vv. 24-42
         (1) Testimony amid opposition, vv. 24-33
         (2) Demand for supreme loyalty in the worker, vv. 34-39
         (3) Assurance of reward in faithful service, vv. 40-42
   4. Continued activity of the King, 11:1

E. Difficulties of the Kingdom, 11:2-30
   1. Perplexity of John the Baptist, vv. 2-15
      a) Reply of the King to John's question, vv. 2-6
      b) Teaching to the people about John, vv. 7-15
   2. Unreceptiveness of the masses, vv. 16-24
      a) Unreasonableness of the generation, vv. 16-19
      b) Impenitence of the favored cities, vv. 20-24
   3. Attitude of the King amid difficulty, vv. 25-30

F. Opposition to the Kingdom, 12:1—16:12
   1. Attacks by Pharisees concerning the Sabbath, 12:1-14
      a) Attack in the grainfield, vv. 1-8
      b) Attack in the synagogue, vv. 9-14
   2. Activity of the King under attack, 12:15-21
   3. Attack by Pharisees concerning exorcism, 12:22-37
      a) Exorcism evoking the attack, vv. 22-24
      b) Reply to the attackers, vv. 25-37
   4. Demand by scribes and Pharisees for a sign, 12:38-45
   5. Interference from the King's family, 12:46-50
   6. Parabolic teaching of the Kingdom in mystery, 13:1-52
      a) Teaching to the multitude by the sea, vv. 1-35
         (1) Parable of the sower and the soils, vv. 1-23
            (*a*) Parable spoken to the crowd, vv. 1-9

(*b*) Explanation for the new method, vv. 10-17
(*c*) Explanation of the parable, vv. 18-23
(2) Parable of the wheat and darnel, vv. 24-30
(3) Parable of the mustard seed, vv. 31-32
(4) Parable of the leaven, v. 33
(5) Fulfilment of Scripture in the method, vv. 34-35
b) Teaching to the disciples in the house, vv. 36-52
  (1) Interpretation of the wheat and darnel, vv. 36-43
  (2) Parable of the buried treasure, vv. 44
  (3) Parable of the costly pearl, vv. 45-46
  (4) Parable of the drag-net, vv. 47-50
  (5) Understanding of the parabolic teaching, vv. 51-52
7. Manifestations of the rejection of the Kingdom, 13:53–14:12
  a) Rejection of the King at Nazareth, 13:53-58
  b) Reaction of terror by the tetrarch, 14:1-12
    (1) Nature of Herod's reaction, vv. 1-2
    (2) Reasons for the reactions, vv. 3-12
      (*a*) Imprisonment of the Baptist, vv. 3-5
      (*b*) Murder of the Baptist, vv. 6-12
8. Activities of the rejected King, 14:13-36
  a) Feeding of the five thousand, vv. 13-21
  b) Walking on the water by Jesus and Peter, vv. 22-33
  c) Healing ministry in Genessaret, vv. 34-36
9. Attack by Pharisees concerning ceremonial purity, 15:1-20
  a) Deputation making the attack, vv. 1-2
  b) Reply exposing the evil of their traditions, vv. 3-9
  c) Teaching concerning true defilement, vv. 10-20
10. Ministry of the King in withdrawal, 15:21-39
  a) Healing of the demonized daughter, vv. 21-28
  b) Healings east of the Sea of Galilee, vv. 29-31
  c) Feeding of the four thousand, vv. 32-39
11. Allied hostility of Pharisees and Sadducees, 16:1-12
  a) Refusal of the requested sign from heaven, vv. 1-4
  b) Warning to the disciples about false teaching, vv. 5-12
G. Success with His subjects, vv. 16:13-20
  1. Testimony to His messiahship, vv. 13-16
  2. Victory revealed to His disciples, vv. 17-20

III. The Cross of the Messianic King, 16:21–27:66
  A. The cross and the King's subjects, 16:21–20:34
    1. The cross and the future glory, 16:21–17:20
      a) Revelation concerning the cross, 16:21-28
        (1) Cross for the King, vv. 21-23
        (2) Cross for His subjects, vv. 24-28
      b) Glorification of the King, 17:1-13
        (1) Account of the transfiguration, vv. 1-8
        (2) Suggestion of the impending cross, vv. 9-13
      c) Healing of the demonized boy, 17:14-20
        (1) Act of healing in power, vv. 14-18
        (2) Reason for the disciples' failure, vv. 19-20
    2. The cross and the demands of daily life, 17:22–19:22
      a) Renewed teaching of the coming cross, 17:22-23
      b) Payment of the temple tax, 17:24-27
      c) Practical instructions for life in the Kingdom, 18:1-35
        (1) Problem of greatness in the Kingdom, vv. 1-6
        (2) Warning concerning offences, vv. 7-14
        (3) Method of settling offences, vv. 15-20
        (4) Measure of mutual forgiveness, vv. 21-35
      d) Healing ministry in Perea, 19:1-2
      e) Pronouncements concerning divorce and marriage, 19:3-12
        (1) Answer to the Pharisees about divorce, vv. 3-9
        (2) Reply to the disciples about marriage, vv. 10-12
      f) Blessing of the little children, 19:13-15
      g) Revelation to the young man seeking eternal life, 19:16-22
    3. Subjects of the Kingdom, 19:23–20:34
      a) Entrance into the Kingdom, 19:23–20:34
      b) Teaching concerning position in the Kingdom, 19:27–20:16
        (1) Promises of reward to loyal subjects, 19:27-30
        (2) Parable of warning against self-seeking, 20:1-16
      c) Announcement of the impending cross, 20:17-19
      d) Selfish request for positions by James and John, 20:20-23

      e) Method of achieving greatness in the Kingdom, 20:24-28

      f) Healing of two blind men at Jericho, 20:29-34

B. Rejection by the Jewish leaders, 21:1—23:39

  1. Public offer of Himself as Messiah, 21:1-11

  2. Authoritative cleansing of the temple, 21:12-17

  3. Symbolic judgment on the fruitless fig tree, 21:18-22

  4. Consecutive attacks by various groups, 21:23—22:40

     a) Question concerning the King's authority, 21:23—22:14

      (1) Attack by the Sanhedrin muzzled, 21:23-27

      (2) Parables exposing the leaders, 21:28—22:14

        (*a*) Parable of the two sons, 21:28-32

        (*b*) Parable of the wicked husbandmen, 21:33-46

        (*c*) Parable of the royal marriage feast, 22:1-14

     b) Question concerning paying tribute to Caesar, 22:15-22

     c) Question concerning the resurrection, 22:23-33

     d) Question concerning the greatest commandment, 22:34-40

  5. The King's counterattack on the leaders, 22:41—23:39

     a) Question concerning Messiah's sonship, 22:41-46

     b) Public denunciation of the scribes and Pharisees, 23:1-39

      (1) Teaching concerning religious authority, vv. 1-12

      (2) Final woes upon the scribes and Pharisees, vv. 13-36

      (3) Sorrowing verdict upon Jerusalem, vv. 37-39

C. Revelation to the disciples about the future, 24:1—26:2

  1. Revelation concerning the near future, 24:1-2

  2. Revelation concerning the distant future, 24:3—25:46

     a) Revelation concerning Israel, 24:3-44

      (1) Portrayal of the future, vv. 3-31

        (*a*) General picture of the future, vv. 3-14

        (*b*) Details of the great tribulation, vv. 15-28

        (*c*) Return of the King in glory, vv. 29-31

      (2) Teaching in view of the future, vv. 32-44

> *b*) Parabolic revelation concerning Christendom, 24:45–25:30
>> (1) Parable of household responsibility, 24:45-51
>> (2) Parable of the waiting virgins, 25:1-13
>> (3) Parable of the talents, 25:14-30
> *c*) Revelation concerning the nations, 25:31-46
3. Revelation about the immediate future, 26:1-2

D. Passion of the King, 26:3–27:66
  1. Preparatory events, 26:3-16
    a) Plotting of the Jewish leaders, vv. 3-5
    b) Anointing for His burial at Bethany, vv. 6-13
    c) Bargain by Judas to betray Jesus, vv. 14-16
  2. Passover with His disciples, 26:17-29
    a) Preparation of the Passover, vv. 17-19
    b) Events at the Passover, vv. 20-29
      (1) Revelation of the betrayer, vv. 20-25
      (2) Institution of the Lord's Supper, vv. 26-29
  3. Warning on the way to Gethsemane, 26:30-35
  4. Scenes in the garden of Gethsemane, 26:36-56
    a) Seasons of prayer in Gethsemane, vv. 36-46
    b) Betrayal and arrest in Gethsemane, vv. 47-56
  5. Trials of Jesus, 26:57–27:31
    a) Appearances before the Jewish court, 26:57–27:2
      (1) Trial before the Sanhedrin at night, 26:57-68
      (2) Three denials by Peter, 26:69-75
      (3) Formal condemnation at dawn, 27:1-2
    b) Remorse and suicide of Judas, 27:3-10
    c) Appearance before the Roman governor, 27:11-26
    d) Mock coronation by the soldiers, 27:27-31
  6. Crucifixion and death of the King, 27:32-56
    a) Cross-bearer for Jesus, v. 32
    b) Mocking of the crucified King, vv. 33-44
    c) Events in connection with His death, vv. 45-56
  7. Entombment of the King, 27:57-66
    a) Burial in the new tomb of Joseph, vv. 27-61
    b) Sealing and guarding of the tomb, vv. 62-66

IV. Triumph of the King, 28:1-20
   A. Confirmation of His resurrection, vv. 1-10
   B. Failure of His enemies, vv. 11-15
   C. Commission by the empowered King, vv. 16-20

A BOOK LIST ON MATTHEW

Albright, W. F., and Mann, C. S. *Matthew*. The Anchor Bible. Garden City, New York: Doubleday, 1971.

A 198-page introduction, forming one-third of the volume, discusses the background problems in detail. Matthew is named as the probable author, since this identification seems most consistent with the Palestinian milieu before A.D. 70. The authors draw upon recent archaeological and critical studies. Prints the authors' translation, followed by notes and comments. Challenging but not always convincing. Shy on the supernatural.

Allen, Willoughby C. "A Critical and Exegetical Commentary on the Gospel According to S. Matthew." In *The International Critical Commentary*. 3d ed. Reprint. Edinburgh: T. & T. Clark, 1957.

An erudite work, most valuable for the advanced student in the study of sources for Matthew. Gives a verse-by-verse translation but presupposes a knowledge of Greek. It has been dubbed as committed to the proposition that Matthew is a by-product of Mark.

Argyle, A. W. "The Gospel According to Matthew." In *The Cambridge Bible Commentary on the New English Bible*. Cambridge: Cambridge U., 1963.

The New English Bible text is printed in sections, followed by brief comments which constitute little more than half of the volume. The meager comments reflect recent scholarly views.

Barclay, William. "The Gospel of Matthew." In *The Daily Study Bible*, vols. 1-2. Philadelphia: Westminster, 1956-57.

Divides the gospel into brief sections intended for daily study. The author follows his own translation; his comments "aim to make the results of modern scholarship available to the non-technical reader in a form that it does not require a theological education to understand." Word studies and refreshing insights abound, with a stress upon the relevance of the gospel for modern life. Liberal in spots.

Barnes, Albert. *Notes on the New Testament, Explanatory and Practical: Matthew and Mark*. Edited by Robert Frew. 1868. Reprint. Grand Rapids: Baker, 1962.

A reprint of a popular conservative commentary of the past century.

Broadus, John A. "Commentary on the Gospel of Matthew." In *An American Commentary.* 1887. Reprint. Philadelphia: Amer. Bapt. Pub. Soc., n.d.

One of the ablest American commentaries on Matthew from the past century and still valuable for the systematic interpretation of the gospel. It is the work of an accomplished conservative scholar.

Bruce, Alexander Balmain. "The Synoptic Gospels." In *The Expositor's Greek Testament,* vol. 1. Grand Rapids: Eerdmans, n.d.

Greek text. Provides introductory material on the synoptics in relation to each other and individually. The notes provide many illuminating insights for the Greek student. Due to its age, it does not reflect the latest insights concerning the Greek.

Carr, A. "The Gospel According to St. Matthew." In *Cambridge Greek Testament for Schools and Colleges.* Cambridge: Cambridge U., 1880.

Greek text. Prints the Greek text of Matthew in the Textus Receptus as edited by Scrivener. The introduction presents the old traditional view concerning Matthean authorship. The notes on the Greek text are selective, placing primary stress on the form and meaning of the original. Briefly alludes to historical matters.

Criswell, W. A. *Expository Notes on the Gospel of Matthew.* Grand Rapids: Zondervan, 1961.

A clear and concise running interpretation by a noted conservative Baptist minister. Views Matthew as the fitting connecting link between the Old and New Testaments. Critical problems are not dealt with. The section-by-section interpretation is adapted to the lay Christian reader.

Dietrich, Suzanne de. *The Layman's Bible Commentary,* vol. 16, *Matthew.* Translated by Donald G. Miller. Richmond, Va.: Knox, 1961.

The work of a scholarly Frenchwoman, largely confined to exposition of the text. The work reflects a spirit of deep devotion. The introduction is brief, giving primary attention to the features and structure of the gospel.

English, E. Schuyler. *Studies in the Gospel According to Matthew.* Grand Rapids: Zondervan, 1935.

A simple and precise interpretation of Matthew from a dispensational viewpoint. Originally prepared as a series of Sunday school lessons for *Revelation Magazine,* the volume presents a challenging study of the gospel for the average reader.

Erdman, Charles R. *The Gospel of Matthew.* Philadelphia: Westminster, 1948.

A well-outlined paragraph-by-paragraph interpretation by a noted conservative Presbyterian teacher and writer. Intended for the lay reader. His understanding of the Olivet Discourse is premillennial.

Fenton, J. C. *The Gospel of St. Matthew.* The Pelican Gospel Commentaries. Baltimore, Md.: Penguin, 1963.

A provocative liberal interpretation intended to bring out the meaning of the original for the modern reader. Gives attention to the theological concepts in the gospel, and reflects modern critical views.

Fieldhouse, Marvin L. "The Book of Matthew (in 84 Lessons)." In *The Missionary's Bible Commentary.* Nagano Ken, Japan: Oriental Bible Study Fellowship, n.d.

A stimulating conservative work by an independent thinker intended for group study of the gospel. The missionary author is deeply concerned to let the authoritative, inspired Word speak for itself and seeks to apply its message to daily life. Does not deal with introductory critical problems. Each lesson consists of an introduction to the section to be studied, expository notes, and a closing thought.

Filson, Floyd V. *A Commentary on the Gospel According to St. Matthew.* Harper's New Testament Commentaries. New York: Harper, 1960.

Contains a new translation by the author, printed section by section and followed by the commentary. This readable commentary is generally conservative in its critical approach, but often leaves unanswered some of the questions which are raised. Critical problems are cautiously dealt with in the introduction.

Gaebelein, A. C. *The Gospel of Matthew.* 2 vols. in 1. New York: Pubn. Office, Our Hope, 1910.

A thoroughly dispensational interpretation of Matthew. It contains many valuable insights into the mission and message of Jesus, in spite of its excessive dispensational stress.

Hendriksen, William. "Exposition of the Gospel According to Matthew." In *New Testament Commentary.* Grand Rapids: Baker, 1973.

A recent, monumental (1000 pages) exposition of Matthew by a mature scholar in the Reformed tradition. Offers a 100-page introduction to the synoptic problem and the gospel of Matthew. Gives the author's own translation, a detailed interpretation of the text, and a brief summary of each section. Amillennial in viewpoint. Deals with critical problems yet the material is readily understandable to the non-specialist.

Hobbs, Herschel H. *An Exposition of the Gospel of Matthew.* Grand Rapids: Baker, 1965.

A popular, sermonic exposition of Matthew by an articulate Baptist pastor. It seeks to unfold the meaning of the text and make it relevant to contemporary life. The author is free to state his own views.

Howard, Fred D. *The Gospel of Matthew.* Shield Bible Study Series. Grand Rapids: Baker, 1961.

An inexpensive, clearly outlined, concisely formulated guide for the study of Matthew in Bible schools and churches. Does not give space to critical problems. Conservative in viewpoint.

Johnson, Sherman E., and Buttrick, George A. "The Gospel According to St. Matthew." In *The Interpreter's Bible,* vol. 7. New York: Abingdon-Cokesbury, 1951.

A twofold approach to Matthew by two noted liberal scholars. The second part, the exposition by Buttrick, is much fuller than the section on exegesis by Johnson, and offers much material for sermonic purposes. The exegesis advocates some conclusions of radical form criticism.

Jones, Alexander. *The Gospel According to St. Matthew: A Text and Commentary for Students.* New York: Sheed & Ward, 1965.

Prints the Revised Standard Version text on the left-hand page and the author's concise comments on the right-hand page. This arrangement is intended to keep the scriptural text before the student. A brief but valuable interpretation by a noted contemporary Roman Catholic biblical scholar.

Lange, John Peter. "The Gospel According to Matthew." In Lange's *Commentary on the Holy Scriptures: Critical, Doctrinal, and Homiletical.* Translated from the German, and edited, by Philip Schaff. Reprint. Grand Rapids: Zondervan, n.d.

Following an introduction of 46 pages, each section is divided into three parts, exegetical and critical, doctrinal and ethical, and homiletical and practical. A wealth of information for those willing to dig into fine print. The approach is evangelical and conservative.

Lenski, R. C. H. *The Interpretation of St. Matthew's Gospel.* Columbus, Ohio: Wartburg, 1943.

A massive interpretation (1181 pages) by an accomplished conservative, amillennial, Lutheran scholar. The author gives his own literal translation, printed in small sections, and a thorough interpretation of the passage on the basis of the Greek. A work of abiding importance, readily useable by the non-Greek student.

Micklem, Philip A. *St. Matthew.* Westminster Commentaries. London: Methuen, 1917.

Prints the text of the English Revised Version at the beginning of each section and uses it as the basis for the comments. The commentary seeks to combine an "acceptance of critical principles with loyalty to the Catholic Faith." Questions the reality of demons.

Morgan, G. Campbell. *The Gospel According to Matthew.* New York: Revell, 1929.

The prince of biblical expositors covers the entire gospel in a series of seventy-three biblical expositions. This volume on Matthew is the best of his expository volumes on the four gospels. Does not deal with critical introductory problems. The volume requires careful and intent reading, and offers many rich spiritual insights into Matthew's gospel.

Morison, James. *A Practical Commentary on the Gospel According to St. Matthew.* 9th ed. London: Hodder & Stoughton, 1895.

The lengthy introduction covers critical problems and supports traditional Matthean authorship. This volume of some 650 closely printed pages offers a thorough interpretation by an accomplished conservative scholar of the previous century. It shows wide acquaintance with the scholarly work on the gospel to his day.

Plummer, Alfred. *An Exegetical Commentary on the Gospel According to S. Matthew.* Reprint. Grand Rapids: Eerdmans, n.d.

Long recognized as an outstanding commentary on Matthew (first published in 1909). It provides a scholarly handling of the critical problems and gives a balanced interpretation of the gospel, for the most part conservative. Does not accept apostolic authorship.

Robinson, Theodore H. "The Gospel of Matthew." In *The Moffatt New Testament Commentary.* 1927. Reprint. New York: Harper & Row, n.d.

A liberal commentary, printing the Moffatt translation, and comforming to the format and general viewpoint of the series to which it belongs. The treatment is suggestive but rather light, especially in sections that are parallel to Mark.

Stagg, Frank. "Matthew." In *The Broadman Bible Commentary,* vol. 8. Nashville: Broadman, 1969.

Prints the Revised Standard Version, but the interpretation is based on a careful study of the original. Seeks to combine a balanced combination of exegesis and exposition, while seeking to show the life-relatedness of the gospel. The author holds that the gospel was written to help the church find its way between Pharisaic legalism and the threat of antinomian libertinism, and holds that the answer lies in obedience to Christ who unites both Jew and Gentile into the new people of God. Outlines the gospel around the "five discourses" of Jesus. Liberal in spots.

Stanton, H. U. Weitbrecht. *The Gospel According to St. Matthew.* The
    Indian Church Commentaries. 1912. Reprint. London: Soc. for Pro-
    moting Christian Knowledge, 1919.

    A verse-by-verse interpretation of the gospel with constant reference
to the religious thought and life of India at the beginning of the twentieth century by a veteran missionary. The treatment, running to some
700 pages, is conservative in viewpoint.

Tasker, R. V. G. "The Gospel According to St. Matthew." In *The Tyndale
    New Testament Commentaries.* Grand Rapids: Eerdmans, 1961.

    A concise, non-technical interpretation of Matthew from a conserva-
tive viewpoint. The volume is devoted almost exclusively to interpretation, with few textual problems considered. The interpretative material
is often quite meager. It is well adapted to use by the general reader
who desires to get the over-all thrust of the gospel.

5

THE GOSPEL ACCORDING TO MARK

An Introduction to Mark

THE ANCIENT CHURCH paid less attention to the gospel of Mark, the shortest and simplest of our four gospels, than to Matthew or Luke. Its comparative neglect is accounted for by the fact that it was commonly regarded as a mere abbreviation of Matthew. The patristic writers seldom quoted Mark, since Matthew and Luke contain almost all of the material found in it, and they accorded preference in quotation to the more comprehensive gospels. Before the nineteenth century comparatively few commentaries were written on the second gospel.

The views of modern critical scholarship, however, have catapulted Mark into the limelight of scholarly interest and critical study. It has become the object of intensive and sustained study in modern times. It is no longer held to be an abridgment of a fuller account but is accepted as an independent work, complete in itself, written with a specific purpose, and eminently suited for an initial study of the gospel story.

The Authorship of the Second Gospel

The second gospel, like its companions, contains no statement of authorship. But the uniform tradition of the early church attributes it to Mark, the apostle Peter's attendant. The correctness of the traditional view concerning its authorship is seldom questioned today.

1. EXTERNAL EVIDENCE

The earliest direct witness to the second gospel and its origin is Papias (*c.* 70-150), bishop of Hierapolis, dating to the first half of the second century. Eusebius in his famous *Ecclesiastical History* quotes the testimony of Papias as follows:

> And the Elder [i.e., the elder John] used to say this: Mark, having become Peter's interpreter, wrote accurately as many things as he remembered, not, indeed, in order, of the things spoken and done by the Lord. For he neither heard the Lord nor did he follow Him, but afterwards, as I said, he followed Peter, who used to give his teachings according to the needs [i.e., of his hearers], but not as though he were making a connected account of the Lord's oracles. So then Mark made no mistake in thus recording some things as he remembered them, for he made it his one concern not to omit anything of the things he heard nor to falsify anything in them.[1]

Several significant assertions concerning the second gospel and its author are made in this ancient testimony, coming from the Roman province of Asia.

1. Mark had not been a personal follower of Jesus.
2. Mark was a companion of Peter and attended his preaching.
3. Mark recorded the things he heard from Peter accurately, but "not, indeed, in order."
4. Mark served as the "interpreter" of Peter's preaching. The intended meaning of "interpreter" (*hermēneutēs*) is not clear. It may mean "translator," and some scholars advocate this meaning. Thus Sloan thinks that "Peter could speak very little Greek" and that Mark "traveled with Peter and translated Peter's addresses and sermons into the Greek."[2] But the view that Peter, who came from bilingual Galilee, could not speak fluent, although unpolished, Greek is highly improbable. Zahn remarks:

> The idea that Mark performed the office of an interpreter, translating Peter's Aramaic discourses into Greek, or what is still more impossible, his Greek sermons into Latin, cannot be held by anyone having any knowledge at all of language conditions in the apostolic age.[3]

Baxter holds to this meaning of the term but views the situation quite differently:

> My own view is that Mark was the compiler-translator of records

---

1. Eusebius *Ecclesiastical History* 3. 39. 15. For the Greek text see Vincent Taylor, *The Gospel According to St. Mark*, pp. 1-2.
2. W. W. Sloan, *A Survey of the New Testament*, p. 15. See also Alfred Wikenhauser, *New Testament Introduction*, pp. 160-61.
3. Theodor Zahn, *Introduction to the New Testament*, 2:443.

already *written* by Peter, in *Aramaic*, many of them written at, or soon after, the actual times of the events and forming a kind of diary.[4]

In support of his view he appeals to the fact that Justin Martyr quoted Mark 3:17 as from the "Memoirs of Peter." But the view that Peter, the former fisherman, as a disciple in fellowship with Jesus, kept such a diary is questionable.

Others think that Mark was an "interpreter" in that he preserved and handed on what he had heard from Peter. Thus Lenski holds that "Mark became the interpreter of Peter to the church at large by putting Peter's words into writing in his Gospel."[5] There were many others who had heard Peter preach and knew what he preached without putting it into writing. In recording Peter's teaching Mark, as the disciple of Peter, explained it to a larger circle. Thus as Peter had treasured up and proclaimed the words of Jesus, "so Mark in his turn did the same for the treasured words of his venerated Rabbi, Peter."[6] "Explained" rather than "translated" seems the probable meaning.

It seems that the direct testimony of John "the elder" is confined to the first sentence quoted by Eusebius. The remainder of the quotation records the personal comment of Papias. But Papias represented himself as transmitting the Johannine tradition. Marxsen stamps the statement as "historically worthless" because he insists that this view of the gospel is inconsistent with the findings of form criticism.[7] But to reject this early tradition leaves us in total darkness, for we possess no earlier tradition and no later variant views. But Papias must have had some known connection with the Johannine tradition; otherwise his stories would have had no meaning. The fact that Eusebius, writing in A.D. 326, quoted Papias' explanation of the origin of Mark's gospel indicates that it commended itself to the judgment of the church. Eusebius apparently knew no other explanation, nor did he feel the need for further explanation. Yet Eusebius was not one to simply accept the tradition because of its antiquity. (He scornfully rejected Papias' views on the millennium.) He accepted the tradi-

4. J. Sidlow Baxter, *Explore the Book,* 5:220.
5. R. C. H. Lenski, *The Interpretation of St. Mark's and St. Luke's Gospels,* p. 9.
6. R. A. Cole, "The Gospel According to St. Mark," in *Tyndale New Testament Commentaries,* p. 36.
7. W. Marxsen, *Introduction to the New Testament,* p. 143.

tional explanation because it commended itself as authentic. The testimony reaches back to apostolic times.

It is obvious that the testimony of "the elder" in defense of Mark's gospel was given in answer to detractors. Questions were being raised about that gospel, its omissions, its failure to record things "in order," as well as the reliability of part of its contents. This implies that at the time these criticisms were being voiced there were other gospels with which it was being compared.

The answer of John the elder, and of Papias, to these criticisms was that the character of Mark's gospel and its limitations were due to its origin. It was in reality the record of the public testimony of the aged Peter. And Peter himself had not always presented his material in chronological order but had shaped it according to the needs of his hearers. This accounted for its omissions as well as its order. Mark had faithfully reproduced the testimony of Peter.

While the Papias tradition asserts that the main source behind the second gospel was the apostle Peter, it holds that its actual author was a person of second rank. This ascription of authorship "would have scarcely been invented for the pleasure of lessening the authority of this Gospel."[8] The only natural explanation is that it was based on known facts.

Other early witnesses support the statement of Papias. In his *Dialogue with Trypho,* Justin Martyr observes that the "Memoirs of Peter" related that Jesus applied the title "Boanerges" to the sons of Zebedee.[9] Since this information is given only in Mark (3:17), the quotation must be from the second gospel. A fragmentary Latin prologue to Mark's gospel, known as the *Anti-Marcionite Prologue* dated around A.D. 160-180, says, "Mark . . . was the interpreter of Peter. After the death of Peter himself he wrote down this same gospel in the regions of Italy."[10] This statement, while in agreement with the testimony of Papias, adds the further assertion that Mark's gospel was composed in Italy after Peter's death.

Irenaeus (*c.* 140-203), bishop of Lyons in Gaul, in *Against Heresies,* written around A.D. 185, says in a passage naming the writers of our four gospels:

8. A. Robert and A. Feuillet, *Introduction to the New Testament,* p. 216.
9. Justin Martyr *Dialogue with Trypho,* chap. 106.
10. For the Latin fragment and an English translation see V. Taylor, *The Gospel According to St. Mark,* p. 3.

> Now after the death [Gr. "exodus"] of these [i.e., Peter and Paul], Mark the disciple and interpreter of Peter, himself also transmitted to us in writing the things preached by Peter."[11]

The context speaks of the work of Peter and Paul in Rome. This testimony affirms that Mark wrote in Rome after the "exodus" of Peter and Paul. The context favors the view that by "exodus" Irenaeus means their "departure" in death, but scholars like Manson[12] who favor a date before the death of Peter hold that it refers to their "departure" from Rome. Either meaning is possible and other evidence must decide the issue.

Clement of Alexandria (*c.* A.D. 195) gives a somewhat different account in two statements preserved by Eusebius. In the work called *Hypotyposes* Clement is quoted as writing:

> When Peter had publicly preached the word in Rome and declared the gospel by the Spirit, those present, of whom there were many, besought Mark, as one who had followed him for a long time and remembered the things said, to record his words. Having done so, he delivered the Gospel to those who had made the request of him. When Peter learned of it, he neither forbade it nor encouraged it.[13]

But in another place Clement is quoted as saying that when Peter learned by a revelation from the Spirit what Mark had done, "he was pleased with the zeal of the men and ratified the writing for use in the churches."[14] It is very probable that Mark undertook the task at the urging of others; that he completed the task during the lifetime of Peter is less certain. The latter point is contrary to the testimony of Irenaeus and the *Anti-Marcionite Prologue* as well as the earlier testimony of Papias if his words "as he remembered them" are taken to mean Mark rather than Peter, as seems most natural.

Eusebius also quoted the testimony of Origen (*c.* A.D. 230) that Mark wrote the second gospel "as Peter guided him."[15] This makes Peter an active participant in its production. This assertion seems to be an embellishment of the early tradition intended to underline the apostolic sanction of this gospel.

11. Irenaeus *Against Heresies* 3. 1. 1.
12. W. T. Manson, *Studies in the Gospels and Epistles*, pp. 38-39.
13. Eusebius *Ecclesiastical History* 6. 14. 6.
14. Ibid., 2. 15. 2.
15. Ibid., 6. 25. 5.

Thus the external evidence concerning the authorship of the second gospel, as written by Mark, "the interpreter of Peter," goes back to the beginning of the second century. It was derived from the three centers of early Christianity: Asia, Rome (with Gaul), and Alexandria. The tradition is strengthened by the fact that there is no reason why the gospel would have been assigned to a minor character like Mark if he did not write it. The ancient caption of this gospel, *Kata Markon,* "according to Mark," likewise supports this uniform tradition (see pp. 47-48). It is perhaps our earliest witness to the authorship of the second gospel.

2. INTERNAL EVIDENCE.

The second gospel contains no explicit testimony concerning the identity of its author. Yet it is generally accepted that its contents do not disagree with external evidence. Certain features are consistent with its traditional association with Peter. Peter's connection with the writing of this gospel is not necessary for its interpretation, but certain features in it take on added interest if that connection is recognized.[16] For example, the addition of the two little words "and Peter" (16:7), found only in Mark, is then freighted with emotional overtones. The connection naturally accounts for the "eyewitness vividness" of many of Mark's episodes. It seems natural that Mark's use of "they" in introducing a story concerning Jesus represents Peter's "we" in reciting an event as the experience of one who had been a disciple of Jesus.[17] The inclusion of Aramaic expressions attributed to Jesus (5:41; 7:11, 34; 14:36), not found in the other gospels, may well be due to the fact that Mark recalled "vividly the tones of the Apostle in relating the Master's solemn words."[18] It has also been noted that this gospel omits incidents which might honor Peter—his walking on the water (Mt 14:28-31), the promise of the keys (Mt 16:17-19), the payment of the temple tribute (Mt 17:24-27)—but elaborates on events that were to his discredit (Mk 8:33; 9:5-6; 14:29-31, 66-72). Peter's traditional connection with this gospel is supported by the fact that it conforms to the outline of the gospel story as given by Peter in Acts 10:34-43.

16. A. T. Robertson, *Studies in Mark's Gospel,* pp. 38-43.
17. See 1:21, 29; 5:1, 38; 6:53-54; 8:22; 9:14, 30, 33; 10:32, 46; 11:1, 12, 15, 27; 14:18, 22, 26, 32.
18. Guy Kendall, *A Modern Introduction to the New Testament,* p. 17.

There is, however, no need to assume that when Mark commenced the writing of his gospel he deliberately restricted himself to a reproduction of Peter's preaching. As a youth Mark had heard the preaching of the apostles in Jerusalem. He was also familiar with the preaching of Paul and Barnabas (Ac 13:5-12; 15:39; Col 4:10-11). The Petrine preaching was, indeed, the main source upon which he drew, but he was well informed about Jesus before he became Peter's assistant.

We accept without hesitation the Marcan authorship of the second gospel. This view does justice to the early and strong external evidence concerning its authorship and is consistent with the internal features of the gospel.

THE AUTHOR OF THE SECOND GOSPEL

The identification of the Mark of Papias with the John Mark of the New Testament has been commonly assumed. Taylor remarks, "Today this view is held almost with complete unanimity."[19] But some objections to the identification have been raised. It is maintained that the name "Marcus" is far too common to allow the identification. It may be readily admitted that the name itself does not establish the validity of the identification. The identification is further questioned because it is not explicitly mentioned until the time of Jerome. It may be replied that the earlier writers took the identification for granted and felt no need to stress it. It has also been asserted that the writer could not have been from Jerusalem, since he apparently was unfamiliar with Palestinian geography. This claim has not been established and it has found little acceptance. The gospel contains nothing that is demonstrably inconsistent with a writer who was a resident of Jerusalem during his youth.

There is no evidence for another Marcus in the Roman church who had the close connection with Peter asserted by Papias and the New Testament. Nor is it evident why the church at Rome should be willing to sanction such a work by an otherwise entirely unknown Christian named Marcus when it was well known that Mark, the cousin of Barnabas (Col 4:10), had the close relations with Peter necessary to produce this gospel. The picture of the New Testament Mark agrees fully with the Papias tradition.

19. Taylor, p. 26.

The assertion of Papias that Mark was not himself a follower of Jesus agrees with the fact that the name of Mark never occurs in the gospels, although it is clear from Acts that John Mark was a resident in Jerusalem. That he was not personally associated with the public ministry of Jesus may have been due to his age at the time or to a lack of personal commitment to Christ.

It seems a natural assumption that the "young man" in Gethsemane (Mk 14:51-52) was Mark himself. It is the most reasonable explanation for the inclusion of this trifling incident which is otherwise quite irrelevant to the story. That Mark did not learn of this unimportant incident from Peter or the other apostles is evident from the fact that in the preceding verse it is recorded that "they all forsook him, and fled" (14:50). Obviously the writer knew about the incident because he had experienced it. It is best understood as "a bit of autobiography embodied in his Gospel"[20] mentioned to indicate his own brief connection with these stirring nocturnal events. This supposition fits all the details. Bickersteth remarks, "The action corresponds with what we know of his [Mark's] character, which appears to have been warm-hearted and earnest, but timid and impulsive."[21] This little incident seems to offer an accurate picture of the early life and character of Mark—impulsively eager to help but fleeing in sudden and complete recoil when unexpected danger looms.

This identification has been stamped as a "completely improbable conjecture."[22] But the rejection of the identification cannot be justly grounded in the remark of Papias that Mark "neither heard nor followed" Jesus, which simply means that Mark himself was not one of Jesus' acknowledged disciples. This brief contact with the horrible events of the closing hours of Jesus' life would naturally make a deep impression on his young soul. Morison indeed thinks that the incident marked "the vital turning point of his spiritual career."[23]

The traditional author of the second gospel is introduced in Acts as "John, whose surname was Mark" (12:12). "John" was a common

20. Manson, p. 35.
21. E. Bickersteth, "The Gospel According to St. Mark," in *The Pulpit Commentary*, 1:5.
22. Werner Georg Kümmel, *Introduction to the New Testament*, p. 69.
23. James Morison, *A Practical Commentary on the Gospel According to St. Mark*, p. xix.

Hebrew name, while "Mark" or "Marcus" was Latin. The use of such a Latin (or Greek) second name was quite common among Greek-speaking Jews. It is inaccurate to call him "John Mark," a combination which the New Testament never uses.

In Acts he is three times identified as bearing both names (12:12, 25; 15:37), twice as John (13:5, 13), and once as Mark (15:39). In the epistles he is always called Mark. The Mark of the epistles is apparently the "John Mark" of Acts because in the epistolary references (Col 4:10; Phile 24; 2 Ti 4:11; 1 Pe 5:13) he is always linked with the same people (Paul, Barnabas, Peter) as in Acts. Either name might be used according to circumstances. In Jewish circles he would appropriately be known as John, but in a Gentile environment he would be called by his Latin name. The fact that his Hebrew name is never used in the epistles shows that the Gentile world was his main sphere of activity.

Mark was the son of a widow whose spacious home in Jerusalem was a meeting place for believers during the early days of the church. When and how Mark was led to personal faith in Jesus Christ is not known. The influence of his pious mother and his contacts with the early Christians in his home were doubtless instrumental in leading him to a personal commitment. His contacts with his noted cousin, Barnabas (Col 4:10), doubtlessly exerted a deep influence on the young man. From Peter's reference to Mark as "my son" in 1 Peter 5:13 it has often been inferred that Mark was converted through his influence. Peter was a frequent visitor to Mark's home as evidenced by the servant girl's reaction to his voice (Ac 12:12-17). Certainly Mark was familiar with the preaching of Peter from early days.

When Barnabas and Saul returned to Antioch from Jerusalem, they took Mark with them (Ac 12:25). Apparently he remained in Antioch until the launching of the first missionary journey when Mark accompanied Barnabas and Saul as their attendant (13:5). For an unstated reason he left the missionary party at Perga and returned to Jerusalem (13:13). Paul felt that Mark's action was unjustified. He vigorously rejected Barnabas' proposal that Mark accompany them on the second journey. The resultant sharp disagreement over Mark led to the separation of Paul and Barnabas. Barnabas and his young cousin sailed to Cyprus, while Paul and Silas travelled through Syria and Cilicia (Ac 15:36-41).

Nothing further is heard of Mark until the time of Paul's first imprisonment in Rome. Paul included greetings from Mark in the letter to the Colossian church (4:10) as well as in the brief letter to Philemon (v. 24). In Philemon Paul included Mark among his fellow workers. Mark had regained Paul's full confidence and was actively collaborating with him. How long he had remained with Barnabas and where he rejoined Paul's work is not known.

When Paul left Rome after his release, Mark apparently remained in that city. Upon Peter's arrival in Rome, Mark joined him. In 1 Peter 5:13 Peter sent greetings to the churches in Asia Minor from the church in Babylon, apparently a cryptic designation for Rome, and added greetings from "Marcus my son." Whether or not Peter meant that Mark was his spiritual son, it does show the close and affectionate relationship between them. The letter apparently was written from Rome not long before Peter's martyrdom during the Neronian persecution.[24]

The last mention of Mark, chronologically, is in 2 Timothy 4:11. Paul requests Timothy to come to him and adds the illuminating order, "Take Mark, and bring him with thee; for he is profitable to me for the ministry." This parting glimpse of Mark shows him to be a valued servant who was willingly devoting his energies to the service of others. He always appears as a subordinate. "He knew how to be invaluable to those who filled the first rank in the service of the Church, and proved himself a true servant of the servants of God."[25]

The Place and Date of the Second Gospel

1. PLACE

The almost uniform testimony of the early witnesses is that Mark's gospel was written in Rome. Mark's presence with Peter in Rome finds confirmation in 1 Peter 5:13, if "Babylon" refers to Rome. The one exception to the traditional testimony is Chrysostom, who associated its composition with Egypt. But it would be incredible to accept the view of Chrysostom (A.D. 347-407) as more reliable *than*

---

24. Concerning the place and date of 1 Peter see Charles Bigg, "A Critical and Exegetical Commentary on the Epistles of St. Peter and St. Jude," in *International Critical Commentary*, pp. 67-80; J. N. D. Kelly, "A Commentary on the Epistles of Peter and of Jude," in *Harper's New Testament Commentaries*, pp. 26-34.
25. Henry Barclay Swete, *The Gospel According to St. Mark*, p. xx.

that of the earlier witnesses. His view seems to be based on a misunderstanding of an ambiguous statement of Eusebius concerning Mark's preaching in Alexandria.[26]

According to the testimony of Clement of Alexandria (see p. 85) this gospel was written in Rome at the request of Roman Christians and delivered to them upon its completion. The contents of the gospel support the view that Mark wrote for Gentile readers in general, and for Roman readers in particular. That the gospel was intended for non-Jewish readers seems evident from the fact that, in contrast to Matthew, "no mention is made of the Law or its connection with the New Covenant (cf. Mt 5, 17-19; 10, 5; 19, 9), little is said about the fulfilment of prophecy (citations made by Jesus: 7, 6; 9, 12; 10, 4ff; 11, 17; 12, 10. 24; 14, 21. 27; made by Mark: 1, 2ff; 14, 49; 15, 28?), or the attack made by Jesus against the scribes (12, 38-40)."[27] Mark carefully explains Jewish customs and terms (cf. 7:3-4; 12:42; 14:12) and translates Aramaic words and sentences whenever they are introduced (cf. 3:17; 5:41; 7:11, 34; 14:36; 15:22, 34). His remark that the Mount of Olives was "over against the temple" (13:3) would be quite superfluous for Jewish readers. Mark uses a number of Latin terms in preference to their Greek equivalents, apparently because they would be more familiar to his readers (cf. 6:27; 7:4; 12:14, 42; 15:15, 16, 39). This observation is most naturally taken as pointing to a Roman readership. A Roman origin seems clearly suggested by the fact that Mark alone identifies Simon of Cyrene as the father of Alexander and Rufus (15:21). This human-interest touch suggests that they were well known to the readers. Romans 16:13 indicates that a certain Rufus was a member of the church at Rome. The common identification of this Rufus with the one in Mark 15:21 is consistent with the traditional origin of Mark. In further support of the Roman destination of Mark, Scroggie observes:

> We must add the general tone of this Gospel, which would be calculated to appeal especially to the Roman mind, as Matthew's does to the Hebrew, and Luke's to the Greek. At any rate, in Rome it 'had a powerful environment in which to take root.'[28]

26. Eusebius *Ecclesiastical History* 2. 16. 1.
27. Robert and Feuillet, p. 218.
28. W. Graham Scroggie, *A Guide to the Gospels*, p. 169.

There seems to be nothing in this gospel which specifically forbids the view that it was written in Rome. This is the most tenable view and is generally accepted today.

2. DATE

The traditional testimony concerning the dating of Mark is divided. Irenaeus, according to the more natural meaning of his testimony, placed it after the death of Peter and Paul. This dating is supported by the *Anti-Marcionite Prologue.* The testimony of Papias is not explicit on this point, but he is generally held to support the position of Irenaeus, since Irenaeus seems to have drawn his testimony from Papias. But Clement of Alexandria and Origen, on the other hand, placed the composition of the gospel during the lifetime of Peter. The latter view makes possible a much wider range in the proposed dating of the gospel.

Robertson feels that "these contradictory traditions leave us free to settle the date of Mark's Gospel apart from the stories in Irenaeus and Clement of Alexandria."[29] Accordingly, the suggested dates for Mark have varied greatly, from A.D. 44 to 130.[30] A. B. Bruce remarks that "the endless diversity of opinion means that the whole matter belongs sharply to the region of conjecture."[31]

Scholars who date the gospel during the lifetime of Peter advocate "the fifties or late forties."[32] That view assumes that Irenaeus' reference to Peter's "exodus" means not his death but his departure from the place where Mark was. This would bring the testimony of Irenaeus into agreement with that of Clement. But it must reject the declaration of the *Anti-Marcionite Prologue.* Such an early date is especially attractive to those who are firmly committed to the priority of Mark's gospel among the synoptics. It opens up the probability of an early date for the gospel of Luke. But such an early date naturally implies a non-Roman origin for Mark's gospel, since Peter apparently did not come to Rome until around A.D. 63. Any date before A.D. 63 thus labors under the burden of accounting for the almost uniform tradition of a Roman origin for Mark's gospel.

29. Robertson, p. 14.
30. See James Moffatt, *An Introduction to the Literature of the New Testament,* p. 213 for a list of authors and dates.
31. Alexander Balmain Bruce, "The Synoptic Gospels," in *The Expositor's Greek Testament,* 1:35.
32. Robert H. Gundry, *A Survey of the New Testament,* p. 81.

If we accept the view of Irenaeus that Mark wrote after the death of Peter, the earliest date for the gospel is the latter half of A.D. 64, the earliest date for the martyrdom of Peter during the Neronian persecution. Thus the gospel has generally been dated between A.D. 65 and 68. Taylor holds that "there is most to be said for the date 65-67."[33] So also Cranfield.[34]

Some scholars advocate a date after A.D. 70.[35] It is held that such a date is necessary to allow time for the church's development of the gospel tradition which was embodied in this gospel.[36] Such an argument has weight only for those who hold that the writer of this gospel simply collected the developing traditions of the early church concerning Jesus. In support of a late date it has been asserted that "the apocalyptic teaching of Mk. xiii, in its present form, suggests an adulteration of Jesus' teaching far beyond that which might be expected of Peter."[37] But this is simply a subjective evaluation based on what is thought that Jesus could or could not have said. No argument as to the date of the gospel can be drawn from Christ's eschatological discourse given in chapter 13 unless we deny Christ's ability to predict the future.

Guthrie points out that the conflict concerning the date in the traditional testimony may be brought into harmony under the assumption that "Mark began his Gospel before and completed it after Peter's death; a suggestion which merits more consideration than it generally receives."[38] Lange, indeed, asserts that there is no contradiction between the statements of Irenaeus and Clement, "as Irenaeus refers not to the commencement, but to the close of its composition."[39] Martindale accepts this reconciliation and thinks that the gospel was completed before Peter's death but was not officially published until after his death in A.D. 64.[40] If we can accept this proposed harmonization of the traditional testimony, we arrive at

33. Taylor, p. 32.
34. C. E. B. Cranfield, "The Gospel According to Saint Mark," in *Cambridge Greek Testament Commentary*, p. 8.
35. B. Harvie Branscomb, "The Gospel of Mark," in *The Moffatt New Testament Commentary*, p. xxxi; Ernest Findlay Scott, *The Literature of the New Testament*, pp. 56-57.
36. D. E. Nineham, "The Gospel of St. Mark," in *The Pelican Gospel Commentaries*, p. 42.
37. Richard Heard, *An Introduction to the New Testament*, p. 56.
38. Donald Guthrie, *New Testament Introduction*, p. 73.
39. John Peter Lange, "The Gospel According to Mark," in *Commentary on the Holy Scriptures: Mark-Luke*, p. 9.
40. C. C. Martindale, *The Gospel According to Saint Mark*, p. xiii.

a fairly specific date for the gospel of Mark. Since Peter was martyred during the Neronian persecution, the earliest possible date would be the latter part of A.D. 64, or in the following year. We suggest a date between the latter part of A.D. 64 and 65 as most probable for the publication of the gospel of Mark.

THE PURPOSE OF THE SECOND GOSPEL

Like the gospel of Matthew, the second gospel contains no statement of purpose. Conclusions concerning its purpose must be based upon an evaluation of its contents and assumed historical setting. Recent studies have resulted in widely differing assessments.[41]

The gospel of Mark is not a biography in the modern sense of the term. It is a historical narrative concerning the person and work of Jesus Christ as the "good news" of salvation. His story constitutes the very heart of Christianity's unique message. Mark introduces Jesus Christ in His official and public career as the busy Servant of the Lord. His initial identification of Jesus as "the Son of God" (1:1) underlines the basic truth that His mighty ministry must be viewed in the light of His unique personality. The busy Servant of the Lord was in truth the Son of God. What He did proved who He was. What He wrought authenticated what He taught. Mark's gospel "presents the history of Christ as the working, manifestation, and influence of the God-man."[42]

As the Son of God this Servant of the Lord revealed His power over the visible and the invisible world. Mark makes few personal comments in recounting the story of Jesus' amazing deeds and arresting teaching. He lets the record produce its own witness to His unique and commanding personality. His mighty and beneficent ministry proclaimed the fact that in Him the kingdom of God was at hand (1:15). Mark's purpose was not merely to tell the story of a matchless religious teacher but to proclaim Jesus Christ as the saving event announced in the Hebrew prophets. His purpose was basically evangelistic, to win converts to the Christian faith. Jesus Christ fully merited being accepted and served as Saviour and Lord.

Mark's account portrays the attracting as well as the repelling

41. For a summary of recent views see Thien An N. Vo, "Interpretation of Mark's Gospel in the Last Two Decades," in *Studia Biblica et Theologica*, 2:37-62.
42. Lange, p. 3.

influence of this mighty Servant of the Lord. Even as the common people thronged Him, the shadow of unbelief and open hostility began to cloud his ministry. What He did as revealing His identity aroused unbelief which deepened into mortal hatred. He was misunderstood, attacked, and rejected by the very people He came to serve and to save.

The hostility against Jesus was initiated and largely led by the religious leaders. It arose when He did not fulfil their expectations concerning the Messiah, which centered on His anticipated glorious rule. The Messianic hope had become intimately entwined with the political and national yearnings of the Jewish people. The prevailing conception practically eliminated any realistic understanding of the Messiah's spiritual saving ministry. Jesus therefore avoided using the term Messiah in reference to Himself. He rather spoke of His identity as the Son of Man and of His coming suffering and death in terms of the Suffering Servant of the Lord. His use of the term Son of Man half concealed and half revealed His identity as the personal Messiah. He thus avoided forcing the people to make a decision concerning His identity as Messiah until He made clear His understanding of the Messianic office. His redemptive mission was inseparably connected with His death and resurrection, events prominent in the gospels. Mark's picture of Jesus Christ is in harmony with the declared purpose of Jesus that "the Son of man came not to be ministered unto, but to minister, and to give his life a ransom for many" (10:45).

The current Messianic concepts did not include the dimension of deity which Christ's ministry clearly demonstrated. It is clear that Jesus understood and used the designation "the Son of man" in the light of Daniel 7:13-14. The prophetic picture conveyed superhuman connotations, depicting One who came with clouds symbolizing deity to exercise everlasting world dominion. The title thus had Messianic implications but the aspect of deity in it was not recognized in current views regarding the Messiah. John 12:34 shows that the crowds in Jerusalem understood Jesus' use of it as a Messianic claim, but they were not able to reconcile their conception of the eternally abiding Messiah with Jesus' reference to death. When at His trial Jesus used the term, with its implied claim to being the peer of God, in His reply to the high priest, the Sanhedrin rejected His claim and condemned

Him for blasphemy (Mk 14:61-64). The true dignity of the Son of man can be fully appreciated only in the light of the fact that He, as Son of God, voluntarily accepted the cross.

The key to Mark's portrayal of the person and work of Jesus is the deliberate contrast drawn between Jesus' personal dignity as the incarnate Son of God and the suffering and rejection which He voluntarily accepted. The portrait contains a remarkable blend of matchless strength and amazing submission. It depicts the achievement of glorious victory through apparent defeat.

In 1901 William Wrede in his book *Das Messiasgeheimnis in den Evangelien* put forth the hypothesis that Jesus' injunctions to silence in Mark (e.g., 5:43; 7:36; 8:30; 9:9) were editorial and unhistorical. They were a literary device, which Mark adopted from the views of the early church. He used it to make it appear that Jesus taught His disciples in private that He was the Messiah, although He actually did not represent Himself as the Messiah.[43] By inventing the "messianic secret" Mark removed a source of embarrassment for the theology of the church by explaining why Jesus was not more generally recognized as Messiah during His lifetime.

Wrede's evaluation of the Marcan account can be viewed only as due to "an illegitimate scepticism regarding the accuracy of reporting in the gospels."[44] Tasker stamps this attack upon the veracity of the gospels as "one of the more perverse features of a certain type of modern Gospel criticism."[45] Wrede's criticism of the Marcan record has strongly influenced gospel studies. It has served to bring into clear prominence the fact that Jesus was reluctant to publicly declare Himself as the Messiah, and He did not sanction noisy acclamation of His Messianic identity by others. But Stonehouse in his discussion of the disclosure of the Messiahship in Mark has shown that the historical account in the gospels has a more natural explanation than the hypothesis of Wrede.[46] In view of the fact that our Lord's own conception of the Messiahship was radically different from that which a public use of the term would suggest to the people, it is understandable that His own explicit claims to Messiahship, at least in public,

43. William Wrede, *The Messianic Secret*, trans. J. C. C. Grieg.
44. Gundry, p. 80.
45. R. V. G. Tasker, "The Gospel According to St. Matthew," in *The Tyndale New Testament Commentaries*, p. 126.
46. Ned B. Stonehouse, *The Witness of Matthew and Mark to Christ*, pp. 50-85.

were made indirectly and with a certain amount of reserve. The Marcan account is best understood as reflecting the historical reality.

Mark's picture of the Lord as the Suffering Servant was a timely message for the suffering church.[47] It was necessary that the church recognize in Him the pattern for its discipleship as well as its salvation. Jesus clearly taught His disciples that the cross was not only for Him, the Messiah, but was also demanded of the Messianic community (8:34-38). The Roman believers who read Mark's gospel, experiencing severe suffering and martyrdom for their Lord, could draw inspiration and courage from the example of their victorious Lord. The Marcan portrait of the Suffering Servant challenged them to find in Him the power to endure and to remain faithful to Him even unto death, if need be. His victory assured them that their cause was not hopeless. This gospel resounded His invitation, "Follow me."

THE CHARACTERISTICS OF THE SECOND GOSPEL

1. BREVITY

Mark is the shortest of the four gospels, being only two-thirds as long as Luke. Its comparative brevity is partly due to Mark's omission of the nativity account as well as the genealogy. (In presenting the story of the Servant of the Lord he did not need to relate His birth or ancestry.) In addition, Mark eliminated all but two of Jesus' long discourses (4:1-34; 13:3-37), and these are considerably shorter than the corresponding sections in Matthew.

2. ACTION

The gospel of Mark is characteristically a book of action. It moves at a breathless pace, portraying Jesus as incessantly active. His work was continuous, persistent, and strenuous; He performed all of His work with dispatch. The Greek adverb *euthus*, translated "immediately, straightway," occurs more often in Mark than in the other three gospels together. He makes frequent use of "and" to tie one event to another. Only Mark records that Jesus was too busy to eat (3:20; 6:31). Repeatedly the crowds jostled Him with their de-

---

47. William L. Lane, "The Gospel According to Mark," in *New International Commentary on the New Testament*, pp. 12-17. For a different proposal concerning the setting and purpose of Mark's gospel see Ralph Martin, *Mark: Evangelist and Theologian*, pp. 156-62.

mands. It has been remarked, "To read this Gospel at a single sitting
is to feel hemmed in by crowds, wearied by their demands, besieged
by the attacks of demons."[48] The miracles of Jesus occupy a prominent place in the record. Eighteen miracles are recorded, two of
which are mentioned only in this gospel (7:31-37; 8:22-26). Mark's
gospel devotes proportionately more space to Christ's miracles than
the other gospels. Mark records comparatively little of Jesus' teaching. He repeatedly mentions the fact that He taught without recording what He taught (1:21, 39; 2:2, 13; 6:2, 6, 34; 10:1; 12:35).
His teaching ministry was an important part of His work as the
Servant of the Lord. Mark does record numerous fragments of discourses that sprang out of His controversies with the religious leaders
(cf. 2:8-11, 17, 19-22, 25-28; 3:23-30; 7:6-23; 10:2-12; 12:1-11, 38-
40). Yet they form an integral part of the event being narrated.

3. VIVIDNESS

This gospel is characterized by the vividness and fullness of its
narratives. Many events which are related in all three synoptics are
told in greatest detail by Mark. These vivid accounts give the impression of having been related by an eyewitness. They contain those
extra touches which suggest the oral reminiscences of a personal ob-
server.

The language is simpler than that of Matthew and Luke. It is
characterized by a roughness of style, "revealed by such things as
broken sentence structure (2:10; 11:32), abundant use of the historical present intermingled with past tenses, parenthetical remarks
(3:30; 7:19), and colloquialisms such as would be expected in popular speech."[49] In many places he uses two expressions when one
would suffice (cf. 1:35; 2:4; 4:5; 9:2; 11:1; 13:1, 19, 35; 14:61).

4. REALISM

Mark records his story with remarkable candor and realism. He
paints no halo over the disciples but frankly records the dullness
which they occasionally displayed (4:13; 6:52; 8:17, 21; 9:10, 32).
He does not withhold the fact that they had even dared to criticize

48. Gerard S. Sloyan, "The Gospel of St. Mark," in *New Testament Reading Guide*,
     p. 7.
49. Everett F. Harrison, *Introduction to the New Testament*, p. 188.

Jesus (4:38; 5:31). The concern of Jesus' family about His mental health is also told with undisguised frankness (3:21, 31-35).

This gospel also portrays Jesus' human reactions and emotions. Hunter remarks, "Mark shows us Jesus, as no other evangelist does, in all His gracious humanity."[50] He mentions Jesus' compassion (1:41; 6:34; 8:2), His sighs (7:34; 8:12), His hunger and weariness (4:38; 6:31; 11:12), His distress and sorrow (14:33-34). He notes His sweeping gaze (3:5, 34; 5:32; 10:23; 11:11), the touch of His hand (1:31, 41; 7:33; 9:27), His warm interest in little children (9:36; 10:14-16). He refers to His anger and displeasure (1:43; 3:5; 9:16; 10:14). Only Mark records how Jesus, on the last journey to Jerusalem, resolutely went before His disciples amid a prevailing feeling of apprehension (10:32). If Mark insists upon the uniqueness of Jesus as the Son of God, he also pictures Him as a sympathetic man who freely mingled with men and shared their feelings, and sufferings. The common people were drawn to Him and heard Him gladly (12:37). Mark takes note of the varied reactions of people to Jesus. They expressed amazement (1:27; 2:12), criticism (2:7), fear (4:41), astonishment (1:22; 6:2; 7:37), as well as bitter hatred (14:1).

Only Mark records that Jesus was known in Nazareth as "the carpenter" (6:3), a comment which throws light upon the obscure years before His public ministry. In several passages Mark notes that Jesus withdrew in the midst of His busy ministry, either to escape His enemies or to refresh His soul through prayer (1:35, 45; 3:7; 6:30-32; 7:24; 8:27; 9:2; 11:11, 19).

5. THEOLOGICAL CONCEPTS

The basic theological concepts in this gospel are those which have characterized the faith of the Christian community from the very first. Its high Christology is thrust upon the reader with the opening identification of Jesus Christ as "the Son of God" (1:1). This assertion concerning His unique nature is shown to be confirmed by the testimony of the Father (1:11; 9:7), by demons (3:11; 5:7), by Jesus Himself (13:32; 14:61-62), and by the centurion who supervised the crucifixion (15:39). This supernatural element manifested itself in His authoritative teaching as well as His miraculous deeds,

---

50. A. M. Hunter, *Introducing the New Testament*, p. 39.

which were almost always performed to meet some specific human need. But Mark stresses Jesus' insistence that the demons not reveal His identity (1:25, 34; 3:12) and the secrecy which He imposed on those whom He healed (1:44; 5:43; 7:36; 8:26). Following Peter's confession (8:29), Jesus charged the disciples not to reveal it to others (8:29-30).

Jesus' insistence upon secrecy and silence was probably due to the prevalence of inadequate and misleading views concerning the Messiah among the Jews. He preferred not to use the title "the Messiah" of Himself because in the thinking of the people the term had become overlaid with connotations that were inimical to His saving mission. In non-Jewish locations (5:19) the demand for secrecy was not insisted upon. Jesus preferred to speak of Himself as "the Son of man," a title found in fourteen passages in this gospel. It carried few undesirable implications in the thinking of the people. Jesus joined it to the concept of the Suffering Servant in the prophet Isaiah. Because of His identity as Son of man He claimed the right to forgive sins (2:10) and to exercise authority as "the Lord of the Sabbath" (2:28). He announced that with His appearing the Kingdom of God was at hand (1:15). In the face of His rejection by the religious leaders He revealed that He would ultimately return in power and glory (9:38; 13:26; 14:62). The fulfillment of His Messianic mission, however, demanded that He first suffer all the things concerning Him foretold by the prophets (8:31; 9:31; 10:33, 45). The passion of our Lord is prominent in this gospel. Two-fifths of its contents are devoted to Jesus' journey to Jerusalem and the events connected with His death and resurrection.

6. GENTILE INTEREST

The second gospel is well suited for Gentile readers. It does not have the strong Jewish-Christian coloring which characterizes Matthew. It does not presuppose a comprehensive knowledge of the Old Testament on the part of its readers. Mark quotes only one Old Testament passage (1:2-3; the quotation in 15:28 is generally omitted as lacking manuscript authority). But Mark notes that Jesus quoted the Old Testament frequently.

Mark's account of the sending out of the Twelve does not mention the prohibition concerning the Samaritans and Gentiles (6:7-11; cf.

Mt 10:5-6). According to Mark's record of Christ's eschatological discourse, the gospel was to be preached to all nations (13:10). Jesus cleansed the Temple to preserve it as "a house of prayer for all the nations" (11:17, NASB). The author of this gospel had learned well the truth that the gospel of Jesus Christ is for all mankind. It is a gospel well suited to appeal to the Roman mind.

7. ORDER OF MATERIAL

It was the testimony of Papias that Mark wrote "accurately" but "not in order." Yet it is commonly accepted today that the material in Mark is more nearly chronological in order than the material in Matthew. Examination of Mark's gospel does not reveal the groupings seen in Matthew; it is more nearly an "unhalting succession of astonishing doings. Mark is the camera-man of the four Gospel-writers, giving us shot after shot of unforgettable scenes.[51] But some grouping is evident. The events in Mark 2:1–3:6 were apparently grouped together by Mark because all of them refer to Jesus' controversies with the scribes and Pharisees.

Obviously the statement of Papias was prompted by a comparison of Mark's order of events with that found in other gospels. Plummer remarks:

> He is evidently contrasting Mark with some other Gospel which he regards as a model, and there is little doubt that the model Gospel is the Fourth. . . . If the Fourth Gospel is written "in order," the Second Gospel is not so written. In this way we get an intelligible meaning for the Presbyter's criticism.[52]

8. ENDING

There is serious manuscript confusion about the ending of Mark. This confusion, centering around 16:9-20 of our canonical gospel, is one of the major textual problems of the New Testament.

The manuscripts show three endings for this gospel. The vast majority of the Greek manuscripts and lectionaries, as well as various ancient versions, contain 16:9-20, known as the "long ending." Tatian used those verses in compiling his *Diatessaron* (c. A.D. 175), and

---

51. Baxter, 5:190.
52. Alfred Plummer, "The Gospel According to St. Mark," in *Cambridge Greek Testament*, p. xxiv.

Irenaeus (*c.* 180) quoted verse 19 as being found at the end of Mark. Whether or not they are accepted as the original ending of the gospel of Mark, these verses form an early and historically credible account of the post-resurrection period.

Over against the voluminous evidence in favor of the long ending stands strong evidence against it. The great uncial manuscripts Aleph and B, both dating from the fourth century, end with verse 8. The scribe of B, contrary to his usual practice, left a blank column at the end with the words "according to Mark." This probably means that he knew of a longer ending but his copy ended with verse 8. Cursive 2386, of the twelfth century, also ends with verse 8. The longer ending is likewise absent in the Sinaitic Old Syriac and in most copies of the Armenian and the Ethiopic versions. A number of cursives include verses 9-20 but add a note expressing uncertainty concerning them. Four uncial manuscripts, dating from the sixth to the eighth or ninth centuries, a cursive manuscript from the thirteenth century, as well as manuscripts in the Sahidic, Ethiopic, Harklean Syriac, and the earliest Bohairic copies have two endings. A shorter ending, following verse 8, reads:

> But they reported briefly to Peter and those with him all that they had been told. And after this, Jesus himself sent out by means of them, from east to west, the sacred and imperishable proclamation of eternal salvation (RSV).

This so-called short ending is followed by verses 9-20. There can be no doubt that this short ending is not original but was a scribal addition prompted by an abrupt ending at verse 8. It was added because the account concluding at verse 8 was felt to be incomplete.

The first known Christian writer to express doubts concerning the long ending was Eusebius of Caesarea (*c.* A.D. 265-340). In his work *Questions and Solutions Concerning the Passion and Resurrection of the Saviour* he remarks that nearly all of the copies of the gospel according to Mark terminated at verse 8. Jerome, writing from Bethlehem in A.D. 406 or 407, made a statement to the same effect. Victor of Antioch (fifth century), the first known commentator on Mark, repeated the statement of Eusebius, and added comments on the longer ending because he found it in very many copies. An Armenian manuscript of the gospels written in A.D. 986 contains a note that

Mark 16:9-20 was "of the presbyter Ariston." This statement of authorship is much too late to be of any authority, but it does bear winess to the view of the scribe that these verses were not from the hand of Mark.

Thus the external evidence concerning the ending of Mark is sharply divided. Evaluations of the internal evidence have likewise resulted in opposing pronouncements.

It is commonly accepted today that the phenomena displayed in these verses indicate a non-Marcan origin. Hort summarizes this unfavorable evidence as follows:

> It does not join to the end of 8, the change of subject being extremely abrupt. The style is wholly unlike that of Mark; we have here not a narrative, but a summary or epitome of events after the Resurrection, covering in a few lines a considerable period: and the writer shews a strong desire to 'point a moral', which is not in the least characteristic of Mark.[53]

But other students, while aware of the difficulties, hold that Mark 16:9-20 is part of the original.[54] They admit that there is a marked difference in style and manner of presentation between these verses and the remainder of the gospel. They hold, however, that the verses are consistent with the writer's special purpose of pointing out the successive steps by which the unwillingness of the apostles to accept the fact of the resurrection was subdued in preparing them for the reception and execution of the Great Commission. Proponents of their authenticity point out that these verses contain some material not found in the other gospels. The fact that there are some apparent discrepancies favors Marcan authorship, for a later compiler would avoid such differences. Thus equally conscientious students differ widely in their evaluation of the actual phenomena. The majority of modern scholars feel that the combined force of the external and internal evidence shuts out the conclusion that the "long ending" is the original conclusion of the gospel of Mark. The "short ending" is obviously unauthentic.

53. A. F. Hort, *The Gospel According to St. Mark*, p. 199. See the full discussion in Brooke Foss Westcott and Fenton John Anthony Hort, *The New Testament in the Original Greek*, vol. 2, appendix, pp. 29-51.
54. John W. Burgon, *The Last Twelve Verses of the Gospel According to S. Mark;* Morison, pp. 446-49, 463-70; Samuel M. Zwemer, *Into All the World*, chap. 5; Lenski, pp. 464-79; Edward F. Hills, *The King James Version Defended!*, pp. 102-13.

Acceptance of the conclusion that the long ending was not written by Mark leaves open two alternative positions: 1) that the gospel, terminating with verse 8, is incomplete; 2) that Mark intended to conclude the gospel with verse 8. Those who accept the former view advance varied conjectures to explain its incompleteness. In the very nature of the case such conjectures cannot be confirmed.

An increasing number of modern scholars incline to the view that Mark intentionally terminated his gospel at verse 8.[55] It is held that such an abrupt ending is consistent with Mark's abrupt style throughout and that this view explains the origin of both the longer and the shorter endings as scribal attempts to provide an acceptable conclusion for what they felt was an incomplete account. There is evidence that an abrupt ending at verse 8 is stylistically possible. The serious objection to this view is that Mark would thus end his story without mentioning any personal appearances of the risen Christ. It leaves unfulfilled the promise of His appearing to His disciples given in verse 7. The existence of two different endings in the manuscripts testifies to the strong conviction held throughout the course of Christian history that to end the gospel at verse 8 is to leave it incomplete.

None of the views proposed to explain the complex phenomena concerning the end of Mark's gospel is without its difficulties. No *mutually* satisfactory solution to the problem has been devised.

An Outline of Mark

Although the gospel of Mark consists largely of a succession of events, it is most readily organized in terms of the geography of Jesus' ministry. It is best to follow this geographical arrangement of the material in an outline. After the introductory section, the material is geographically grouped—Galilee, Galilee and surrounding areas, journey to Jerusalem, Jerusalem.

The theme of the gospel may be stated as "The Servant of Jehovah."

(This outline is reproduced from the author's volume *Mark: A Portrait of The Servant*, pp. 20-23.)

---

55. See the references in Kümmel, pp. 71-72. For a full presentation of this view see Ned Bernard Stonehouse, *The Witness of Matthew and Mark to Christ*, chap. 4.

I. Coming of the Servant, 1:1-13
   A. Title of the book, v. 1
   B. Ministry of the baptist, vv. 2-8
   C. Baptism of Jesus, vv. 9-11
   D. Temptation by Satan, vv. 12-13

II. Ministry of the Servant, 1:14—13:37
   A. Ministry in Galilee, 1:14—4:34
      1. Summary of the preaching, 1:14-15
      2. Call to four fishermen, 1:16-20
      3. Ministry in Capernaum, 1:21-34
         a) Excitement in the synagogue, vv. 21-28
         b) Healing of Peter's mother-in-law, vv. 29-31
         c) Healing ministry at sundown, vv. 32-34
      4. Tour of Galilee, 1:35-45
         a) Departure from Capernaum, vv. 35-39
         b) Cleansing of a leper, vv. 40-45
      5. Conflicts with the scribes, 2:1—3:6
         a) Paralytic forgiven and healed, 2:1-12
         b) Call of Levi and his feast, 2:13-17
         c) Question about fasting, 2:18-22
         d) Controversies about Sabbath observance, 2:23—3:6
            (1) Plucking of grain on the Sabbath, 2:23-28
            (2) Man with the withered hand, 3:1-6
      6. Ministry to the multitudes, 3:7-12
      7. Appointment of the twelve, 3:13-19*a*
      8. Mounting opposition to Jesus, 3:19*b*-35
         a) Anxiety of His friends, 19*b*-21
         b) Charge of collusion with Beelzebub, vv. 22-30
         c) Identity of His true kindred, vv. 31-35
      9. Parabolic teaching to the crowd, 4:1-34
         a) Setting for the teaching, vv. 1-2
         b) Content of the teaching, vv. 3-32
             (1) Parable of the sower, vv. 3-20
            (2) Responsibility of the hearers, vv. 21-25
            (3) Parable of the seed growing, vv. 26-29
            (4) Parable of the mustard seed, vv. 30-32
         c) Summary of the parabolic section, vv. 33-34

B. Withdrawals from Galilee, 4:35–9:50
    1. First withdrawal and return, 4:35–6:29
      a) Stilling of the tempest, 4:35-41
      b) Cure of the Gerasene demoniac, 5:1-20
      c) Two miracles upon returning, 5:21-43
        (1) Plea of Jairus, vv. 21-24
        (2) Woman with the flow of blood, vv. 25-34
        (3) Raising of Jairus' daughter, vv. 35-43
      d) Rejection of Jesus at Nazareth, 6:1-6
      e) Mission of the twelve, 6:7-13
      f) Reaction of Antipas to the reports about Jesus, 6:14-29
        (1) Excited reaction of Herod Antipas, vv. 14-16
        (2) Explanatory account of John's death, vv. 17-29
    2. Second withdrawal and return, 6:30–7:23
      a) Feeding of the five thousand, 6:30-44
      b) Walking on the water, 6:45-52
      c) Ministry of healing among the people, 6:53-56
      d) Controversy concerning defilement, 7:1-23
        (1) Condemnation of human tradition, vv. 1-13
        (2) Source of true defilement, vv. 14-23
    3. Third withdrawal and return, 7:24–8:13
      a) Appeal of the Syrophoenician woman, 7:24-30
      b) Cure of the deaf stammerer, 7:31-37
      c) Feeding of the four thousand, 8:1-10
      d) Request for a sign from heaven, 8:11-13
    4. Fourth withdrawal and return, 8:14–9:50
      a) Warning concerning leaven, 8:14-21
      b) Blind man at Bethsaida, 8:22-26
      c) Confession of Peter, 8:27-30
      d) Announcement concerning the cross, 8:31–9:1
        (1) Coming passion foretold, 8:31-32*a*
        (2) Rebuke to Peter, 8:32*b*-33
        (3) Teaching about cross-bearing, 8:34–9:1
      e) Transfiguration on the mount, 9:2-8
      f) Discussion concerning Elijah, 9:9-13
      g) Cure of the demoniac boy, 9:14-29
      h) Renewed teaching about the cross, 9:30-32

   i) Teaching in Capernaum to the disciples, 9:33-50
    (1) Question of greatness, vv. 33-37
    (2) Mistaken zeal of John, vv. 38-41
    (3) Seriousness of sin, vv. 42-50
 C. Journey to Jerusalem, 10:1-52
  1. Departure from Galilee, v. 1
  2. Teaching concerning divorce, vv. 2-12
  3. Blessing of little children, vv. 13-16
  4. Question concerning eternal life, vv. 17-22
  5. Discussion about wealth and reward, vv. 23-31
  6. Third announcement of the passion, vv. 32-34
  7. Problem of position among the disciples, vv. 35-45
   a) Request of James and John, vv. 35-40
   b) Teaching to the twelve, vv. 41-45
  8. Healing of the Jericho beggar, vv. 46-52
 D. Ministry in Jerusalem, 11:1–13:37
  1. Preparatory events, 11:1-25
   a) Entry into Jerusalem as Messiah, vv. 1-11
   b) Cursing of the fig tree, vv. 12-14
   c) Cleansing of the Temple, vv. 15-19
   d) Lesson from the withered fig tree, vv. 20-25
  2. Public teaching in Jerusalem, 11:27–12:44
   a) Questions by the enemies, 11:27–12:34
    (1) Question of authority, 11:27–12:12
     (*a*) Questioners silenced, 11:27-33
     (*b*) Questioners exposed, 12:1-12
    (2) Question of tribute, 12:13-17
    (3) Question about the resurrection, 12:18-27
    (4) Question about the first commandment, 12:28-34
   b) Counterattack by Jesus, 12:35-40
    (1) Question concerning Messiah's sonship, vv. 35-37
    (2) Condemnation of the scribes, vv. 38-40
   c) Commendation of the widow's giving, 12:41-44
  3. Eschatological discourse to the disciples, 13:1-37
   a) Prediction about the Temple, vv. 1-2
   b) Question by the four disciples, vv. 3-4
   c) Prophetic answer to the disciples, vv. 5-37

(1) Warnings to the disciples, vv. 5-13
    (*a*) Perils from the character of the age, vv. 5-8
    (*b*) Personal danger amid persecution, vv. 9-13
(2) Sign of the end and the Advent, vv. 14-27
    (*a*) End-time crisis, vv. 14-23
    (*b*) Return of the Son of man, vv. 24-27
(3) Concluding instructions, vv. 28-37
    (*a*) Lesson from the fig tree, vv. 28-29
    (*b*) Date of the consummation, vv. 30-32
    (*c*) Need for watchfulness, vv. 33-37

III. Self-Sacrifice of the Servant, 14:1–15:47
    A. Foes and friends of Jesus, 14:1-11
        1. Plotting of the Sanhedrin, vv. 1-2
        2. Anointing in Bethany, vv. 3-9
        3. Treachery of Judas, vv. 10-11
    B. Passover observance, 14:12-25
        1. Preparation for the Passover, vv. 12-16
        2. Announcement of the betrayal, vv. 17-21
        3. Institution of the Lord's Supper, vv. 22-25
    C. Garden of Gethsemane, 14:26-52
        1. Revelation on the way, vv. 26-31
        2. Agony in the garden, vv. 32-42
        3. Betrayal and arrest, vv. 43-50
        4. Young man who fled, vv. 51-52
    D. Trials of Jesus, 14:53–15:20*a*
        1. "Trial" before the Sanhedrin, 14:53-65
        2. Three denials by Peter, 14:66-72
        3. Trial before Pilate, 15:1-15
        4. Mockery by the soldiers, 15:16-20*a*
    E. Account of the crucifixion, 15:20*b*-41
        1. Road to Golgotha, vv. 20*b*-22
        2. Crucifixion and first three hours, vv. 23-32
        3. Last three hours and death, vv. 33-39
        4. Women watching from afar, vv. 40-41
    F. Burial of the body, 15:42-47

IV. The Resurrection of the Servant, 16:1-20
    A. Women coming to the empty tomb, vv. 1-8

B. Longer ending of Mark, vv. 9-20
  1. Appearings of Jesus, vv. 9-14
  2. Commission to His followers, vv. 15-18
  3. Ascension of the Lord Jesus, vv. 19-20

A BOOK LIST ON MARK

Alexander, J. A. *Commentary on the Gospel of Mark.* 1858. Reprint. Grand Rapids: Zondervan, n.d.

A comprehensive, conservative interpretation of Mark's gospel by a New Testament scholar who was one of the greatest of his day. Based on sound scholarship, the volume offers a careful unfolding of the meaning of the gospel text. Surprisingly fresh in spite of its age.

Barnes, Albert. *Notes on the New Testament, Explanatory and Practical: Matthew and Mark.* Edited by Robert Frew. 1868. Reprint. Grand Rapids: Baker, 1962.

Blunt, A. W. F. "The Gospel According to Saint Mark." In *The Clarendon Bible.* Oxford: Clarendon, 1929.

Prints the English Revised Version. Has a long section on introductory problems. A scholarly but thoroughly liberal interpretation.

Branscomb, B. Harvie. "The Gospel of Mark." In *The Moffatt New Testament Commentary.* London: Hodder & Stoughton, 1937.

Moffatt translation. A readable, scholarly liberal commentary, conforming to the viewpoint and format of the series to which it belongs.

Bruce, Alexander Balmain. "The Synoptic Gospels." In *The Expositor's Greek Testament,* vol. 1. Grand Rapids: Eerdmans, n.d.

Clarke, W. N. "Commentary on the Gospel of Mark." In *An American Commentary.* 1881. Reprint. Philadelphia: Amer. Bapt. Pubn. Soc., n.d.

An older conservative commentary that still has value for a careful study of the text of the gospel. Fully comments on but does not accept the canonical ending as from the hand of Mark.

Cole, R. A. "The Gospel According to St. Mark." In *The Tyndale New Testament Commentaries.* Grand Rapids: Eerdmans, 1961.

A recent, conservative commentary well suited to the average lay reader. Unfolds the meaning of the gospel in a non-technical manner. Valuable introductory material.

Cranfield, C. E. B. "The Gospel According to Saint Mark." In *Cambridge Greek Testament Commentary.* 3d impression. Cambridge: Cambridge U., 1966.

Greek text. An important modern commentary on the Greek text by a noted British scholar. It is generally conservative in tone and rejects the more radical views of modern scholars.

Earle, Ralph. "The Gospel According to Mark." In *The Evangelical Commentary on the Bible*. Grand Rapids: Zondervan, 1957.

Includes the author's own literal translation. Contains a very full bibliography. The commentary, revealing the author's own wide acquaintance with the literature on the second gospel, was written not for the advanced student but rather the lay Bible student. The interpretation, consistently conservative, is concise yet quite full.

English, E. Schuyler. *Studies in the Gospel According to Mark*. New York: Pubn. Office "Our Hope," 1943.

A comprehensive, warm-hearted treatment of Mark's gospel by a well-known contemporary premillennial Bible teacher. Defends the Marcan origin of the canonical ending of the gospel.

Erdman, Charles R. *The Gospel of Mark*. Philadelphia: Westminster, 1917.

A valuable paragraph-by-paragraph interpretation adapted to the lay reader. It is free from all technicalities and is conservative and reverent in its treatment of the scriptural text.

Gould, Ezra P. "A Critical and Exegetical Commentary on the Gospel According to St. Mark." In *The International Critical Commentary*. Edinburgh: T. & T. Clark, 1896.

Greek text. A scholarly older commentary, best suited for students familiar with Greek. It contains much valuable material, although not one of the outstanding volumes in the series to which it belongs. Generally quite conservative in its viewpoint.

Grant, Frederick C., and Luccock, Halford E. "The Gospel According to St. Mark." In *The Interpreter's Bible*, vol. 7. New York: Abingdon-Cokesbury, 1971.

The material on Mark by two noted liberal scholars falls into two sections. The exegesis by Grant is meager and generally disappointing. The exposition by Luccock provides rich material for contemporary preaching.

Hiebert, D. Edmond. *Mark: A Portrait of the Servant*. Chicago: Moody, 1974.

A phrase-by-phrase study of Mark from a conservative viewpoint. A systematic unfolding of the meaning of Mark through a treatment of grammatical, historical, and theological matters to illuminate the text.

Hunter, A. M. *The Gospel According to Saint Mark*. Torch Bible Commentaries. London: SCM, 1949.

A brief, pithy commentary that lays chief emphasis on the religious and theological meaning rather than on a critical analysis of the Marcan text. Generally quite conservative in its viewpoint.

Johnson, Sherman E. *A Commentary on the Gospel According to St. Mark.* Black's New Testament Commentaries. London: Adam & Charles Black, 1960.

Prints the author's own translation. An up-to-date commentary on Mark based on modern critical opinions. It is skeptical about the historicity of many of the sayings and events in the gospel.

Jones, Alexander. *The Gospel According to St. Mark: A Text and Commentary for Students.* New York: Sheed & Sheed, 1963.

Prints the Revised Standard Version in addition to the author's comments, thus intentionally keeping the scriptural text before the student in his study. The work of a well-known Roman Catholic scholar, this brief commentary is intended for the ordinary Bible student and contains little that is distinctive of the author's church connections. Among other things the introduction contains a unique circular chart of the contents of the gospel.

Lane, William L. "The Gospel According to Mark." In *The New International Commentary.* Grand Rapids: Eerdmans, 1974.

A massive exposition (650 pages) by an erudite conservative scholar. Seeks to present the meaning of Mark's gospel as a creative literary work. Makes available to the reader a condensation of the wealth of contemporary scholarship relating to this gospel found in journals and monographs.

Lange, John Peter. "The Gospel According to Mark." In Lange's *Commentary on the Holy Scriptures: Critical, Doctrinal, and Homiletical.* Translated from the German, with additions, by Philip Schaff. Reprint. Grand Rapids: Zondervan, n.d.

Conforms to the pattern of the author's commentary on Matthew.

Lenski, R. C. H. *The Interpretation of St. Mark's and St. Luke's Gospels.* Columbus, Ohio: Lutheran Book Concern, 1934.

One of the most thorough conservative commentaries on Mark published in the present century. The work of an accomplished Lutheran scholar. Prints the author's own literal translation. Is based on a thorough study of the original Greek, but is readily usable by the non-Greek student. Highly rewarding for a careful interpretation of the text of Mark.

Lindsay, Thomas M. *The Gospel According to St. Mark.* Handbooks for Bible Classes and Private Students. Edinburgh: T. & T. Clark, 1883.

An older treatment of Mark from a conservative viewpoint. Well adapted to the lay reader and still valuable for its fine comments and historical material.

Morgan, G. Campbell. *The Gospel According to Mark.* New York: Revell, 1927.

A series of thirty sermons on texts, which form the center of an exposition of a longer paragraph. The messages cover almost all of the gospel. Characterized by the famous expository preacher's insights into Scripture, yet not up to the high standard of his series on Matthew.

Morison, James. *A Practical Commentary on the Gospel According to St. Mark.* 8th ed. London: Hodder & Stoughton, 1896.

A thorough discussion of introductory problems in the 80-page introduction. This thorough, scholarly, conservative commentary is still of great value. It reveals the author's wide acquaintance with the literature on Mark to his own day. Contains a thorough study of the problems concerning the canonical ending of the gospel and strongly defends its Marcan origin.

Nineham, D. E. *The Gospel of St. Mark.* The Pelican Gospel Commentaries. Reprint. 1963. Baltimore, Md.: Penguin, 1967.

A scholarly work that thoroughly applies the views of form criticism to this gospel. Prints the text of the Revised Standard Verson. The author is skeptical of the historicity of much of the contents of Mark.

Plummer, A. "The Gospel According to St. Mark." In *Cambridge Greek Testament for Schools and Colleges.* 1914. Reprint. Cambridge: Cambridge U., 1938.

Greek text. A volume of continued usefulness for the Greek student by a noted British scholar of the past generation. Generally conservative in viewpoint.

Rawlinson, A. E. J. *St. Mark.* Westminster Commentaries. 2d ed. London: Methuen, 1927.

Prints the English Revised Version (1881). Good introductory section. The commentary is most helpful for the more advanced student. Valuable for references to rabbinical material. Liberal in spots.

Riddle, Matthew B. "The Gospel According to Mark." In *The International Revision Commentary on the New Testament.* New York: Scribner, 1881.

A commentary based on the Revised Version (1881) when it first came out. A clear, concise, conservative commentary on the biblical text.

Salmond, S. D. F. *St. Mark.* The Century Bible. Edinburgh: T. C. & E. C. Jack, n.d.

Prints the English Revised Version. A compact yet remarkably full interpretation of the gospel by a conservative scholar of a past generation.

Schweizer, Eduard. *The Good News According to Mark.* Translated by
Donald H. Madvig. Richmond, Va.: Knox, 1970.

The text quoted is from *Good News for Modern Man,* published by
the American Bible Society. The commentary, the work of a liberal
German scholar, employs a basic form- and redaction-critical approach
in examining the contents of Mark. His position is somewhat less radical than that of Bultmann. The author has an involved German style.

Swete, Henry Barclay. *The Gospel According to St. Mark.* 2d ed. Reprint.
London: Macmillan, 1905.

Greek text. One of the best older commentaries for the Greek student. Gives a full introduction, and a full and balanced interpretation
of the text. Cites classical sources. A monumental work, of great value
in spite of its age.

Taylor, Vincent. *The Gospel According to St. Mark.* 2d ed. New York:
St. Martin's, 1966.

Greek text. A monumental 700-page volume, thoroughly abreast of
recent critical scholarship on this gospel. Taylor follows a form critical
approach, but generally defends the historicity of the material in Mark.
Important introduction of 149 pages. Invaluable for the advanced student. Liberal in places.

Wuest, Kenneth S. *Mark in the Greek New Testament for the English
Reader.* Grand Rapids: Eerdmans, 1950.

Intended to make available to the English reader something of the
riches of the original Greek by means of an expanded translation and
comments on the Greek text. Does not deal with critical problems.

6

THE GOSPEL ACCORDING TO LUKE

An Introduction to Luke

The Student who has thoroughly familiarized himself with the first two gospels cannot fail to be impressed with the fact that the third gospel has various characteristic features of its own. It is not simply a monotonous repetition of the same story. Luke's portrait of Jesus Christ is distinctive. "In Matthew He is Israel's *King;* in Mark He is Jehovah's *Servant;* in Luke He is the perfect *Man.*"[1]

The gospel of Luke is the longest and most comprehensive of the four gospels. It is also the longest book in the New Testament. Its beautiful hymns and the superb stories from the lips of Jesus, unique to this gospel, have made it a favorite with countless readers. Its attractive literary features justify the comment of a French rationalistic critic (Ernest Renan) that this gospel is "the most beautiful book ever written."

The Authorship of the Third Gospel

Although the name of the author nowhere appears in it, the third gospel does not present itself as an anonymous work. In his prologue the author refers to himself in saying, "it seemed good to me also" (1:3), and it is certain that Theophilus, the original recipient of the gospel, knew the writer's identity. In fact, it must have been common knowledge from the very beginning. Since the name of the author cannot with unquestioned certainty be deduced from the contents of his work, the uniform traditional ascription of it to Luke must represent information known from the first century.

1. External Evidence

The uniform testimony of Christian tradition, dating back to early

1. J. Sidlow Baxter, *Explore the Book,* 5:229.

times, names Luke as the author of the third gospel. Guthrie remarks, "At no time were any doubts raised regarding this attribution to Luke, and certainly no alternatives were mooted. The tradition could hardly be stronger."[2]

Among the fragments that have survived from the writings of Papias there is nothing concerning the authorship of the third gospel. (Concerning the dating of Papias, see p. 48.) But this does not prove that Papias was unfamiliar with the tradition or rejected it. Eusebius quotes his testimony concerning the authorship of the first and second gospels, but quotes nothing from Papias concerning the third gospel. Godet concludes, "All that can reasonably be inferred from this silence is, that Eusebius had not found anything of interest in Papias as to the origin of Luke's book."[3] The obvious implication is that Papias had nothing new to add to the view current in his day concerning the authorship of the third gospel.

Although he does not name Luke as the author, Justin Martyr (*c.* A.D. 100-165) in his *Dialogue with Trypho* quotes Luke 22:44 (chap. 103) and 23:46 (chap. 105). Justin refers to the gospels as the "Memoirs" composed "by His apostles and those who followed them" (chap. 103). It seems highly probable that by "those who followed them" Justin refers to Mark and Luke whom Justin regarded as the disciples of Peter and Paul.

The earliest witnesses that name Luke as the author belong to the latter part of the second century A.D. But the subsequent testimony is so strong and uniform that it may be fairly surmised that the Lucan tradition was well known before that date.

The so-called *Muratorian Canon*, which is dated between A.D. 160 and 200 and apparently represents the views held at Rome, says, "The third book of the Gospels Luke compiled in his own name from reports, the physician whom Paul took with him after the ascension of Christ, as it were for a traveling companion; however, he did not himself see the Lord in the flesh and hence begins his account with the birth of John as he was able to trace (matters) up."[4]

2. Donald Guthrie, *New Testament Introduction*, p. 99.
3. F. Godet, *A Commentary on the Gospel of St. Luke*, 1:15.
4. For the Latin text, see F. F. Bruce, *The Acts of the Apostles*, p. 1. For an English translation of the canon, see Kirsopp Lake and Silva Lake, *An Introduction to the New Testament*, pp. 279-81.

Irenaeus in his noted work *Against Heresies* (*c.* A.D. 185) says, "Luke, the companion of Paul, put down in his book the Gospel which Paul preached."[5] He calls Luke "the follower and disciple of the apostles,"[6] and remarks that Luke was Paul's co-worker in the gospel, and inseparable from him.[7]

Tertullian of Carthage (*c.* A.D. 150-222) in his work *Against Marcion* names the gospels of John and Matthew as written by apostles and those by Luke and Mark as by "apostolic men"[8] and remarks that the reading of the gospel of Luke was an established practice in the apostolic churches.[9] He declares that Marcion accepted only the gospel of Luke, although he mutilated it, because it was written by the companion of Paul.[10]

Origen in his *Commentary on Matthew* (*c.* A.D. 230) is quoted by Eusebius as saying, "The third, according to Luke, the Gospel commended by Paul, which was written for the converts from the Gentiles."[11] Origen's teacher, Clement of Alexandria (*c.* 155-216), in *The Stromata* quotes Luke 3:1-2, 23 as being "written in the Gospel of Luke."[12]

Similar testimony to the Lucan authorship of the third gospel is given by Eusebius[13] and Jerome.[14]

The *Anti-Marcionite Prologue* to the third gospel, generally dated A.D. 160-180 and accepted as independent of Irenaeus, contains one of the fullest statements of the tradition concerning the third gospel and its author. It gives the following account:

> Luke is a man from Antioch, Syria, a physician by profession. He was a disciple of the apostles, and later he accompanied Paul until his martyrdom. Having neither wife nor child, he served the Lord without distraction. He fell asleep in Boeotia at the age of eighty four, full of the Holy Spirit.
>
> Moved by the Holy Spirit, Luke composed all of this Gospel in the

5. Irenaeus *Against Heresies* 3. 1. 1.
6. Ibid., 3. 10. 1.
7. Ibid., 3. 14. 1.
8. Tertullian *Against Marcion* 4. 2.
9. Ibid., 4. 5.
10. Ibid., 4. 1.
11. Eusebius *Ecclesiastical History* 6. 25. 6.
12. Clement of Alexandria *The Stromata* 1. 21. 145.
13. Eusebius *Ecclesiastical History* 3. 4. 7.
14. Jerome *Lives of Illustrious Men* 7.

districts around Achaia although there were already Gospels in existence—one according to Matthew written in Judea and one according to Mark written in Italy. He reveals this fact in the prologue: that other Gospels were written before his and that it was imperative that an account of the divine plan be set forth for the Gentile believers. This was necessary in order that they might neither be distracted by Jewish myths nor, deceived by heretical and vain phantasies, depart from the truth.

Therefore, right at the beginning Luke took up the birth of John because this was a most necessary matter. John is the beginning of the Gospel. He was the forerunner of the Lord and his partner in the preparation of the gospel, in the administration of the baptism, and in the fellowship of the Spirit. The prophet with this ministry is mentioned in the Twelve (Minor Prophets).

Afterwards the same Luke also wrote 'the Acts of the Apostles'.[15]

Although the above account of Luke and his gospel is exceptionally circumstantial, some have questioned its general reliability. Since it was composed at a time when the Marcionite dispute was still a vital concern, it is unlikely that the author of this prologue would have made erroneous statements which the opposite side could readily attack. It can be accepted as embodying the tradition concerning the third gospel commonly held around the middle of the second century and earlier.

The testimony of all the early witnesses not only named Luke as the author of the third gospel but also asserted that he wrote Acts. This testimony to the Lucan authorship of the third gospel comes from all parts of the Christian world. The author is uniformly identified as a physician and companion of Paul. In summarizing the external evidence Plummer remarks, "In the literature of that period it would not be easy to find a stronger case."[16] If the tradition were not based on known facts dating from the first century, it is difficult to see why this gospel, which was known and treasured in the early church, would have been ascribed to a comparatively minor character like Luke.

15. As quoted in E. Earle Ellis, "The Gospel of Luke," in *The Century Bible: New Edition*, p. 41.
16. Alfred Plummer, "A Critical and Exegetical Commentary on the Gospel According to S. Luke," in *The International Critical Commentary*, p. xvi.

2. INTERNAL EVIDENCE

The internal evidence concerning the authorship of the third gospel begins with its classic prologue:

> Forasmuch as many have taken in hand to draw up a narrative concerning those matters which have been fulfilled among us, even as they delivered them unto us, who from the beginning were eyewitnesses and ministers of the word, it seemed good to me also, having traced the course of all things accurately from the first, to write unto thee in order, most excellent Theophilus; that thou mightest know the certainty concerning the things wherein thou wast instructed (1: 1-4).

From this passage we may draw several inferences about its author:

1. He was not an eyewitness of the events recorded in his gospel.
2. He was acquainted with earlier accounts.
3. He had used his opportunities to receive personal information from those who "from the beginning were eyewitnesses, and ministers of the word."
4. The results of his own careful research had stimulated him to write his gospel.
5. He was a man of scholarly methods and could claim thoroughness, accuracy, and reliability for his production.
6. He was a man of considerable literary ability. This is evident from the balanced literary structure of the prologue. It suggests that the author was familiar with the classical writers, such as Herodotus, Thucydides, and Polybius.

The prologue to the third gospel thus supplies us with information about the writer, but does not identify him.

The external evidence asserts a common authorship for the third gospel and the Acts. The internal evidence is consistent with this assertion. This unity of authorship is evident from the following:

1. Both books are dedicated to the same man, Theophilus (Lk 1: 1-4; Ac 1:1-5).
2. Acts explicitly refers to the former treatise; the summary of the nature of that work fits the third gospel (Ac 1:1-4).
3. The two books show strong similarities in language, style, and

arrangement. Plummer asserts, "This similarity is found to exist in such a multitude of details (many of which are very minute), that the hypothesis of careful imitation by a different writer is absolutely excluded."[17]

4. Acts effectively picks up the account exactly where the third gospel ends. The gospel forms the foundation for the story recorded in Acts. Acts forms the natural continuation of the gospel story and in reality completes it. Goodspeed points out that "the Gospel of Luke does not reach the goal it sets itself—the impartation of the Spirit to the disciples," and notes that the promise of Jesus in 24:49 finds its fulfillment only in the second chapter of Acts.[18] This connection between Luke and Acts has a clear parallel in the opening sentences of the two parts of Josephus' work *Against Apion.*

Today, the virtual consensus of critical opinion is that the third gospel and Acts come from the same hand and were intended to form a single work on the beginnings of Christianity. The common modern designation "the Luke-Acts narrative" recognizes this unity of plan and purpose for the third gospel and the Acts of the Apostles. Each part is long enough to fill a papyrus scroll of convenient length. The two books were given to the public as separate scrolls, and each volume was sufficiently complete to be used alone. But in the author's conception and purpose they belonged together. Because they are so closely connected, the evidence concerning authorship derived from the Acts has a bearing upon the third gospel.

3. INTERNAL EVIDENCE CONCERNING THE AUTHORSHIP OF ACTS

The "we-sections" in Acts (16:10-17; 20:5–21:18; 27:1–28:16) were written by a friend and traveling companion of Paul. The sudden change to the first person plural in these sections is most naturally interpreted to mean that the author thus intended to indicate his personal presence in those parts of his narrative. This interpretation is the fair and logical inference drawn by the ordinary reader and is consistent with the author's use of the first person singular in the opening paragraphs of both of his books (Lk 1:1-4; Ac 1:1-5).

17. Ibid., p. xi.
18. Edgar J. Goodspeed, *An Introduction to the New Testament,* p. 181.

The author of the we-sections wrote the entire book of Acts. A comparison of the characteristics of the we-sections with the remainder of the book clearly points to a common authorship. The unity of the book has been effectively demonstrated by the investigations of Hawkins[19] and Harnack.[20] Plummer summarizes, "That the 'we' sections are by the same hand as the rest of the book is shown by the simple and natural way in which they fit into the narrative, by the references in them to other parts of the narrative, and by the marked identity of style."[21] It has been pointed out that peculiarities of vocabulary and style evident throughout the book are numerous in the we-sections. Harnack concludes his detailed investigation of the Greek of the we-sections in relation to the rest of Acts with the remark, "All the observations which we have made in regard to their vocabulary, style, and subject-matter—observations which bring home to us the absolute impossibility of separating the 'we' sections from the work as a whole—remain unaffected in their convincing force."[22] This unity of authorship for the book of Acts establishes that its author was a close friend and companion of Paul.

Opponents of the traditional view, however, assert that these we-sections were portions of a travel document by a companion of Paul which the author of the Acts later utilized in writing his book.[23] But such a view is highly questionable. Goodspeed sets forth three objections to this view: (1) There is no evidence that the ancients kept diaries. (In the case of Xenophon we have a literary man making travel notes for his own later use, just as Luke seems to have done.) (2) It is highly unlikely that such a diary by a companion of Paul would have survived for thirty or more years and then fallen into the hands of a man who conceived the idea of writing a history of those travels. (3) It is not explained why this writer in using that diary would mistakenly copy the first person plural unaltered in seventy-seven instances; such a crude blunder is inconsistent with his careful use of the material elsewhere. Goodspeed's conclusion is:

> The idea that the We-sections were drawn by the author from some-

---

19. John C. Hawkins, *Horae Synopticae*, pp. 182-89.
20. Adolf Harnack, *Luke the Physician*, pp. 26-120.
21. Plummer, p. xiii.
22. Harnack, p. 120.
23. H. Windisch, "The Case Against the Tradition," in *The Beginnings of Christianity*, F. J. Foakes Jackson and Kirsopp Lake, eds., 2:343-45.

body else's diary must be given up, simply because it involves such a series of improbabilities, none of which have been grappled with, much less answered, by its advocates. The We-sections thus resume their normal place as the most important guide to the authorship of the book, showing conclusively that it was written by a companion of Paul.[24]

Paul's companion may be identified as Luke the physician. The we-sections contain specific information concerning this companion: (1) He first joined Paul's company, or first revealed his presence with the missionary party, at Troas. (2) He worked with Paul during the mission at Philippi. (3) He reappeared as a companion of Paul following his visit to Philippi on the way to Jerusalem during the third missionary journey. (4) He traveled with Paul to Jerusalem where Paul was imprisoned. (5) After Paul's two-year imprisonment at Caesarea, during which there is no definite indication concerning the whereabouts of the writer, he accompanied Paul to Rome, experiencing the shipwreck enroute.

References to various companions of Paul in these we-sections at once distinguish the author from other of Paul's close companions. Other well-known companions appearing in the Pauline epistles do not fit into the pattern set by these we-sections and can be located elsewhere at one time or another. Of the known close companions of Paul only Titus and Luke are never named in Acts. That Titus is not named is strange, but no one has ever seriously suggested that Titus was the author of Luke-Acts. This leaves only Luke as the probable author, and he is strongly supported by the external evidence. Wikenhauser holds that in the light of the internal evidence "the scientifically correct course is to accept tradition"[25] since Luke meets all the requirements. Plummer concludes, "If antiquity were silent on the subject, no more reasonable conjecture could be made than 'Luke the beloved physician'. He fulfills the conditions."[26]

Valid confirmatory evidence that the author was Luke the physician is provided by the medical language in the Luke-Acts narrative. Although this argument has been exaggerated, the point is still valid. In his book *The Medical Language of St. Luke*, William Hobart com-

24. Goodspeed, pp. 201-2.
25. Alfred Wikenhauser, *New Testament Introduction*, p. 208.
26. Plummer, p. xiii.

pares the writings of Luke with those of the leading Greek physicians (Galen, Hippocrates, Dioscorides, Aretaeus). He concludes that the author of Luke-Acts was a man at home in the language of Greek medicine, indicating that he was a physician.[27] While Hobart claimed too much, his basic conclusion received the firm support of Harnack[28] and Zahn.[29] But Cadbury has shown that most of Hobart's examples can be paralleled by examples drawn from other educated non-medical Greek writers of the period.[30] Cartledge feels that Cadbury has "completely wrecked Hobart's proof." [31] But Creed is more cautious when he remarks, "He has not demolished the relevance of *some* of the evidence which has been collected, and in a few cases he has unduly depreciated the force of the medical parallels."[32] Robertson shows through a comparison of the accounts in Mark and Luke that the writer of the third gospel had an interest in medicine.[33] Cadbury's work offered a necessary corrective to the claims of Hobart and set his findings in proper perspective. Lenski concludes, "The upshot of the matter is that the medical science in Luke's time had not developed specialized foreign terms, but used the ordinary Greek world language. Luke did not parade his medical learning before his readers. What he did was to write with more exactness about diseases and medical matters. Only in a quiet and refined way does Luke betray himself as a physician."[34] Robertson further points out that Paul and the author of Hebrews were well educated, yet the writings of neither reveals the medical interests reflected in the Luke-Acts narrative.[35] We may agree with Harrison's judicious conclusion, "The net result of the various investigations is that the language of Luke-Acts is thoroughly compatible with the authorship of a medical man, but does not prove that he must have been a physician."[36]

The historical aspects of the Luke-Acts narrative may confidently

27. William Kirk Hobart, *The Medical Language of St. Luke.*
28. Harnack, pp. 175-98.
29. Theodor Zahn, *Introduction to the New Testament*, 3:146-48.
30. H. J. Cadbury, *The Style and Literary Method of Luke*, pp. 39-72; *The Beginnings of Christianity*, 2:349-55.
31. Samuel A. Cartledge, *A Conservative Introduction to the New Testament*, p. 71.
32. John Martin Creed, *The Gospel According to St. Luke*, p. xix.
33. A. T. Robertson, *Luke the Historian in the Light of Research*, pp. 90-98.
34. R. C. H. Lenski, *The Interpretation of St. Mark's and St. Luke's Gospels*, p. 487.
35. Robertson, p. 11.
36. Everett F. Harrison, *Introduction to the New Testament*, p. 199.

be accepted as in full agreement with the uniform external tradition naming Luke the physician as the author.

Within recent times liberal scholars have vigorously renewed their attacks upon the traditional authorship on theological grounds. Their objections are based on the alleged theological differences between Luke-Acts and Paul.

It is maintained that there is a contradiction between Paul's view of the Mosaic law and the view of Acts. The main point is that Acts does not stress the characteristic Pauline emphasis upon the Christian's freedom from the law. This, it is asserted, shows that the author of Acts cannot have been a close companion of Paul. Acts gives no hint of the theological tension over circumcision reflected in Galatians, and the Acts account of Paul's attitude toward circumcision as seen in the case of Timothy (Ac 16:3) contradicts Galatians. To this argument Guthrie replies, "While it cannot be denied that the Lucan picture differs from Paul's, it cannot be asserted that the two pictures contradict one another. There is no ground for demanding that Luke must present Paul's theology in his historical book in precisely the same form as Paul presents it in his pastoral and didactic letters."[37]

It is insisted that the Areopagus speech in Acts 17 presents a theological view foreign to Paul's teaching as revealed in his letters. Objection is also made to Paul's speech at Pisidian Antioch (Ac 13:16-41). It is felt that Luke could not have attributed such a speech to Paul. In reply it may be said that it is unjustified to insist that Paul's missionary addresses conform to the pattern and viewpoint of his letters to believers. Such objections to Lucan authorship of Acts fail to take into account the historical situation as depicted by the author. The only Pauline speech in Acts which bears any analogy to the situation behind the letters of Paul is his speech to the Ephesian elders (Ac 20:17-35) and the contents of this speech reflect most closely Paul's language and thought in his letters.

It is held that a close companion of Paul could not have written Acts because the portrait of Paul therein is so different from the man who appears in the epistles. Differences in emphasis are admitted but there are no proven contradictions. Guthrie observes, "It is not so unusual for a close companion to paint a portrait of a person which

37. Guthrie, p. 107.

differs from that person's self-disclosures."[38] Such differences as exist have no real bearing on the question of the Lucan authorship of Luke-Acts. They only prove the independence of Luke as a writer.

Opponents of the traditional view concerning the authorship of Luke-Acts give little weight to the uniform and strong external evidence and focus upon internal difficulties. The discussion of these difficulties, whether basically historical or theological, has contributed to a richer understanding of the Lucan writings. But it has not been agreed that the difficulties which have been advanced necessitate a rejection of the traditional view. Guthrie notes that the "advocates of Lucan authorship are not only in the majority, but are also drawn from widely differing schools of theological opinion."[39]

We conclude that there is far stronger evidence for retaining the traditional view than for rejecting it. We concur with the assertion of Ellis, "Apart from the major Pauline letters the authorship of no section of the New Testament is as well supported as that of the two volumes to Theophilus by Luke the physician and companion of Paul."[40]

THE AUTHOR OF THE THIRD GOSPEL

The name "Luke" is familiar to every reader of the Bible, yet it occurs only three times in the entire New Testament (Col 4:14; Phile 24; 2 Ti 4:11). The widespread familiarity with his name is not attributable to the few references to him in the Pauline epistles but rather to the association of his name with the third gospel and the Acts. Luke has the honor of being the largest contributor to the New Testament from the standpoint of length. His two books, the longest in the New Testament, constitute about twenty-eight percent of its entire contents. Luke has the distinction of being the first Christian historian. Luke and Acts have been of incalculable importance for the furtherance of the cause of Christianity.

1. SCRIPTURAL DATA

The three occurrences of Luke's name in the Pauline epistles confirm that he was a beloved friend and co-worker with the apostle to

38. Ibid., pp. 108-9.
39. Ibid., p. 109. See the references cited in n. 5, pp. 109-10.
40. Ellis, p. 52.

the Gentiles. All three references connect his name with Paul while the apostle was a prisoner in Rome. "Luke, the beloved physician" is mentioned in Colossians 4:14 as sending greetings to the Colossian church, while in Philemon he is connected with three other companions characterized as "my fellowlabourers" (v. 24). These two references, included in writings which belong to the time of Paul's first Roman imprisonment, establish that Luke was a physician by profession and that he was actively associated with Paul in the furtherance of the gospel.

The third occurrence of Luke's name, "Only Luke is with me" (2 Ti 4:11), belongs to the time of Paul's second Roman imprisonment. The words are a loving tribute to Luke's steadfast loyalty to Paul in the face of great stress and personal danger.

Further information concerning Luke's story can be gleaned from his indirect references to himself in the we-sections of Acts. They reveal that he was Paul's travelling companion during parts of Paul's missionary journeys. The dropping of the "we," however, does not prove that he was no longer with Paul. In Acts 28 the "we" is dropped as soon as the party reaches Rome, but we know from Paul's letters that Luke remained with Paul in Rome during at least part of his imprisonment there.

Luke reveals his presence with Paul at Troas on the second missionary journey with the words, "Concluding that God had called us to preach the gospel unto them" (16:10, NASB). This statement establishes that he felt himself included in the call to preach the gospel to the Macedonians. His participation in the service by the riverside at Philippi (Ac 16:13) gives a glimpse of his active part in the work there. In narrating Paul's work after leaving Philippi Luke drops the "we." Apparently Luke remained at Philippi to continue his medical practice and to guide the young church.

The reappearance of "we" indicates that Luke rejoined Paul when Paul left Philippi for Jerusalem on the third missionary journey (Ac 20:5–21:18). The "we" is not used in regard to Paul's conference with James in Jerusalem, but Luke obviously remained in Jerusalem during the days that followed, culminating in Paul's arrest and consequent two-year imprisonment at Caesarea (Ac 21:17–26:32). Nothing is mentioned of Luke's activities during those two years, but it is natural to assume that he was among the friends who were allowed to minister to the imprisoned apostle (Ac 24:23).

When Paul journeyed from Caesarea to Rome as a prisoner Luke was one of two friends who accompanied him (Ac 27:1—28:16), as indicated by the use of "we" in the narrative. With the arrival of the party in Rome the "we" is dropped. How long Luke remained with Paul in Rome is not known. The fact that he was not mentioned in the letter to the Philippians most naturally suggests that he was not with Paul when that letter was written. When and where he rejoined Paul during the second Roman imprisonment is not known (2 Ti 4:11).

2. NATIONALITY

The nationality of Luke has been disputed. Some scholars, like Albright,[41], Arndt,[42] and Reicke,[43] hold that Luke was a Hellenistic Jew. Advocates of this view identify Luke with the Lucius of Cyrene in Acts 13:1. Although the name offers no objection, being only a variant form, this proposed identification is highly improbable. Blair points out that the author of Acts, "who seems studiously to avoid direct reference to himself, would hardly have flatly named himself in Acts 13:1."[44] There is no firm scriptural evidence, nor tradition, to link Luke with Cyrene. The attention given by Luke to New Testament prophets and prophecy does not warrant Ellis' conjecture that "Luke was a Christian prophet with contacts among others exercising the same gift" in the Antioch church.[45]

It is commonly held that Luke was a Gentile. This seems to be a necessary conclusion based on Paul's reference to him in Colossians 4:14. In verses 10-14 six persons send greetings, and they are named in two groups. The three men named in verses 10-11 are identified as "of the circumcision" with the appreciative comment, "These only are my fellow workers unto the kingdom of God." Paul next mentions three other companions, Epaphras, Luke, and Demas. Certainly Epaphras, a native of Colossae (v. 12), was a Gentile. If Luke were

41. W. F. Albright, *History, Archaeology and Christian Humanism*, p. 296.
42. William F. Arndt, *The Gospel According to St. Luke*, pp. 2-3.
43. Bo Reicke, *The Gospel of Luke*, pp. 21-22.
44. E. P. Blair, "Luke (Evangelist)," in *The Interpreter's Dictionary of the Bible*, 3:179.
45. Ellis, p. 54.

Jewish, Paul would not have failed to name him in the former group, since the appreciative comment concerning his Jewish co-workers would in that case be a direct slap at Luke as one who had brought no cheer to Paul's heart. But any such suggestion is inconsistent with Paul's warm personal commendation of Luke as "the beloved physician." Luke, most naturally, did not belong to those "of the circumcision." If this conclusion is correct, then Luke was the only non-Jewish contributor to the New Testament.

Luke's non-Jewish background seems to reveal itself in Acts 1:19. In referring to Akeldama, "the field of blood," he slips in the words "in their language" (the language of the Jews). Grosheide holds that Luke's describing the inhabitants of Malta (Melita) as "barbarians" (Ac 28:2, 4) indicates that he was a Gentile. He asserts, "At the time no Jew would employ this word for these people who were Phoenicians, and thus related to the Jews."[46] Luke's feeling for the sea, which is evident from his graphic descriptions of sea voyages, especially in Acts 27, points to his non-Jewish origin; Jews, at least during the Roman period, did not find the sea congenial. Harrison points to Luke's obvious fondness for city centers "since this was the geographical unit of significance among the Greeks but not among the Hebrews."[47] In view of the evidence, we conclude that Luke was a Gentile rather than a Hellenistic Jew.

Luke apparently was a native Greek. Rackham holds that his Greek origin is reflected "by his ready pen, his versatility, and not least by his interest in the sea."[48] It is not certain whether he was a free Hellene or a Greek slave set free by his master. The latter is quite probable, since in wealthy Roman families the part of the family doctor was often committed to a trusted slave or freedman. If Luke was a freedman it is likely that he was set free with Roman citizenship.

3. BIRTHPLACE

Luke's native city cannot be determined from his writings. Different conclusions have been drawn from inferences based on Acts, but

46. F. W. Grosheide, "Acts of the Apostles," in *The Encyclopedia of Christianity,* 1:47.
47. Harrison, p. 198.
48. Richard Belward Rackham, "The Acts of the Apostles," in *Westminster Commentaries,* p. xxviii.

the most probable suggestion is Antioch of Syria. Codex Bezae (D) contains an interesting we-section in Acts 11:28: "And there was much rejoicing; and when we were gathered together one of them stood up and said." While the evidence is too slender to prove this we-section as authentic, it obviously embodies an early tradition connecting Luke with the church at Antioch. The *Anti-Marcionite Prologue* asserts that Luke was "a man from Antioch, Syria."[49] Eusebius and Jerome likewise name Antioch of Syria as Luke's place of residence. The author of Acts certainly reveals a deep interest in that city (cf. 11:19-30; 13:1; 14:26-28; 15:22, 30-35; 18:22). The only deacon whose place of origin Luke mentioned was Nicolaus of Antioch (6:5). Antioch would naturally be mentioned because of the important part that it played in the spread of Christianity beyond Jerusalem. But Luke's record includes trifling touches which seem to indicate personal familiarity with the scenes. The evidence is not sufficient to be absolutely convincing but does strongly suggest that Luke was born and reared in Antioch of Syria.

4. CONVERSION

Where and how Luke became a Christian can only be conjectured. If he was a native of Antioch it is quite probable that he was won to Christ during the missionary work among the Greeks in that city described in Acts 11:20-21. If the we-section in Acts 11:28 in Codex D embodies a reliable tradition, then Luke was a member of the church in that city. He apparently was converted directly from heathenism. Since Paul did not group him with those "of the circumcision" (Col 4:10-14) it is clear that Luke had not previously received circumcision as a proselyte to Judaism. He may, however, have belonged to the class of God-fearing Gentiles who frequented the synagogues as "proselytes of the gate," a class frequently mentioned in Acts. Nowhere is there any hint that Luke was Paul's convert. If the tradition that Luke was a member of the church at Antioch is correct, he must have been converted before Paul was brought to Antioch by Barnabas (Ac 11:20-26).

---

49. See quote from the *Anti-Marcionite Prologue*, pp. 116-17. Also see F. F. Bruce, *The Acts of the Apostles*, pp. 6-7.

5. CONJECTURES

It has been conjectured that "the brother" mentioned in 2 Corinthians 8:18 whom Paul sent with Titus from Macedonia to Corinth to expedite the collection was Luke. His "praise in the gospel" had made him well-known in all the churches. This suggestion, as old as Origen, was embodied in the scribal subscription added to 2 Corinthians stating that the epistle "was written from Philippi, a city of Macedonia, by Titus and Lucas." Although it has received numerous supporters, it must remain an unverified conjecture.[50] It apparently originated in the mistaken notion that "the gospel" here has reference to a written gospel (the gospel of Luke).

Ramsay[51] and others,[52] in adopting the suggestion that "the brother" in 2 Corinthians 8:18 is Luke, conclude that Luke was the physical brother of Titus. In support they maintain that this most naturally explains why the name "Titus" is not mentioned in Acts. This omission is indeed noteworthy in view of the importance of Titus for Paul's work as seen in the Pauline epistles. The suggestion is plausible but is not supported by Paul's expression "the brother." While the original may bear such a meaning, more probably it designates this individual as a fellow Christian. Kelly well points out that if the expression meant his brother after the flesh "the object and character of the association would have been frustrated by selecting one so near to Titus."[53] The purpose in sending this brother with Titus was to shield him against insinuations of unworthy dealings in connection with the collection money.

It has been conjectured that Luke was one of the "seventy" (Lk 10:1-7), or that he was the companion of Cleopas on the Emmaus Road (Lk 24:13-33); but these conjectures are ruled out if Luke was a Greek. That he was one of the Greek proselytes who applied to Philip to be introduced to Jesus during Passion Week (Jn 12:20-21) is highly improbable, although not impossible. Any personal contact on the part of Luke with the earthly life of Jesus seems clearly

---

50. For a survey of conjectures about the identity of this "brother" see Philip E. Hughes, "Commentary on the Second Epistle to the Corinthians," in *New International Commentary*, pp. 312-16.
51. W. M. Ramsay, *St. Paul the Traveller and the Roman Citizen*, pp. 59, 390.
52. Harrington C. Lees, *St. Paul's Friends*, p. 89; A. Souter, "Luke," in *Dictionary of Christ and the Gospels*, 2:84.
53. William Kelly, *Notes on the Second Epistle of Paul the Apostle to the Corinthians*, p. 169.

excluded by his statement in the prologue that he did not witness the events recorded in his gospel. Clearly Luke belonged to the second generation of Christians.

A tradition as old as the sixth century claims that Luke was a painter and painted a picture of Mary the mother of Jesus. Whether or not the tradition is an accurate recollection of Luke's varied gifts, it is clear that Luke was able to paint vivid word-pictures. His beautiful pen-portraits have exerted a profound influence on Christian art through the centuries.

The Intended Readers of the Third Gospel

Luke formally dedicates both of his books to a certain man named Theophilus (Lk 1:1-4; Ac 1:1-5), concerning whom we know nothing beyond what may be gleaned from these dedicatory remarks. His name, which means "friend of God," does not justify the opinion of some that Luke used it symbolically for believers generally, like the English "dear Christian reader." The address, "most excellent Theophilus" (Lk 1:3), indicates that he was an actual person of high social standing. In Acts 23:26; 24:3; 26:25 the title is used of the Roman governors of Judea, but the designation might also be applied to an individual of great wealth or social prominence. Whatever the position of Theophilus, it is clear that Luke meant to dedicate his work to him. Such dedications were common. It was the custom for a book thus dedicated to become the property of the one to whom it was dedicated with the understanding that the recipient assumed the responsibility for its publication.

While writing for the personal benefit of Theophilus (Lk 1:4), Luke clearly intended for his work to have a much wider circulation. It may be assumed that Theophilus was a Gentile, although the name was common among Jews as well as Gentiles.[54] Theophilus was representative of the larger circle of Gentile readers for whom it was intended.

Various features of the gospel indicate that it was intended for Gentile readers. Luke substitutes Greek words for Aramaic terms. In the list of the Twelve Matthew uses "the Cananaean" (10:4), but Luke changes this to "the Zealot" (6:15). He avoids the Jewish address "rabbi" which would be puzzling to non-Jewish readers,

54. Plummer, p. v.

although Matthew and Mark readily used it.* He omits the Semitic "hosanna," used by both Matthew and Mark, from his account of Jesus' triumphal entry into Jerusalem (Lk 19:29-44). Matthew uses the Aramaic "Golgotha" for the place of crucifixion (27:33), while Luke uses the Greek term *kranion*, meaning "skull" (23:33).

Luke explains Jewish customs and localities. Thus he refers to both Nazareth and Capernaum as "a city of Galilee" (1:26; 4:31), since the location of these towns might not be known to non-Palestinian Gentiles. He likewise mentions the country of the Gerasenes "which is over against Galilee" (8:26); the low mountain on the eastern side of Jerusalem "that is called Olivet" (21:37); the feast of unleavened bread "which is called the Passover" (22:1); Arimathaea "a city of the Jews" (23:51); and Emmaus, "which was threescore furlongs from Jerusalem" (24:13).

Luke quotes a number of passages from the Old Testament, but as Plummer points out, "they are found mostly in the sayings of Christ (iv. 4, 8, 12, 18, 19, 26, vi. 4, vii. 27, viii. 10, xiii. 19, 28, 29, 35, xviii. 20, xix. 46, xx. 17, 37, 42, 43, xxi. 10, 24, 26, 27, 35, xxii. 37, 69, xxiii. 30, 46) or of others (i. 15, 17, 37, 46-55, 68-79, ii. 30, 31, 32, iv. 10, 11, x. 27, xx. 28)."[55] Unlike Matthew, Luke places little emphasis on the fulfillment of prophecy; for Jewish readers this was a subject of vital concern, but for Gentile readers it would be of lesser interest.

In the third gospel, unlike the other synoptics, there is a definite effort to relate the historical events occurring in Palestine to the larger Roman historical situation. Luke connects the events recorded to the reigns of the Roman emperors (2:1; 3:1). This seems to point to a Gentile trying to set the story in a historical context familiar to Gentile readers.

The evidence supports the conclusion that Luke's gospel was written for people of Gentile origin. They probably had some familiarity with the Old Testament through the Septuagint version but were not conversant with the Aramaic language. Guthrie concludes, "The Gospel may therefore be said to be designed for all who in the non-

---

*In the New Testament "rabbi" occurs only in the gospels. It occurs four times in Mt (23:7—doubled in T. R., 8; 26:25, 49); three times in Mk (9:5; 11:21; 14:45—doubled in T. R.); absent in Lk; eight times in Jn (1:38, 49; 3:2, 26; 4:31; 6:25; 9:2; 11:8).

55. Ibid., p. xxxiv.

Christian world were not averse to Christianity and were genuinely interested in having a historical account of its origins."[56]

THE PURPOSE OF THE THIRD GOSPEL

Unlike Matthew and Mark, Luke specifically states his purpose, "that thou mightest know the certainty concerning the things wherein thou wast instructed" (Lk 1:4). Guthrie well observes, "Where an author specifically states his own intention, that must always be given more weight than any scholarly conjectures."[57]

Luke's stated purpose is to give Theophilus a comprehensive, accurate, historical account of the matters concerning Christianity in order that he may be assured of the reality of the things which he has been taught. His ultimate aim is to convey these truths to Gentile readers and to awaken and deepen their faith in Jesus as the God-sent Saviour for all mankind. Thus Luke may appropriately be called "the historical Evangelist."

Luke's description of his work (Lk 1:1-3) makes it clear that he means to write a historical account. But Luke does not write simply as an impartial historian; his real aim is to bear witness to the validity of the Christian faith which centers in the unique person of Jesus. For Luke, as for the other evangelists, the story of Jesus' saving mission logically culminates in His death and resurrection. This is the very heart of the evangelistic message of the early Christian preachers, and Theophilus has already received instruction concerning these Christ-centered events. Luke's comprehensive, thorough, accurate, and orderly account centering in the person of Jesus is well suited to assure Theophilus, and others like him, of the reality of the teaching.

In setting forth his story of Jesus Luke reveals the methods of a careful historian. His accuracy and trustworthiness as a historian have been thoroughly vindicated.[58] But Luke's own statement of purpose indicates that there is a theological motive behind his work. His aim is to bear evangelical witness to the unique person whom he portrays. Contemporary Lucan studies tend to stress Luke's theological contribution. But to speak of his theological contribution must not be taken to demand that he altered his sources in order to

---

56. Guthrie, p. 96.
57. Ibid., p. 93.
58. Robertson, chaps. 9, 13-16; I. Howard Marshall, *Luke: Historian and Theologian*, chap. 3.

conform them to his own theology. "His earnest desire to be a witness is inseparable from his belief in the historical truth of his material, and his belief in this truth is an indispensable factor to account for his desire to bear witness to it."[59] Luke is interested in bringing out the theological significance of the historical events which he relates. He does so by his own particular style and his choice and arrangement of the material which he presents. This may be illustrated by the prominence which he gives to Jerusalem in 9:51–18:14. This material is peculiar to Luke, depicting Jesus' steadfastness in moving toward Jerusalem in order to die there. In that fact Luke sees the central significance of his story. His theology is summarized in the statement that "the Son of man came to seek and to save that which was lost" (Lk 19:10). He died that He might redeem not only the people of Israel but all mankind. All four gospels indicate that the good news of salvation in Christ is for all mankind, but this fact is most emphatically set forth in the third gospel. "In Luke Christ is not the Messiah of the Old Testament, or the Servant of God, so much as the Saviour of all mankind, the Satisfier of humanity's need."[60]

In view of the close connection between the third gospel and the Acts, an apologetic purpose is often posited for the gospel of Luke. It may be assumed that any apologetic purpose clearly discernible in Acts also underlies Luke. It is commonly accepted that Acts was intended to offset any charges that Christianity was politically antagonistic to the Roman administration. It is assumed that Luke had a similar purpose in writing the story of the founder of Christianity. Thus Gilmour asserts that Luke's first objective was "to show that Christianity was not a subversive sect."[61] Luke's statement of his purpose (Lk 1:4) indicates that such an apologetic purpose was not the primary, although it may well have been a secondary, aim. Luke's account of the trial before Pilate makes it clear that Jesus Himself, the founder of Christianity, was innocent of any wrongdoing toward the Roman authorities. Pilate thrice announced the innocence of Jesus (23:4, 14, 22) and Luke specifically notes that Pilate's order to

59. A. R. C. Leaney, "A Commentary on the Gospel According to St. Luke," in *Harper's New Testament Commentaries*, p. 8.
60. William Evans, *The Gospels and the Acts of the Apostles*, p. 124.
61. S. MacLean Gilmour, "The Gospel According to St. Luke" in *The Interpreter's Bible*, 8:7.

have Jesus crucified was simply a concession to the unrelenting demands of Jesus' enemies (23:20-24). But this in itself does not demonstrate an apologetic purpose for the third gospel, since evidence for Jesus' innocence is found in the other gospels also.

THE SOURCES OF THE THIRD GOSPEL

Those who accept the Bible as the Word of God believe that Luke wrote his gospel under divine inspiration. But Luke states in his prologue that he diligently investigated the historical facts before he recorded them. That negates the view that he received his information directly through divine revelation. As one who had not personally witnessed the story recorded in his gospel, Luke depended on others for the historical information. His frank statement that he used sources is the mark of an honest historian. He indicates that he had access to both written and oral sources of information.

Luke had almost unparalleled opportunities to obtain authentic information concerning the story of Jesus Christ, and his writings prove that he made diligent and faithful use of those opportunities. For a number of years he had been in direct contact with the apostle Paul who in turn had been in direct contact with Peter, James, John, and others who had known the Lord Jesus personally (Gal 1:18-19). Luke himself had contacts with many eyewitnesses. On the way to Jerusalem with Paul he met such people as Philip, Agabus, and Mnason (Ac 21:8-16). Upon arrival in Jerusalem he had opportunity to meet James and numerous other members of the early church (Ac 21:17–23:22), many of whom must have cherished vivid memories of their experiences in relation to Jesus. They must have been eager to share with Luke their knowledge of events involving Jesus. Luke's remark that he received information from "eyewitnesses and ministers of the word" points to men who had not only witnessed these things but were also active in proclaiming the message. They did not keep their blessed knowledge of Jesus to themselves but freely shared it with others.

Apparently Luke remained in Palestine during Paul's two-year imprisonment in Caesarea (Ac 24:23-27). Luke must have used the time to travel extensively in Palestine in search of further information. He would not only talk with the leaders but would endeavor to gain additional information from any believers who remembered their personal contacts with Jesus some thirty years before. Various individuals would recall listening to the gracious teaching of Jesus or recite the thrill of His healing ministries. Luke's referring to various women by name suggested that he visited women who were closely connected with the story of Jesus (Lk 8:1-3; 24:10). It is not improbable that Luke personally visited Mary the mother of Jesus, who apparently was living in the care of the apostle John. Certainly his infancy narrative (Lk 1-2) was drawn from a special source. He relates the nativity story from Mary's standpoint and includes numerous reminiscences which only a loving mother would be able to supply.

Luke indicates in the prologue that he had access to various written accounts of the story of Jesus (Lk 1:1-2), but he does not give his personal evaluation of these accounts. He does not describe the nature and scope of these written accounts, but to imply that he disapproved of them or found them inadequate is unwarranted. They did serve to stimulate his own research. The identity of the written sources used by Luke has been thoroughly debated in discussions of the synoptic problem. Current synoptic views generally accept the gospel of Mark as one of these sources. It is less probable that he had access to the gospel of Matthew. The material common to the first and the third gospels not found in Mark is generally held to have been derived from a common source, usually designated as *Q* (*Quelle*). But nearly half of the material in Luke's gospel is not included in either Matthew or Mark. Aside from the infancy narrative (chaps. 1-2), Luke has two blocks of material (Lk 6:20—8:3; 9:51—18:14) which are distinctive to his gospel. Luke's source for this material is one of the great literary problems connected with his gospel.

Although we have not identified Luke's sources, we are sure that he had authentic information and that he used it with the utmost care. He went about his work systematically, and, under the inspiration of the Holy Spirit, produced a gospel that forms one of the priceless treasures of the New Testament.

THE DATE AND PLACE OF THE THIRD GOSPEL

1. DATE

The third gospel does not contain specific information to which we

136 An Introduction to the New Testament

can appeal as unmistakable evidence for a precise date. Suggestions for the date of composition range from A.D. 50 to 150. The date assigned to the gospel is related to the date accepted for Acts, since it was written before Acts (Ac 1:1-2).

The radical critics have advocated a date some time after A.D. 100. This view is based on the claim that the writer of the third gospel depended on known late sources. J. Knox suggests a date in the middle of the second century on the ground that the third gospel in its present form represents an enlargement of a gospel used by Marcion.[62] But such a view is highly improbable. The orthodox opponents of Marcion's heretical views charged that Marcion mutilated the third gospel. They maintained that Marcion's gospel was based on the canonical gospel of Luke. If this claim had been a known error, however, it is certain that Marcion's supporters would have countered it. Orthodox apologists confidently appealed to our four gospels in rejecting the views of Marcion. But "it is difficult to believe that the defenders of the faith would have based their attack on so insecure a foundation as the antiquity and apostolicity of the four Gospels if Knox's theory is correct."[63] Marcion sought to purge Jewish elements from his gospel and therefore did not accept the nativity accounts as given in Luke. Ellis points out that our gospel of Luke cannot be simply an enlargement of an anti-Jewish work since the first two chapters of Luke "are essential to the basic plan of the Gospel."[64]

Such a second century dating also confronts historical difficulties. Thus Plummer observes, "The historical atmosphere of the Acts is not that of A.D. 95-135. In the Acts the Jews are the persecutors of the Christians; at this late date the Jews were being persecuted themselves."[65]

Such a late date also makes questionable the author's assertion that he had consulted eyewitnesses of the events recorded. Opportunities to consult those who had been eyewitnesses and active preachers would be scarce indeed by that time.

The evidence of modern comparative historical grammar also militates against a second century dating. It has long been recognized

62. John Knox, *Marcion and the New Testament*, pp. 110-12.
63. Guthrie, p. 111.
64. Ellis, p. 55.
65. Plummer, p. xxxi.

that the Greek of the New Testament differs from classical Greek. The massive evidence from the papyri and the inscriptions which archaeology has brought to light have established that the New Testament was written in the Greek commonly used in the first century. In fitting the Greek of the New Testament into the historical development of the Greek language, comparative grammar points to the conclusion that the books of the New Testament were written during the first century.

A date around the close of the first century has been advocated on the ground that Luke drew upon *Antiquities of the Jews* by Josephus, which was published around A.D. 94. This claim has not proved convincing to scholars and is seldom pressed today.[66] The claim for Lucan dependence on Josephus turns primarily on the references to Lysanias as tetrarch of Abilene (Lk 3:1-2). While there are coincidences between Luke and Josephus, the divergences are so great as to render highly improbable the assumption that Luke copied from Josephus. The divergences prompted Schürer to comment, "Either Luke had not read Josephus, or he had forgotten all about what he had read."[67] The natural explanation seems to be that Luke differed from Josephus because he was following independent reliable sources. Ramsay has shown that archaeological evidence supports Luke's reference to Lysanias as tetrarch some time between A.D. 14 and 29.[68]

A number of scholars advocate a date between A.D. 70 and 80. Advocates of a date after the destruction of Jerusalem in A.D. 70 give much weight to Luke's formulation of the eschatological picture in Luke 21. Thus Streeter maintains that a comparison of Luke 21:20 with Mark 13:14 shows that Luke deliberately altered the eschatological picture in Mark because he already knew what had happened when he wrote.[69] That Luke's account is different and more explicit than Mark's does not prove that Luke wrote after the fall of Jerusalem. Such an argument turns Christ's prediction into a prophecy after the event. Such a claim can have no weight for those

66. H. J. Cadbury, "Subsidiary Points," in *The Beginnings of Christianity*, 2:355-58.
67. Emil Schürer, *Zeitschrift für wissenschäftliche Theologie*, 19(1876):582, quoted by Norval Geldenhuys, "Commentary on the Gospel of Luke," in *New International Commentary*, p. 31, n. 2.
68. W. M. Ramsay, *The Bearing of Recent Discoveries on the Trustworthiness of the New Testament*, pp. 297-300.
69. Burnett Hillman Streeter, *The Four Gospels: A Study of Origins*, p. 540.

who accept the ability of Christ to predict the future and believe that the gospel writers are reliable witnesses. While Christ's words in Luke 21:20 and Mark 13:14 are commonly taken as relating to the same event, the difference in the signs would rather suggest that the two passages refer to two different times. The statement in Luke specifically records the sign preceding the fall of Jerusalem, while the sign in Mark relates to the eschatological end.

The currently favored solution to the synoptic problem holds that Luke made use of Mark's gospel. Since Mark is generally dated around A.D. 65-68, it is held that Luke must be dated a little after A.D. 70, thus allowing sufficient time for the writing of the third gospel. But Guthrie remarks, "Whether Luke used Mark as a written source or not, no great interval need have separated them, for if he did use Mark he may well have gained access to it very soon after it was written."[70] From Colossians 4:10-14 it is certain that Luke and Mark were personally acquainted and were together in Rome. The publication of Mark's gospel could not have long remained unknown to Luke. Geldenhuys indeed asserts, "It is quite possible that Luke could, even within the first few weeks after Mark had written his gospel, have borrowed it from him to use it for the composition of his own Gospel."[71] Thus it is not necessary to assume a time interval between the two gospels which would push the third gospel after A.D. 70.

Other scholars advocate a date before the fall of Jerusalem, around A.D. 60-64. This dating is directly tied to an early dating for Acts. It is held that the most natural explanation for the fact that Acts does not mention the death of Paul (*c*. A.D. 65 or early 66), is that it had not yet happened. It is further urged that the absence of any mention of such important events as the burning of Rome in A.D. 64 and the destruction of Jerusalem in A.D. 70 means that these events had not yet taken place when Luke wrote. Further, it is alleged that if the writer of Acts had known the epistles of Paul to the Corinthians and the Galatians, he would have inserted some things or made some further explanations. Luke, it is felt, may have remained personally unacquainted with these letters if he wrote before A.D. 61, but it is quite improbable that he would have remained

70. Guthrie, p. 113.
71. Geldenhuys, p. 34.

unacquainted with them if he wrote as late as 75 or 80. A strong point in favor of this early date is the fact that during Paul's two-year imprisonment at Caesarea (Ac 24:27) Luke would have had ample opportunity to carry out his investigations and write his gospel. That Luke did use the time to make his investigations seems unquestionable, but it does not prove that he put his gospel into final form during that time. It is possible that he began writing at Caesarea and finished later, at Rome, or elsewhere.

The arguments for such an early date are plausible, but do not amount to positive proof. The fact that Luke did not record the death of Paul does not prove that it had not yet taken place. Acts is not a complete story and the open-ended termination of the book may be purposeful. If Luke's intention in writing Acts was to establish the political innocence of Christianity, his omission of the Neronian persecution of the church and the death of Paul are understandable.

There is thus no data which demands a precise date for Luke's gospel. A date before the beginning of the Neronian persecution is possible if it is accepted that Luke did not use Mark, or if an earlier date for Mark is adopted. Neither alternative is free of difficulties. If Luke did use Mark's gospel, the earliest possible date, under our view concerning Mark, would be A.D. 65; no long interval between the publication of Mark's gospel and the writing of the third gospel need be postulated. Since Luke must certainly have been collecting material for his gospel before he came to Rome, it seems but natural that he would discuss with Mark any matters concerning which Mark could offer information. If Luke did make use of Mark, he could well have issued his own gospel within a year after the appearance of the second gospel, even if he was not in Rome at the time of writing. Thus we may postulate a date of A.D. 66 or early 67. Such a date would be in harmony with the implied position of Irenaeus that Luke's gospel was written after the death of Paul.[72]

2. PLACE

The traditional evidence concerning the place of writing is meager and is not uniform. The *Anti-Marcionite Prologue* states that Luke wrote his gospel in Achaia. Jerome in his preface to his commentary

72. Irenaeus *Against Heresies* 3. 1. 1.

on Matthew mentions "Achaia and Boeotia," but in his later *Lives of Illustrious Men* (8) he assumes a Roman origin. None of the other early sources mentions the place where the third gospel was written. In later minuscle manuscripts both Rome and "Attica belonging to Boeotha" are mentioned.[73]

The contents of the third gospel do not offer any data for a specific place of origin beyond the fact that it was obviously addressed to non-Palestinian readers. "The peculiarities of its diction," Plummer declares, "point to a centre in which Hellenistic influences prevailed."[74] This would not automatically rule out Rome, but a native Greek area would seem more probable.

Modern guesses about the place of writing have included Caesarea, Rome, Asia Minor (Ephesus, specifically), Greece, probably Corinth, and even the Decapolis. It is possible that Luke began his two-part work in Caesarea or Rome but gave it final form and published it in Greece. We can be certain only that Luke wrote somewhere outside Palestine.

THE CHARACTERISTICS OF THE THIRD GOSPEL

1. COMPREHENSIVENESS

The gospel of Luke is distinguished by the comprehensive scope of its contents. Luke's statement in the prologue that he had "traced the course of *all things* accurately *from the first*" (italics added) indicates that he aimed at presenting the story of Jesus in its total sweep. Chronologically his gospel covers a longer period of time than any of the others.† His narrative begins fifteen months before the birth of Jesus (1:5, 26), whereas Matthew begins less than six months before His birth (1:18-25). Luke also carries his story further than the other gospels; he does not conclude with the resurrection but ends with an account of His ascension and the response of the disciples to that event (24:50-53).

The third gospel also contains an impressively large amount of material not found in any of the other gospels. Six of the twenty

73. Zahn, 3:8.
74. Plummer, p. xxxii.

†The narrative of each gospel picks up Jesus' biography at a different point. Luke begins fifteen months before the birth of Jesus (1:5, 26); Mt begins less than six months before the birth of Jesus (1:18 with Lk 1:26, 56); Mk begins with the public ministry of John the Baptist (1:1-4); Jn begins at least forty days after the baptism of Jesus (1:19, 29, 35, 43 as related to the period of the temptation).

miracles recorded in this gospel are peculiar to Luke, while nineteen of the thirty-five parables in the third gospel are not found in the others. Luke's nativity stories are entirely different from those in Matthew. The two large blocks of material which are peculiar to Luke (6:20–8:3; 9:51–18:14) contain some of our most precious gospel treasures. We owe our possession of this rich material to Luke's diligent research and his desire to give a comprehensive account of the story of Jesus.

2. PRAISE AND THANKSGIVING

This is the gospel of song and thanksgiving. Only Luke records the four beautiful songs connected with the nativity events, commonly known as the *Magnificat* (1:46-55), the *Benedictus* (1:68-79), the *Gloria in Excelsis* (2:14), and the *Nunc Dimittis* (2:29-32). These canticles, which are largely drawn from the character and contents of the Hebrew psalms, are the first Christian hymns. Scroggie comments, "Luke is the first great Christian hymnologist, not as a creator, but as a preserver of sacred songs."[75]

Luke begins and ends his gospel with a scene of worship in the temple (1:9; 24:53). It contains repeated references to "glorifying," "praising," or "blessing" God. The words "rejoice" and "joy" appear more often than in the other gospels. This joy is connected with the experience of salvation (15:7, 10, 22-24; 19:6). This joy is felt in heaven as well as on earth.

3. PERFECT HUMANITY

The third gospel portrays Jesus as the perfect man. Luke makes abundantly clear His supernatural origin and His right to the throne of David, but his "central conception of Jesus is that He is the friend and brother of man—the representative of universal humanity."[76] His gospel gives the fullest account of Jesus' birth, childhood, and normal development as a human being. Whereas Matthew traces His genealogy back to Abraham, Luke traces it back to Adam, thus connecting Jesus with the entire human race. Luke's nativity stories make very real the true humanity of Jesus.

Luke's account of Jesus' ministry often touches on His humanity.

75. W. Graham Scroggie, *A Guide to the Gospels*, p. 371.
76. Herbert L. Willett and James M. Campbell, *The Teachings of the Books*, p. 62.

Nazareth is referred to as the town "where he had been brought up" (4:16). He began His ministry "in the power of the Spirit" (4:14). He shared the common social life (7:34-36; 10:38-42; 11:37; 14:1-24; 19:1-10). He felt the strain of living as a wandering teacher with no place to lay His head (9:58); He broke into a tearful lament over the city of Jerusalem which rejected Him (13:34; 19:41); as He prayed in the garden, He agonized so sorely that His "sweat became as it were great drops of blood" (22:44); in His death He cried, "Father, into thy hands I commend my spirit" (23:46). Only Luke informs us that Jesus verified the reality of His resurrection-body by inviting His followers to "handle" Him, and ate a piece of "broiled fish" before them (24:39-43). Of the various titles applied to Jesus, the one that seems most suited to embody Luke's portrait of Him is "the Son of man." "Jesus was not merely *a* son of man; he was *the* son of man, the ideal man, in whom all human perfectibility is summed up."[77] Jesus shared our human nature in everything except sin (Heb 4:15).

Luke's portrait of Jesus was ideally suited to the Greek mind. The Greek ideal was human excellence, the perfect individual. In his gospel Luke shows that Jesus fulfilled this ideal in the highest and most absolute sense. He was the answer to the aspirations of the Greek. "Here was a perfect man, a human as well as divine Saviour who was worthy of their acceptance, faith, and worship."[78]

4. SAVIOUR FOR ALL

This gospel stresses the fact that the salvation offered in Christ is equally available to all men. All four gospels quote from Isaiah 40: 3-5, but only Luke extends the quotation to include the announcement that "*all flesh* shall see the salvation of God" (3:4-6, italics added). Luke records the aged Simeon's dcelaration that the child Jesus would be "a light for revelation to the Gentiles" as well as the glory of Israel (2:32). Jesus is pictured as being sympathetic toward and offering forgiveness to all sinners without reference to their race or position. Luke records that Jesus used two illustrations from the Old Testament to demonstrate God's grace toward non-Israelites, the sending of Elijah to the Gentile widow in Zarephath and the cleansing of Naaman the Syrian leper (4:25-28). Luke makes it clear that

77. Ibid.
78. Evans, p. 124.

admission to the Kingdom of God is open to all, "to the Samaritan (ix. 51-56, x. 30-37, xvii. 11-19) and the Gentile (ii. 32, iii. 6, 38, iv. 25-27, vii. 9, x. 1, xiii. 29, xxi. 24, xxiv. 47) as well as the Jew (i. 33, 54, 68-79, ii. 10); to publicans, sinners, and outcasts (iii. 12, 13, v. 27-32, vii. 37-50, xv. 1, 2, 11-32, xviii. 9-14, xix. 2-10, xxiii. 43) as well as the respectable (vii. 36, xi. 37, xiv. 1); to the poor (i. 53, ii. 7, 8, 24, iv. 18, vi. 20, 21, vii. 22, xiv. 13, 21, xvi. 20, 23) as well as to the rich (xix. 2, xxiii. 50)."[79] Christ Himself is recorded as declaring that He came "to seek and to save that which was lost" (19:10) and directed that "repentance and remission of sins should be preached in his name unto all the nations" (24:47).

For Luke Christianity had universal significance. He clearly shared the viewpoint of Paul, his friend and companion, as evidenced in his broad outlook on the world and understanding of the gospel as relevant for all men.

5. INTEREST IN PEOPLE

This gospel reflects Luke's interest in people. Because he believed in the universal power of the gospel, Luke focused attention upon its impact on the lives of various individuals. Jesus' three famous parables in chapter 15, unique to this gospel, stress His concern for individuals. Luke notes that Jesus was frequently surrounded by great crowds who were amazed at His words (5:26; 7:16-17; 11:14; 13:17; 14:25), but, unlike Matthew (9:36; 15:32), Luke "does not speak of Jesus' compassion on the multitude. This is reserved for individuals."[80]

This gospel vividly depicts individual men and women. Luke's ability to draw word pictures is evident in his description of the godly priest Zacharias (1:5-23, 57-79), the extortionate tax collector Zacchaeus (19:1-10), and the mourning Cleopas and his companion on the Emmaus road (24:13-33). Women play a more prominent role in Luke's gospel than in any of the other gospels. His opening section recounts the exciting experiences of Elizabeth, an aged handmaid of the Lord, in relation to the unique privilege accorded to Mary, her cousin (1:24-56), as well as the spiritual insight of the aged prophetess Anna (2:36-38). His gospel also tells the story of

79. Plummer, p. xlii.
80. Harrison, p. 206.

the widow of Nain whose dead son was restored to her by Jesus (7:
11-18); the repentant sinful woman in the house of Simon the Pharisee (7:36-50); the women who ministered to Jesus of their material
means (8:1-3); Martha and Mary of Bethany whose hospitality Jesus
enjoyed (10:38-42); the hunchbacked woman healed in the synagogue (13:10-13); the women of Jerusalem bewailing Jesus on His
way to the cross (23:27-31); as well as the prominent part played by
the women in the resurrection events (24:1-11). Because of this
prominence given to women the third gospel has aptly been characterized as "the gospel of womanhood." Luke's high esteem for wom-
en stands in contrast to the low view of women which characterized
the prevailing Greek and Jewish schools of thought.

Luke's interest in people also extends to children and young people. Only Luke describes the childhood of John the Baptist and
Jesus. Luke notes three times that an individual young person was
an "only" child (7:12; 8:42; 9:38).

6. DOMESTIC INTEREST

Luke also reveals interest in the domestic side of life. In his gospel
Jesus is portrayed as enjoying social fellowship in the homes of
friends and followers: the meal in the home of Martha and Mary
(10:38-42), His visit in the home of Zacchaeus (19:1-10), and the
supper in the home of the two Emmaus disciples (24:29-31). Jesus
readily associated with publicans and sinners at table, for which He
was criticized (15:2). Luke alone recounts that on three separate
occasions Jesus accepted an invitation to dine with a Pharisee (7:36;
11:37; 14:1). Jesus used the domestic setting to reach people re-
gardless of their sex, background, or social status.

Luke's domestic interest is also reflected in many of Jesus' parables
which he records. They refer to various home-connected activities,
such as supplying a belated traveler with needed food (11:5-8); an
innkeeper tending a wounded man (10:35); a woman putting leaven
in dough (13:21), patching clothes (5:36), or sweeping her house in
search of a lost coin (15:8); rejoicing at the return of the prodigal
(15:20-24); or a servant tending to the needs of his master (17:7-9).

7. ECONOMIC INTERESTS

Both poverty and wealth appear in this gospel. Luke's narrative demonstrates God's graciousness to the poor and humble. Mary celebrated this fact in her song (1:50-53); Christ was born of humble parents and amid circumstances of deep poverty (2:6-7, 22-24); the humble shepherds were given the angelic announcement of the birth of the Saviour (2:8-20); Jesus announced that He came to evangelize the poor (4:16-18); He gave His beatitude on the poor (6:20), and commended the sacrificial giving of the poor widow (21:1-4). In the discourses and parables of Jesus recorded by Luke emphasis is often laid on wealth, its use and abuse (6:24-25; 12:13-34; 14:12-24; 16:1-31; 18:18-30). But Luke does not simply condemn the possession of material means. He also gives instances in which it was used for commendable ends (8:1-3; 21:1-4).

8. PRAYER

The third gospel is the gospel of prayer. In keeping with his emphasis on the perfect humanity of Jesus, Luke mentions nine occasions when Jesus prayed. Seven are found only in this gospel: 1) at His baptism (3:21); 2) after a day of miracles (5:16); 3) before choosing the Twelve (6:12); 4) before revealing His coming passion to the disciples (9:18-22); 5) at the transfiguration (9:29); 6) at the return of the Seventy (10:17-21); 7) before teaching His disciples how to pray (11:1); 8) in Gethsemane (22:39-46); 9) on the cross (23:34, 46). Luke alone records Jesus' declaration to Peter that He had prayed for him that his faith would not fail (22:31-32). Luke preserves two parables by Jesus devoted to the subject of prayer: the parables of the importunate widow (18:1-8), and the Pharisee and the Publican (18:9-14).

9. HISTORICAL CONTEXT

A distinctive feature of Luke's gospel is that he devotes attention to the larger historical setting of his story. He shows his historical interest in synchronizing the events in Palestine with what was going on elsewhere in the Roman Empire. He gives the historical framework for his account of the nativity events (1:5; 2:1) as well as the commencement of the public ministries of John and Jesus (3:1-2).

10. LANGUAGE AND STYLE

This gospel reveals the remarkable literary versatility of its author.

Plummer observes, "He can be as Hebraistic as the LXX, and as free from Hebraisms as Plutarch. And, in the main, whether intentionally or not, he is Hebraistic in describing Hebrew society, and Greek in describing Greek society."[81] The prologue (1:1-4) is a carefully balanced sentence constructed in accordance with classical Greek patterns, revealing Luke's cultural background. But without warning, he changes to a style with a strong Semitic flavor in relating the infancy narratives. The remainder of the gospel is written in good Koine Greek, the language commonly used throughout the Empire.[82] As an artist Luke chose a style which would harmonize with the life situation being dealt with. The variableness in his style may well be due to his faithfulness to his sources. There is nothing in his gospel which could not have been the work of a capable scholar who was himself steeped in the language of the Septuagint and was fully at home in the prevailing culture and language of his day.

Luke's style is simple and dignified. He reveals a strong power of accurate observation, a vividness of description, and the ability to delineate a character or paint a scene with a few vigorous lines or words. "He possesses the art of composition. He knows not only how to tell a tale truthfully, but how to tell it with effect."[83]

Luke had a remarkably large vocabulary, the largest of any New Testament writer. In his gospel and the Acts there are some eight hundred words which do not occur elsewhere in the New Testament.[84] He also employs a wide variety of expressions and constructions more often than any other writer.[85] He also shows a fondness for compound words. Clearly he must have been a man of remarkable skill and thorough training, just as the tradition concerning him asserts.

AN OUTLINE OF LUKE

The gospel of Luke presents the story of Jesus in its full historical sweep. The main divisions relate the story in chronological sequence and conform to the broad outlines of the story as presented in the

81. Plummer, p. xlix.
82. Cf. Creed, pp. lxxvi-lxxxiv; Plummer, pp. xlviii-lxiii.
83. Plummer, p. xlvi.
84. Joseph Henry Thayer, *A Greek-English Lexicon of the New Testament*, pp. 699-703; Plummer, p. lii.
85. Plummer, pp. liii-lxvii.

other synoptics. This gospel portrays the person of Jesus as a member of humanity who lived the perfect and representative life as the Son of Man. His self-sacrifice qualified Him to be the Saviour of mankind.

The theme of the gospel may be stated as "The Son of Man, the Saviour of Mankind."

I. Prologue, 1:1-4

II. Advent of the Son of Man, 1:5—2:52
    A. Annunciations in preparation, 1:5-56
        1. Announcement of the forerunner's birth, 5-25
          a) Character of Zacharias and Elisabeth, 5-7
          b) Promise to the father of a son, 8-23
          c) Conception of the son, vv. 24-25
        2. Annunciation to Mary, vv. 26-28
        3. Visit of Mary to Elisabeth, vv. 39-56
          a) Prophetic words of Elisabeth, vv. 39-45
          b) Song of Mary, vv. 46-55
          c) Summary of the visit, vv. 56
    B. Birth of the forerunner, 1:57-80
        1. Birth and naming of the child, vv. 57-66
        2. Song of the father, vv. 67-79
        3. Summary concerning the boy, v. 80
    C. Nativity of the Saviour, 2:1-20
        1. Journey to Bethlehem and the birth, vv. 1-7
        2. Revelation to the shepherds, vv. 8-20
    D. Infancy of the Saviour, 2:21-39
        1. Circumcision and naming of Jesus, v. 21
        2. Presentation in the temple, vv. 22-39
          a) Offerings according to the law, vv. 22-24
          b) Recognition of the Saviour, vv. 25-39
            (1) Song and prophecy of Simeon, vv. 25-35
            (2) Testimony of Anna, vv. 36-39
    E. Development of the Son of man, 2:40-52
        1. Development as a child, v. 40
        2. Significance of His first Passover, vv. 41-50
        3. Development from boyhood to manhood, vv. 51-52

III. Presentation of the Son of Man, 3:1—4:13
    A. Preparation by the forerunner, 3:1-20
        1. Beginning of John's ministry, vv. 1-6
        2. Preaching of John, vv. 7-14
        3. Announcement about the coming Christ, vv. 15-17
        4. Summary of the story of John, vv. 18-20
    B. Identification at the baptism, 3:21-22
    C. Genealogy of the Son of man, 3:23-38
    D. Victory over the tempter, 4:1-13

IV. Ministry of the Son of Man, 4:14—21:38
    A. Ministry mainly in Galilee, 4:14—9:50
        1. Beginnings of the ministry, 4:14-44
           a) Summary of the activity, vv. 14-15
           b) Rejection of Nazareth, vv. 16-30
           c) Ministry in Capernaum, vv. 31-41
               (1) Activity in the synagogue, vv. 31-37
               (2) Healing of Simon's mother-in-law, vv. 38-39
               (3) Ministry to many after sundown, vv. 40-41
           d) Ministry beyond Capernaum, vv. 42-44
        2. Course of the Galilean ministry, 5:1—8:56
           a) Call to four fishermen, 5:1-11
           b) Cleansing of a leper, 5:12-16
           c) Healing demonstrating authority to forgive sin, 5:17-26
           d) Problem of feasting and fasting, 5:27-39
               (1) Call and feast of Levi, vv. 27-32
               (2) Question about fasting by John's disciples, vv. 33-
                   39
           e) Controversies concerning Sabbath observance, 6:1-11
               (1) Plucking of grain on the Sabbath, vv. 1-5
               (2) Healing of a man's hand on the Sabbath, vv. 6-11
           f) Message of the Kingdom, 6:12-49
               (1) Choice of the Twelve, vv. 12-16
               (2) Ministry to the multitude, vv. 17-19
               (3) Sermon to the disciples, vv. 20-49
                   (*a*) Qualifications for admission, vv. 20-26
                   (*b*) Laws of life in the kingdom, vv. 27-45
                     i) Law of love, vv. 27-35

ii) Law concerning judgment of others, vv. 36-45

(c) Test of obedience for professed members, vv. 46-49

g) Manifestations of His power, 7:1-17
   (1) Healing of the centurion's servant, vv. 1-10
   (2) Raising of the widow's dead son, vv. 11-17

h) Relations to His forerunner, 7:18-35
   (1) Answer to the question from John, vv. 18-23
   (2) Testimony of Jesus to John, vv. 24-30
   (3) Estimate of that generation, vv. 31-35

i) Anointing by a sinful woman, 7:36-50

j) Companions on His tour of Galilee, 8:1-3

k) Parables concerning the kingdom, 8:4-18
   (1) Parable given to the multitude, vv. 4-8
   (2) Parable explained to the disciples, vv. 9-15
   (3) Parable of the lamp, vv. 16-18

l) Revelation concerning spiritual kinship, 8:19-21

m) Miracles demonstrating His authority, 8:22-56
   (1) Stilling of the storm at sea, vv. 22-25
   (2) Deliverance of the Gerasene demoniac, vv. 26-39
   (3) Double miracle upon returning to Galilee, vv. 40-56
      (a) Plea of the synagogue ruler, vv. 40-42
      (b) Healing of a woman with a hemorrhage, vv. 43-48
      (c) Raising of the daughter of Jairus, vv. 49-56

3. Work of Jesus with the twelve, 9:1-50
   a) Mission of the twelve in Galilee, vv. 1-6
   b) Perplexity of Herod the tetrarch, vv. 7-9
   c) Feeding of the five thousand, vv. 10-17
   d) Confession by Peter concerning Jesus, vv. 18-20
   e) Revelation of the coming Passion, vv. 21-26
   f) Transfiguration on the mount, vv. 27-36
   g) Healing of the demoniac boy, vv. 37-43a
   h) Renewed announcement of His Passion, 43b-45
   i) Lessons for the disciples, vv. 46-50
      (1) Lesson concerning greatness, vv. 46-48

(2) Lesson concerning tolerance, vv. 49-50
B. Ministry on the way to Jerusalem, 9:51–19:28
   1. First stage of the journey, 9:51–13:21
      a) Rejection by a Samaritan village, 9:51-56
      b) Testing of three candidates for discipleship, 9:57-62
      c) Mission of the seventy, 10:1-24
         (1) Commission to the seventy, vv. 1-16
            (*a*) Instructions for their work, vv. 1-11
            (*b*) Fate of the impenitent cities, vv. 12-16
         (2) Reaction upon their return, vv. 17-24
            (*a*) Response to their report, vv. 17-20
            (*b*) Prayer of thanksgiving, vv. 21-22
            (*c*) Privilege of His disciples, vv. 23-24
      d) Reply to a lawyer's questions, 10:25-37
      e) Visit in the home of Martha and Mary, 10:38-42
      f) Lessons on prayer, 11:1-13
         (1) Model prayer, vv. 1-4
         (2) Parable of importunate praying, vv. 5-8
         (3) Efficacy of prayer, vv. 9-13
      g) Controversy concerning exorcism of demons, 11:14-36
         (1) Reactions to the expulsion of a demon, vv. 14-15
         (2) Refutation of a blasphemous charge, vv. 16-26
         (3) Correction of a woman's emotional response, vv. 27-28
         (4) Rebuke to the demands for a sign, vv. 29-36
            (*a*) Blindness of the sign-seekers, vv. 29-32
            (*b*) Parable of the lamp in explanation, vv. 33-36
      h) Condemnation of ritualism and hypocrisy, 11:37-54
         (1) Criticism addressed to the Pharisees, vv. 37-44
         (2) Criticism addressed to the lawyers, vv. 45-52
         (3) Reaction to the criticism, vv. 53-54
      i) Teachings to various groups, 12:1-59
         (1) Disciples: exhortation to fearless witness, vv. 1-12
         (2) Crowd: warning against covetousness, vv. 13-21
         (3) Disciples: responsibilities of discipleship, vv. 22-53
            (*a*) Warning against anxiety, vv. 22-34
            (*b*) Exhortation to readiness, vv. 35-40
            (*c*) Admonition to faithfulness, vv. 41-48

(*d*) Reminder of His divisive influence, vv. 49-53
(4) Multitudes: interpreting the signs of the time, vv. 54-59
j) Call to repentance, 13:1-9
  (1) Lesson from current tragedies, vv. 1-5
  (2) Parable of the fig tree in a vineyard, vv. 6-9
k) Conflict with a synagogue ruler, 13:10-21
  (1) Healing of a hunchbacked woman, vv. 10-13
  (2) Refutation of the ruler's objection, vv. 14-17
  (3) Parables of the kingdom, vv. 18-21
2. Second stage of the journey, 13:22—17:10
  a) Danger of exclusion from the kingdom, 13:22-30
  b) Message to Herod and the lament over Jerusalem, 13:31-35
  c) Guest in the home of a Pharisee, 14:1-24
    (1) Healing of a man with dropsy, vv. 1-6
    (2) Advice to invited guests, vv. 7-11
    (3) Advice about the choice of guests, vv. 12-14
    (4) Parable of the great supper, vv. 15-24
  d) Warning about the cost of discipleship, 14:25-35
  e) Trilogy of parables on the lost, 15:1-32
    (1) Occasion for the parables, vv. 1-2
    (2) Parable of the lost sheep, vv. 3-7
    (3) Parable of the lost coin, vv. 8-10
    (4) Parable of the lost sons, vv. 11-32
      (*a*) Prodigal son, vv. 11-24
      (*b*) Self-righteous elder son, vv. 25-32
  f) Teaching concerning the use of wealth, 16:1-31
    (1) Parable of the unjust steward, vv. 1-13
      (*a*) Statement of the parable, vv. 1-8
      (*b*) Application of the teaching, vv. 9-13
    (2) Reply to the Pharisees' reaction, vv. 14-18
    (3) Story of the rich man and Lazarus, vv. 19-31
  g) Teaching concerning offenses and service, 17:1-10
    (1) Warning against offenses, vv. 1-4
    (2) Responsibility of the servant, vv. 5-10
3. Third stage of the journey, 17:11—19:28
  a) Healing of ten lepers, 17:11-19

   b) Teaching about the coming of the kingdom, 17:20-37
    (1) Answer to the Pharisees, vv. 20-21
    (2) Teaching to the disciples, vv. 22-37
   c) Teaching on the proper use of prayer, 18:1-14
    (1) Parable of the widow and the unjust judge, vv. 1-8
    (2) Parable of the Pharisee and the Publican, vv. 9-14
   d) Response of Jesus to little children, 18:15-17
   e) Encounter with the rich young ruler, 18:18-30
    (1) Failure of the ruler to pay the price, vv. 18-23
    (2) Discussion of the case with the disciples, vv. 24-30
   f) Third announcement of His Passion, 18:31-34
   g) Events at Jericho, 18:35–19:27
    (1) Healing of the blind beggar, 18:35-43
    (2) Conversion of Zacchaeus, 19:1-10
    (3) Parable of the pounds, 19:11-27
   h) Completion of the journey to Jerusalem, 19:28

 C. Ministry in Jerusalem, 19:29–21:38
  1. Triumphal entry into Jerusalem, 19:29-44
   a) Manner of the entry, vv. 29-38
   b) Refusal to stop the jubilation, vv. 39-40
   c) Prediction of the destruction of Jerusalem, vv. 41-44
  2. Cleansing of the temple, 19:45-46
  3. Attempts to trap Jesus by various questions, 19:47–20:40
   a) Setting for the attempts, 19:47-48
   b) Question concerning His authority, 20:1-18
    (1) Questioners disarmed by His counterquestion, vv. 1-8
    (2) Questioners exposed by His parable, vv. 9-16
    (3) Questioners warned of their fate, vv. 17-18
   c) Question about the tribute money, 20:19-26
   d) Question about the resurrection, 20:27-40
  4. Counterattack on the Jewish leaders, 20:41-47
   a) Question concerning Messiah's sonship, vv. 41-44
   b) Warning against hypocritical scribes, vv. 45-47
  5. Commendation of a widow's giving, 21:1-4
  6. Disclosures to the disciples concerning the future, 21:5-36
   a) Coming destruction of the temple, vv. 5-7

b) Teaching concerning the end, vv. 8-28

    (1) Character of the age, vv. 8-11

    (2) Difficulties ahead for them, vv. 12-19

    (3) Fall of Jerusalem and the fate of the nation, vv. 20-24

    (4) Coming of the Son of Man in glory, vv. 25-28

c) Exhortation to hope and vigilance, vv. 29-36

7. Summary of the ministry in Jerusalem, 21:37-38

V. Passion of the Son of Man, 22:1–23:56

  A. Conspiracy against Jesus, 22:1-6

    1. Plotting of the chief priests and scribes, vv. 1-2

    2. Agreement of Judas to betray Jesus, vv. 3-6

  B. Events in connection with the last supper, 22:7-38

    1. Preparation for the Passover, vv. 7-13

    2. Institution of the Lord's Supper, vv. 14-20

    3. Announcement of the betrayer's presence, vv. 21-23

    4. Response to the dispute about greatness, vv. 24-30

    5. Prediction of Peter's denials, vv. 31-34

    6. Warning about the impending new condition, vv. 35-38

  C. Events on the Mount of Olives that night, 22:39-53

    1. Agony in prayer, vv. 39-46

    2. Betrayal and arrest, vv. 47-53

  D. Three denials of Peter, 22:54-62

  E. Trial before the religious leaders, 22:63-71

    1. Mistreatment of Jesus, vv. 63-65

    2. Official condemnation after dawn, vv. 66-71

  F. Trial before the civil authorities, 23:1-25

    1. Accusations against Jesus before Pilate, vv. 1-7

    2. Examination before Herod Antipas, vv. 8-12

    3. Continuation of the case before Pilate, vv. 13-25

        a) Efforts of Pilate for acquittal, vv. 13-16‡

        b) Surrender of Pilate to the Jews' demands, vv. 18-25

  G. Events on the way to the crucifixion, 23:26-32

    1. Cross-bearer for Jesus, v. 26

    2. Lament of the daughters of Jerusalem, vv. 27-31

    3. Malefactors led out with Jesus, v. 32

---

‡Verse 17 is inserted by many ancient manuscripts.

H. Scene on Calvary, 23:33-49
1. Crucifixion and mockery of Jesus, vv. 33-38
2. Reactions of the two malefactors, vv. 39-43
3. Events connected with the death of Jesus, vv. 44-49
I. Burial of Jesus, 23:50-56

VI. Triumph of the Son of Man, 24:1-53
A. Discovery of the empty tomb, vv. 1-12
1. Experience and report of the women, vv. 1-11
2. Visit to the tomb by Peter, v. 12
B. Appearances of the living Jesus, vv. 13-49
1. Appearance to the two Emmaus disciples, vv. 13-35
a) Discussion on the road, vv. 13-27
b) Recognition at table, vv. 28-32
c) Return to Jerusalem with their report, vv. 33-35
2. Appearance to the disciples in Jerusalem, vv. 36-49
a) Proof of His resurrection given the disciples, vv. 36-43
b) Final instruction to the disciples, vv. 44-49
C. Ascension of the risen Lord, vv. 50-53

A BOOK LIST ON LUKE

Arndt, William F. *The Gospel According to St. Luke.* St. Louis: Concordia, 1956.
A thorough exposition by a conservative Lutheran scholar. The author gives his own translation which is intended to be accurate rather than readable. Each section receives a general exposition which is followed by illuminating notes on the Greek text. The 500-page volume offers a careful unfolding of the gospel.
Balmforth, Henry. "The Gospel According to Saint Luke in the Revised Version." In *The School Clarendon Bible.* Oxford: Clarendon, 1930.
Prints the entire gospel as a unit, followed by a concise exposition in a verse-by-verse treatment. While accepting the basic doctrines of the virgin birth and the resurrection, the stance is generally liberal.
Barclay, William. "The Gospel of Luke." In *The Daily Study Bible.* Philadelphia: Wesminster, 1953.
Prints the author's own translation. A series of popular studies whose strong point is word study. Contains good illustrative material. Part of the author's interpretation follows a liberal position.
Bowie, Walter Russel. *The Compassionate Christ: Reflections from the Gospel of Luke.* New York: Abingdon, 1965.

Devotional comments on the gospel of Luke by a noted liberal scholar. The treatment is section-by-section; it does not attempt to make a detailed commentary but rather aims to picture the compassionate Christ as Luke sought to portray Him.

Browning, W. R. R. *The Gospel According to Saint Luke.* Torch Bible Commentaries. London: SCM, 1960.

Brief comments by a liberal British scholar. Accepts views of form criticism, but seeks to avoid its extremely negative results. The notes are based on the Revised Standard Version, but only phrases from it are included with the comments.

Bruce, Alexander Balmain. "The Synoptic Gospels." In *The Expositor's Greek Testament,* vol. 1. Reprint. Grand Rapids: Eerdmans, 1970.

Burton, Henry. "The Gospel According to St. Luke." In *The Expositor's Bible,* vol. 5. Reprint. Grand Rapids: Eerdmans, 1956.

A practical, warm-hearted exposition by a conservative scholar. Although written during the nineteenth century, it is rich in its interpretative contents, as, for example, on chapter 15.

Caird, G. B. *The Gospel of St. Luke.* The Pelican Gospel Commentaries. Baltimore: Penguin, 1968.

A thoroughly liberal interpretation by a British scholar who views the gospel in the light of contemporary critical and theological studies. Of real value to the discerning student.

Creed, John Martin. *The Gospel According to St. Luke.* 1930. Reprint. London: Macmillan, 1957.

Greek text. A well-known commentary on Luke by a British liberal scholar. The introduction of eighty pages gives a thorough treatment of critical problems. Suitable for the advanced, discerning student.

Danker, Frederick W. *Jesus and the New Age According to St. Luke: A Commentary on the Third Gospel.* St. Louis: Clayton, 1972.

An up-to-date, provocative treatment of the third gospel by an accomplished liberal Lutheran scholar. Places strong emphasis on the apocalyptic aspects of Luke's thought. This commentary provoked controversy before it was published and contributed to the termination of a series for which it was originally intended. Suggested for the discerning reader.

Ellis, E. Earle. *The Gospel of Luke.* The Century Bible, New Edition. London: Nelson, 1966.

The 60-page introduction brings the reader up to date on modern critical studies on Luke. Prints the Revised Standard Version at the top of the page and gives a verse-by-verse treatment. At the beginning of each section attention is called to the structure of the passage and its teaching. The notes are often disappointingly meager. The interpretation is liberal in some spots.

Erdman, Charles R. *The Gospel of Luke.* Reprint. Philadelphia: Westminster, 1936.

A devotional and practical exposition, in paragraph form, by a conservative Presbyterian scholar.

Farrar, F. W. "The Gospel According to St. Luke." In *Cambridge Greek Testament for Schools and Colleges.* 1884. Reprint. Cambridge: Cambridge U., 1903.

Greek text. The work of a famous British scholar of the past century. In spite of its age, the phrase-by-phrase treatment is worth consulting.

Ford, D. W. C. *A Reading of Saint Luke's Gospel.* Philadelphia: Lippincott, 1967.

The author, an Anglican leader in church extension, approaches Luke's gospel primarily with a view to the preacher's need. The exposition centers on the theme of mission and the author attempts to find contemporary meaning without straining the text.

Geldenhuys, Norval. "Commentary on the Gospel of Luke." In *The New International Commentary on the New Testament.* Grand Rapids: Eerdmans, 1954.

One of the very best recent conservative commentaries on the third gospel. Prints the English Revised Version (1881) by paragraphs with numerous footnotes on the text in the light of the Greek; these notes appear after the exposition of the respective section treated. Contains an important introduction, a good bibliography, and important special notes, plus an important excursis on "the Day and Date of the Crucifixion."

Gilmour, S. MacLean; Bowie, Walter Russell; Knox, John; Buttrick, George Arthur; and Scherer, Paul. "The Gospel According to St. Luke." In *The Interpreter's Bible,* vol. 8. New York: Abingdon, 1952.

In conformity with the series to which it belongs, the material is in two parts, the exegesis by Gilmour and the exposition by the other writers. The exegesis, liberal in its slant, is quite brief; the exposition contains much material for sermonic purposes.

Godet, Frederic. *A Commentary on the Gospel of St. Luke.* Trans. E. W. Shalders. 2 vols. Edinburgh: T. & T. Clark, 1881.

An exhaustive, technical commentary by a conservative French theologian of the past century. Godet's theological and critical conservatism is clearly revealed in this work on Luke. Of abiding value in spite of its age.

Harrington, W. J. *The Gospel According to St. Luke: A Commentary.*
Westminster, Md.: Newman, 1967.

A non-technical commentary by a Roman Catholic scholar intended
for the serious Bible student. The author places special emphasis on the
material peculiar to Luke while pointing to the similarities of Luke to
the other gospels.

Hobbs, Herschel H. *An Exposition of the Gospel of Luke.* Grand Rapids:
Baker, 1966.

A paragraph-by-paragraph exposition of Luke by a well-known
Southern Baptist pastor-scholar. Does not deal with critical problems,
but does make repeated reference to the original Greek. Well adapted
to the lay reader.

Leaney, A. R. *A Commentary on the Gospel According to St. Luke.*
Harper's New Testament Commentaries. New York: Harper, 1958.

Prints the author's own translation. A scholarly liberal commentary
which is skeptical of the accuracy of parts of this gospel.

Lenski, R. C. H. *The Interpretation of St. Mark's and St. Luke's Gospels.*
Columbus, Ohio: Lutheran Book Concern, 1934.

(Reprinted in 1946 as a volume separate from Mark with the Wartburg Press imprint.)

Luck, G. Coleman. *Luke: The Gospel of the Son of Man.* Everyman's
Bible Commentary. Chicago: Moody, 1960.

A concise, conservative presentation of the contents of the gospel in
one hundred easy-to-read pages. Well suited for the student making an
initial study of this gospel.

Manson, William. "The Gospel of Luke." In *The Moffatt New Testament
Commentary.* London: Hodder & Stoughton, 1930.

Prints the Moffatt translation. A readable liberal commentary which
follows the format and the general viewpoint of the series to which it
belongs.

Miller, Donald G. *The Layman's Bible Commentary,* vol. 18, *Luke.* Richmond, Va.: Knox, 1959.

A non-technical commentary, printing the Revised Standard Version,
which deals with the gospel by sections. This compact volume presents
the historical Christian faith in a non-dogmatic way. Well suited to the
lay reader.

Morgan, G. Campbell. *The Gospel According to Luke.* New York: Revell, 1931.

A series of expository lectures on the gospel by this prince of expository preachers. Valuable for its exegetical insights.

Owen, John J. *A Commentary, Critical, Expository, and Practical, on the Gospel of Luke.* New York: Leavitt & Allen, 1864.

An old but still useful conservative commentary on Luke. Comments on Quirinius (p. 28) reflect the difficulties of the conservative interpreter before the latest information became available. Devotes twenty two-column pages to the exposition of chapter 15.

Plummer, Alfred. "A Critical and Exegetical Commentary on the Gospel According to S. Luke." In *The International Critical Commentary.* Reprint. Edinburgh: T. & T. Clark, 1896.

Greek text. A recognized classic on the Greek text of Luke. It offers an exhaustive introduction of 75 pages and a thorough treatment of the gospel on the basis of the original. Invaluable for the student able to handle Greek.

Ragg, Lonsdale. *St. Luke.* Westminster Commentaries. London: Methuen, 1922.

A careful and reverent treatment of Luke's gospel by a conservative British scholar. Prints the English Revised Version (1881).

Rice, John R. *The Son of Man: A Verse-by-Verse Commentary on the Gospel According to Luke.* Murfreesboro, Tenn.: Sword of the Lord, 1971.

A devotional commentary by a forthright, conservative Bible teacher and evangelist. Well suited for lay readers and those seeking inspirational material on this gospel.

Summers, Ray. *Commentary on Luke.* Waco, Texas: Word, 1972.

A full yet non-technical commentary on Luke by an accomplished Southern Baptist professor, well suited to the average Bible student. A distinctive feature of the volume is the comparison of the newly discovered gospel according to Thomas with parallel material in Luke. Summers accepts a date around A.D. 80 for Luke and stresses that Luke shows how Jesus' teaching indicated that some time would elapse before His return in glory.

Talbot, Malcolm O. "Luke." In *The Broadman Bible Commentary,* vol. 9. Nashville, Tenn.: Broadman, 1970.

The Revised Standard Version is printed at the beginning of each paragraph into which the gospel is divided. Lucan authorship is accepted as the best "working hypothesis" and the gospel is dated around A.D. 80-85. Seeks to keep a balance between exegesis and exposition. Has a detailed outline of the gospel. Liberal in spots.

Van Oosterzee, John James. "The Gospel According to Luke." In Lange's *Commentary on the Holy Scriptures.* Translated from the 1861 edition by Philip Schaff, with additions. Reprint. Grand Rapids: Zondervan, n.d.

In keeping with the series to which it belongs, the massive material is presented in three parts: exegetical and critical, doctrinal and ethical, and homiletical and practical. Conservative in viewpoint. Valuable for those willing to dig into its vast stores of material, much of which is definitely dated.

7

A SURVEY OF THE SYNOPTIC PROBLEM

THE TERM "synoptic gospels," refers to the first three gospels and distinguishes them from the fourth gospel. The word "synoptic" comes from the Greek *sunoptikos,* meaning "seeing the whole together, taking a comprehensive view." It implies that Matthew, Mark, and Luke are so similar that they may appropriately be regarded as portraying the life of Jesus from a common viewpoint. A rapid perusal of these gospels shows that they share numerous features that are not a part of the fourth gospel. The use of the term "synoptic" dates from the time of J. J. Griesbach (1745-1812). In 1774 he had these gospels printed in three parallel columns so that the common passages stood side by side. He entitled his volume a *synopsis,* a conspectus. Numerous such synopses, or harmonies, have been produced since that time.

The synoptic problem concerns the literary relationship of these three gospels. The problem is compounded by the mixture of widespread agreements and striking divergences within the gospels. The problem is, in the words of Kümmel, "How is the remarkable, complex commingling of agreements and disagreements among Matthew, Mark, and Luke to be explained?"[1] Proposed solutions to the problem seek to clarify the origin and literary relationships of these gospels.

The investigation of the problem is properly a matter for the trained scholar, but the ordinary reader cannot afford to remain uninformed about it. Scroggie appropriately points out two extreme attitudes to be avoided: "(a) indifference to what can be known of the composition and construction of these Gospels; and (b) such occupation with the pursuit of this inquiry that one's appreciation of and subjection to what is written is endangered."[2]

1. Werner Georg Kümmel, *Introduction to the New Testament,* p. 35.
2. W. Graham Scroggie, *A Guide to the Gospels,* p. 83.

THE EXISTING SYNOPTIC PHENOMENA

1. AGREEMENTS

The synoptics show remarkable agreements in that, at least in numerous sections, their contents can readily be arranged in parallel columns. All three agree conspicuously in their overall selection of materials.

The synoptics agree in presenting the story of Jesus under the same broad chronological outline: the period of preparation, the ministry in Galilee, the ministry on the way to Jerusalem, and the ministry in Jerusalem culminating in Jesus' death and resurrection. Much of the narrative material is common to all three, while numerous events are related in two parallel accounts. Taking Mark as a basis of comparison, we see that almost all of its material appears in the other two. Approximately 30 verses from Mark are not paralleled in Matthew; Mark 6:45–8:26 has no parallel in Luke.

In addition to agreeing in their overall framework, the synoptics frequently follow the same order of events. Their sequence of events may lead to a climax with all terminating the thread of events at the same place; and then after a certain interval they again take up the narrative at the same juncture of events. Whenever Matthew or Luke diverges from the order in Mark, the other remains in general agreement with Mark. Parallel episodes are usually reported in the same order.

The synoptics reveal instances of remarkable agreement in the literary formulation of their accounts.[3] They may reveal close agreement in the structure of the event recorded. In the story of the paralytic let down through the roof, all three break their narratives by inserting a parenthesis at exactly the same place (Mt 9:6; Mk 2:10; Lk 5:24). In identifying John the Baptist all three quote Isaiah 40:3 and all three agree in departing from the Septuagint in their quotation (Mt 3:3; Mk 1:3; Lk 3:4). They reveal a common usage of rare words which are not found elsewhere in the New Testament; in their versions of "the Lord's Prayer" both Matthew (6:11) and Luke (11: 3) use the word "daily" (*epiousion*) which thus far has been found only once in secular Greek. In his book *Horae Synopticae* J. C. Hawkins lists identities of language in the synoptics in the construction

3. For details see X. Leon-Dufour, in A. Robert and A. Feuillet, *Introduction to the New Testament*, pp. 256-58.

of sentences, in single words and short phrases, as well as longer passages in which many words are identical.[4]

2. DIFFERENCES

The synoptic gospels also display striking divergences, which are all the more remarkable because on the whole these gospels are so similar.

Each gospel contains material that is peculiar to it. This is especially true of Matthew and Luke. The birth stories in Matthew and Luke are entirely different (Mt 1:18–2:23; Lk 1:5–2:52). Both gospels give genealogies (Mt 1:1-17; Lk 3:23-38), but their lists are different and they appear in different contexts. Only Matthew records the incident of Peter walking on the water (14:28-31) and the coin in the fish's mouth (17:24-27), while the material in Luke 9: 51–18:14 is unique to the third gospel. Each gospel contains events and discourses which do not appear in the others.

Using a percentage basis, Westcott tabulated the peculiarities and coincidences of the four gospels as follows:[5]

Gospel	Peculiarities	Coincidences
Mark	7	93
Matthew	42	58
Luke	59	41
John	92	8

There are often marked differences in the parallel accounts of a specific event. Luke's order of the three temptations of Jesus in the wilderness (4:1-13) differs from the order given in Matthew (4:1-11), while Mark says nothing about the different temptations (1:12-13). In recounting the healing of a centurion's servant at Capernaum Matthew pictures the centurion as personally bringing his request to Jesus (8:5-13), while Luke relates that the centurion made his request through Jewish elders sent to intercede on his behalf (7:1-10). Matthew's record of the "Sermon on the Mount" (chaps. 5-7) is considerably longer than the sermon recorded in Luke (6:20-49), but some of the material in Luke is not found in Matthew's account.

Certain episodes are transposed and related in a different context.

4. John C. Hawkins, *Horae Synopticae,* pp. 54-67.
5. Brooke Foss Westcott, *An Introduction to the Study of the Gospels,* p. 195.

Matthew and Luke place the healing of the centurion's servant in a different historical context. Sayings of Jesus which appear in a certain connection in one gospel are quoted in quite a different connection in another gospel. Parts of the material which Matthew includes in the Sermon on the Mount are placed in different though similar connections by Luke. All the gospels have accounts of events in connection with Passion Week, yet they contain numerous differences and no two record exactly the same series of events.

A comparison of the contents of the synoptic gospels reveals both close resemblances and striking divergences. Says Leon Dufour, "This phenomenon is unique in the world of letters; and it poses this question: What mutual relations do these writings have, one to another?"[6]

The Reactions to the Problem

The early Church was not oblivious to these phenomena, but there was no serious attempt to explain their origin. Since all three gospels were accepted as authentic and authoritative accounts, interest centered on efforts to harmonize them. This interest expressed itself in Tatian's *Diatessaron* (c. A.D. 160) which endeavored to unify the four gospels by constructing from them one continuous narrative of the Good News. Even after the separate gospels displaced the *Diatessaron* in the Eastern Church, the interest continued to center on harmonization of the accounts without serious attempts to solve the questions of their origins and relationships.

In A.D. 400 Augustine broke new ground with his book, *On the Harmony of the Evangelists* (*De consensu evangelistarum*), in which he expressed his opinion on the literary relationship of the gospels. Accepting that the sequence of their origin was Matthew, Mark, Luke, he postulated that the later writers did not write without knowledge of their predecessors, even though each followed an independent course in his narrative. He held that Mark was an abbreviated edition of Matthew. But Augustine's main concern was to answer pagan allegations that the gospels contain contradictions; he expressed his opinion concerning their origins only in passing.

It was not until the eighteenth century, with the upsurge of ra-

6. Leon-Dufour, p. 251.

tionalism, that critical attention began to center on endeavors to find an explanation for the phenomena displayed by the synoptics through investigations of their origins. In the last quarter of the eighteenth century three proposed solutions to the synoptic problem were published. In 1778 G. E. Lessing advanced the hypothesis that these three gospels were translations of one Aramaic source; in 1789 J. J. Griesbach advanced the theory of interdependence, assigning priority to Matthew and holding that Mark was an abridgment of Matthew and Luke; finally in 1796 G. Herder insisted that an "oral gospel" was the source of all the synoptics. The three component elements, namely documentary sources, interdependence, and oral tradition, have continued to play a part in the various hypotheses that have since been advanced in endeavors to solve the synoptic problem.

THE COURSE OF THE SYNOPTIC DISCUSSION

1. EARLY PROPOSALS

Early attempts to explain the synoptic problem gave rise to four major explanations, the elements of which were developed in different directions and sometimes blended.

a. *Primitive gospel theory.* In 1778, Lessing suggested that the three synoptic gospels drew their material from a primitive gospel (*Urevangelium*), no longer extant, which was probably written in Aramaic.[7] This original source was identified with the *Gospel of the Nazarenes* which, according to Jerome, was still current in the sect of the Nazarenes in the fourth century. J. G. Eichhorn took up this suggestion in 1794 and further elaborated it in 1804.[8] His complicated and rather artificial theory proposed that there were several recensions of this primitive gospel between the original and our synoptics. He held that the original Aramaic gospel was recast, enlarged, and abbreviated so that no less than nine different gospels, in Aramaic or Greek, lay behind our canonical gospels. A. B. Bruce remarks, "By this flight into the dark region of conjectural recensions, whereof no trace remains, the *Urevangelium* hypothesis was

---

7. G. E. Lessing, *Neue Hypothese über die Evangelisten als bloss menschliche Geschichtesschreiber.*
8. J. G. Eichhorn, *Über die drei ersten Evangelien; Einleitung in das Neue Testament*, vol. 1.

self-condemned to oblivion."[9] The theory is without historical support and is highly improbable. It cannot, for example, account for the fact that Matthew and Luke have two entirely different genealogies.

b. *Interdependence theory.* In 1789 Griesbach, following the suggestion of Augustine, advocated the view that the origin of the synoptics can be explained on the basis of mutual literary dependence.[10] According to this theory the second writer drew upon the work of the first, and the third writer used the work of the preceding two. The first writer apparently depended on oral tradition, while the other two availed themselves of his written work. Griesbach suggested a Matthew–Luke–Mark sequence, whereas Augustine had conjectured a Matthew–Mark–Luke sequence. This theory makes possible six permutations, and every one of them has been advocated.* Views concerning the source of the borrowing depend on the predilections of the individual advocates. This theory would explain the common material and the uniformity in the sequence of much of that material, but it does not account for the striking differences between them, or explain why each writer omits information included by the others. Moreover, the wide diversity among suggestions regarding order of sequence has done much to weaken its credibility.

In 1835 C. Lachmann noted that Matthew and Luke agree in order only when they hold to Mark's sequence.[11] This suggests that both Matthew and Luke are anchored in the gospel of Mark. Lachmann's observation prepared the way for the widely accepted priority of Mark advocated in more recent source criticism theories.

c. *Oral tradition. theory.* In 1796 J. G. Herder insisted that only an "oral Gospel" lay behind our synoptic gospels, and that no written sources had been used.[12] In 1818 J. K. L. Gieseler gave systematic

9. Alexander Balmain Bruce, "The Synoptic Gospels," in *The Expositor's Greek Testament*, 1:6-7.

10. J. J. Griesbach, *Commentatio qua Marci euangelium totum e Matthaei et Lucae commentariis decerptum esse monstratur.*

*Henry Clarence Thiessen, *Introduction to the New Testament*, lists the following permutations and their advocates: "Matthew, Mark, Luke: Grotius, Mill, Wetstein, Hug, Greswell; Matthew, Luke, Mark: Griesbach, Fritzsche, Meyer, De Wette, Baur; Mark, Matthew, Luke: Storr, Weisse, Wilke; Mark, Luke, Matthew: Hitzig, Bruno Bauer, Volkmar; Luke, Matthew, Mark: Evanson; Luke, Mark, Matthew: Vögel" (p. 104).

11. C. Lachmann, "De ordine narrationum in evangeliis synopticis," *Theologische Studien und Kritiken*, 8:570ff.

12. J. G. Herder, *Von der Regel der Zustimmung unserer Evangelien.*

166 An Introduction to the New Testament

exposition to this view.[13] He held that a uniform presentation of the gospel developed very early through the apostles' frequent repetition of the story of Jesus in Jerusalem. This oral gospel was originally in Aramaic. With the spread of the gospel to the Gentiles it was translated into Greek, but continued to be transmitted orally. The transplanting of the gospel into a Gentile environment naturally brought some changes in presentation and emphasis consistent with the interests and needs of Gentile audiences. This basic Aramaic gospel and its Greek translations formed the main source for the synoptic gospels, each evangelist using the material according to his own purpose and audience. Thus Matthew produced the gospel with its original Palestinian emphasis. Mark, under the influence of the preaching of Peter, recorded a modified Palestinian gospel, while Luke reflected the Pauline emphasis. Literary differences in the synoptics were attributed to the differences in training and background of the evangelists.

With varied modifications, the oral tradition theory received widespread support during the nineteenth century. Leading exponents of the view were B. F. Westcott[14] and Arthur Wright.[15]

Differences may be accounted for by the supplements made by individual apostolic witnesses, the different emphases that arose as the gospel spread among the Gentiles, and the purpose of the individual writer in the choice of his material. The oral theory rightly emphasizes the fact that for some time the gospel material was transmitted by word of mouth. Precisely how long this oral period lasted is a matter of conjecture.

In support of the oral theory the following arguments have been advanced: (1) This view is thoroughly consistent with the practice prevalent among the rabbis of transmitting their teaching orally.[16] (2) It recognizes that "the simple character of the culture possessed by the early Christians in Palestine" did not early call for a written form of the gospel.[17] The apostolic witnesses memorized their material and the common people did not need books. (3) Zahn further

---

13. J. K. L. Gieseler, *Historisch-kritischer Versuch über die Entstehung und die frühesten Schicksale der schriftlichen Evangelien.*
14. Brooke Foss Westcott, *An Introduction to the Study of the Gospels.*
15. Arthur Wright, *The Composition of the Four Gospels.*
16. Westcott, pp. 167-68.
17. Theodor Zahn, *Introduction to the New Testament,* 2:409.

holds that it is in keeping with "the way the words and deeds of Jesus are introduced" in these gospels.[18] (4) The New Testament writers and the postapostolic literature are silent regarding the use of written sources behind our gospels.[19] The remark of Papias (c. 70-150), as quoted by Eusebius,[20] reveals that until the second century, preference was given to oral apostolic sources (see pp. 199-200).

The theory that our gospels were wholly dependent upon oral tradition is not without its difficulties. Clogg remarks, "On this hypothesis agreement would have been expected at the critical points of our Lord's Ministry, whereas, in fact, the most remarkable instances of it are in quite unimportant details: in the narrative of the Passion and the Resurrection, where closest agreement would be expected, there are remarkable differences."[21] Scott further asserts that the oral theory "cannot possibly account for the freedom with which the evangelists vary the order of their record. They must have worked with written documents to which they could refer at leisure, taking a piece from one and a piece from another, and transposing where they thought fit. Writing from their memories, they could never have exercised this freedom."[22] An exclusively oral theory does not give sufficient recognition to the early existence of written accounts. In the preface to his gospel (Lk 1:1-3) Luke points to the oral testimony of eyewitnesses as sources for his written account. But he also admits that numerous written accounts were in existence at the time. How soon such written accounts began to appear is not known. Tools and techniques were available, even in Palestine, to use in recording the teachings and deeds of Jesus almost immediately, perhaps even in shorthand on the scene.[23]

An exclusively oral theory has no leading advocates today. But even if the oral tradition theory does not present an adequate picture, it does make contributions important to a balanced view of gospel origins.

18. Ibid.
19. Ibid., 2:408-9.
20. Eusebius *Ecclesiastical History* 3. 39. 4.
21. Frank Bertram Clogg, *An Introduction to the New Testament*, p. 182.
22. Ernest Findlay Scott, *The Literature of the New Testament*, p. 28.
23. Cf. W. Harold Mare, "The Role of the Note-Taking Historian and His Emphasis on the Person and Work of Christ," *Journal of the Evangelical Theological Society*, 15(Spring, 1972):110-11, and sources cited.

d. *Fragmentary hypothesis.* In 1817 Friedrich Schleiermacher advanced the suggestion that our gospels did not derive from one primitive gospel of comprehensive character, but rather had been compiled from a large number of short written accounts.[24] He found his point of departure in Luke's reference to numerous written accounts which existed prior to his own gospel (Lk 1:1-3). Schleiermacher held that these accounts were brief records of particular events or themes which had been written down by various eyewitnesses. These accounts recorded particular miracles, discourses or parables, or various incidents connected with Jesus. A large number of these fragmentary accounts were later collected by the writers of our gospels from which they constructed their larger, coherent story. When they employed the same fragments their accounts agreed in content and style; when they used different fragments their records necessarily diverged. Insofar as Schleiermacher's theory recognizes that many written accounts existed before our canonical gospel of Luke was written it is on the right track. His theory is unable, however, to explain the remarkable similarities evidenced in vocabulary and sequence of events. The hypothesis does open up the position that our gospels contain collected materials of different origin which were given editorial arrangement in their composition. During the present century Schleiermacher's theory has experienced something of a revival in connection with form criticism.

2. DOCUMENTARY SOURCE THEORIES

Documentary theories assume the existence of a written source or sources behind the synoptic gospels. Such theories vary in complexity, from the assumption of a single document to the postulation of multiplied documents. The initial documentary theory, the *Primitive Gospel* theory, postulated one common source for all three of our gospels. The inadequacy of the view naturally led to more complex and sophisticated views.

a. *Two-Document theory.* This theory has its roots in the observation of Lachmann that Mark seems to determine the order of events in Matthew and Luke (see page 165). This observation was developed by others and led eventually to the two-source theory which was popularized through the work of H. J. Holtzmann and

24. Friedrich Schleiermacher, *Über die Schriften des Lukas: Ein kritischer Versuch,* vol. 1.

Bernard Weiss.[25] The theory in essence assumes that two literary sources account for the origin of the synoptic gospels. It combines the common source theory and the interdependence theory. It has enjoyed widespread recognition during the last hundred years.

The theory may be summarized as follows: The first source is our gospel of Mark or a prior document very similar to the canonical Mark. Mark is accepted as the foundation of Matthew and Luke, since they incorporate almost all of Mark, and Mark's sequence of events in the life of Jesus seems to have a governing influence on the order in Matthew and Luke. Matthew and Luke also utilized another common written source, commonly called *Q*, from the German word *Quelle* (source). This second source is postulated from the fact that Matthew and Luke have about 250 verses of common material which is not found in Mark. But there has been no general agreement as to the exact nature of this second source. Some hold that it consisted only of Jesus' sayings, while others have held that it contained narratives as well as sayings. The existence of *Q* as a historical document is admittedly hypothetical; it is an assumption felt necessary to account for the material common to Matthew and Luke.

The two-document theory requires acceptance of Marcan priority. It reverses the view of the early church which assigned priority to Matthew, a view commonly held until the early part of the nineteenth century. Arguments in favor of Marcan priority are:[26]

(1) The proportion of Mark included in Matthew and Luke. About ninety percent of Mark is paralleled in Matthew, about fifty percent in Luke. Only about four paragraphs in Mark have no parallels in Matthew or Luke.†

(2) The chronological order of Mark dominating Matthew and Luke. The three gospels follow the same broad chronological outline, but there are definite divergences in detail. In the material common to all three, Matthew and Luke agree with each other only insofar as

---

25. H. J. Holtzmann, *Die synoptischen Evangelien, ihr Ursprung und ihr geschichtlicher Charakter;* Bernard Weiss, *Lehrbuch der Einleitung in das Neue Testament,* Eng. trans., *A Manual of Introduction to the New Testament,* 2 vols.

26. See the summary of arguments in Bruce M. Metzger, *The New Testament: Its Background, Growth, and Content,* pp. 80-83.

†Three reports in Mark have no parallels in Matthew or Luke: 4:26-29, the parable of the seed growing by itself; 7:31-37, the healing of a deaf man in Decapolis; 8:22-26, the healing of a blind man in two stages at Bethsaida. Also three very short texts have no parallels: 3:20-21, the comment of friends that Jesus was beside Himself; 9:49, the comment about everyone being salted with fire; 14:51-52, the young man in Gethsemane.

they agree with Mark; where they depart from Mark each goes his own way.[27] They do not *together* leave Mark's sequence as might have been expected, at least occasionally, if they did not both draw on Mark's sequence. Wikenhauser notes that "all the non-Marcan material is put into Mark's framework as insertions."[28]

(3) The implications of the literary features. A comparative study of the three gospels suggests that Mark is the more primitive account. Mark's detailed accounts with their repetitions and redundancies are reported in Matthew and Luke in more concise form. Mark's rough and impromptu style, suggestive of an oral account, is polished by Matthew and Luke.[29]

(4) The greater historical candor of Mark's gospel. Mark's references to the human emotions of Jesus as well as his candid portrayal of the failures of the disciples are apparently modified or toned down in the other synoptics. This is held to be evidence of increasing reverence for Jesus and honor for the disciples. The tendency of Matthew and Luke to moderate unfavorable features is felt to be more understandable if viewed in the light of Marcan priority.

(5) The less explicit accounts in Mark. There are a few passages in Mark which are briefer and less explicit than parallel accounts in Matthew or Luke. Mark's account of Peter's great confession at Caesarea Philippi is very brief and less explicit than the fuller accounts in Matthew and Luke. It is held to be more probable that the story was expanded than that it was abbreviated. Hence Mark's account must have been produced earlier.

Obviously, some of the phenomena mentioned above might receive different explanations, but the majority of scholars today consider the arguments to be of sufficient weight to establish the priority of Mark. It is today commonly accepted as one of the few reliable results achieved by the long and complicated synoptic debate.[30]

27. Compare the tabulation of the order of events in Kümmel, pp. 46-48.
28. Alfred Wikenhauser, *New Testament Introduction*, p. 241.
29. Burnett Hillman Streeter, *The Four Gospels: A Study of Origins*, pp. 162-64; Hawkins, pp. 139-42.
30. See the selected list of advocates in William Hendriksen, "Exposition of the Gospel According to Matthew," *New Testament Commentary*, p. 36, and pp. 36-47 for his own favorable discussion. For a popular presentation of Marcan priority see George Eldon Ladd, "More Light on the Synoptics," *Christianity Today*, March 2, 1959, pp. 12-16. For a categorical rejection see John R. Ludlum, Jr., "New Light on the Synoptic Problem," *Christianity Today*, 10 November and 24 November 1958; John R. Ludlum, Jr., "Are We Sure of Mark's Priority?" *Christianity Today*, 14 September and 28 September, 1959.

The assumed priority of Mark is not without its difficulties. A serious problem for this view is Luke's omission of all the material found in Mark 6:45—8:26. If Luke based his gospel on Mark, what accounts for this striking omission? Several explanations have been conjectured, among them that Luke accidentally or deliberately omitted the material, or that he used a mutilated copy of Mark or an earlier recension of Mark (*Ur-Markus*). These suggestions mitigate but do not really explain the omission.

A further difficulty with the view that Matthew and Luke used Mark is the fact that Matthew and Luke in a number of passages agree against Mark. Scholars are not agreed on the exact number of such instances.[31] Hawkins lists twenty-one and concludes that "it seems almost impossible that Matthew and Luke could have accidentally concurred in making them."[32] Several explanations have been suggested. Lake and Lake conclude that most of these agreements of Matthew and Luke against Mark may "be regarded as a natural coincidence in literary correction" but admit that there remain "a few passages which cannot be so explained."[33] But if Mark was a common source for Matthew and Luke, would they be likely to correct Mark in the same way? Streeter claims that the difficulty may be eliminated by textual criticism.[34] But it is questionable that such a sweeping resort to textual emendation in Mark is warranted. Others suggest that the difficulty can be met by accepting the existence of an earlier recension of Mark (*Ur-Markus*) from which they copied their records. But this suggestion has never gained wide acceptance and is generally questioned today. Leon-Dufour remarks that in the "effort to resolve a small anomaly, it complicated the entire synoptic situation still more."[25]

The theory of Marcan priority also faces the objection that it makes Matthew dependent upon Mark for material describing events which he himself had experienced. This objection lacks force for those who reject apostolic authorship for the first gospel. But those who accept apostolic authorship for our canonical Matthew must deal with it.

31. Leon-Dufour, pp. 271-73.
32. Hawkins, pp. 208-12.
33. Kirsopp Lake and Silva Lake, *An Introduction to the New Testament*, pp. 6-7.
34. Streeter, pp. 295-331.
35. Leon-Dufour, p. 272.

It is difficult to understand why Matthew, who could record from personal observation almost all that is contained in his gospel, would depend upon a non-eyewitness for his material. The difficulty is relieved by the explanation that Matthew wrote an Aramaic account which was earlier than Mark's gospel. Later he prepared our canonical Matthew for a wider circle of readers as a satisfactory representative of or replacement for his earlier work (see pp. 54-55). But the objection concerning Matthew's dependence on Mark is fully met only if it is assumed that Mark somehow was dependent upon this earlier Aramaic work of Matthew. Those who accept apostolic authorship of the first gospel and yet accept Marcan priority remember that this objection is used by critics to discredit apostolic authorship (see pp. 57-59). They admit a difficulty but hold that it is not as serious as it sounds. They hold that at most Matthew used Mark as a source but did not slavishly depend upon it. He shaped and rearranged it to further his own purpose. He made use of Marcan material for his own purpose since his apostolic experience enabled him to recognize the authenticity of the material. Such a view mitigates the difficulty but does not wholly remove it.

The consensus of twentieth century opinion regards the priority of Mark as an axiom in synoptic study. It is accepted as explaining more problems than it creates. But within recent decades Marcan priority has been challenged by some scholars. In 1951 Butler attacked the two-document hypothesis and defended the Augustinian theory that the order of composition was Matthew–Mark–Luke.[36] Farmer in his probing volume, *The Synoptic Problem: A Critical Analysis,* points out the inadequacies of the two-document hypothesis and concludes that the actual order in which the synoptics were written was Matthew–Luke–Mark.[37] A different view of priority was advanced recently by Robert Lindsey. As a result of his efforts to translate Mark from Greek to Hebrew, he found himself forced to the conclusion that Mark, due to the frequency of non-Hebraic expressions in it, could not have been written first. He found that Luke contains almost none of these non-Hebraic expressions so

---

36. B. C. Butler, *The Originality of St. Matthew: A Critique of the Two-Document Hypothesis.*
37. William R. Farmer, *The Synoptic Problem: A Critical Analysis.*

·common in Mark, and concluded that Luke is the earliest of the synoptics.[38]

These divergent views reveal that the assumed priority of Mark has not solved the actual problem of the literary order of these gospels and is not as certain as its advocates suggest. Leon Dufour indeed surmises, "It is possible that the day will come when the absolute priority of Mk will be regarded as an *a priori* position in an obsolete stage of criticism."[39]

There has been much discussion concerning the identity and contents of *Q*, the second source in the two-document theory.[40] Theoretically the source of the non-Marcan material common to Matthew and Luke may have been oral tradition, or one of them may have drawn upon the other, but these hypotheses are commonly discarded in favor of a second documentary source. It has been debated whether this source should be identified with the *logia* of Matthew mentioned by Papias (see pp. 48-49). Some think that *Q* consisted entirely or almost completely of Jesus' sayings, while others hold that it also contained narrative material. Moffatt lists no less than sixteen different proposed reconstructions of the contents of *Q*.[41] It has become clear that its contents cannot be held to be homogeneous, which has led to the suggestion that this source must be divided into two or more documents. This multiplication of supposed sources behind *Q* has created dissatisfaction with the entire *Q* theory. There are not wanting today voices which reject the whole *Q* hypothesis.[42] The concept can at best be regarded as a working hypothesis. Surburg reminds us that "the source 'Q' has never been found nor is there a reference to its existence in the literature of the church."[43] It is a creation of modern scholarship. Reginald Fuller concludes that it is best to regard *Q* as a "layer of tradition" rather than a single document.[44] Such a concession in effect evaporates the second element in the two-document theory.

38. Robert Lisle Lindsey, *A Hebrew Translation of the Gospel of Mark: Greek-Hebrew Diglot with English Introduction*, pp. 9-84.
39. Leon-Dufour, p. 277.
40. See the summary in Donald Guthrie, *New Testament Introduction*, pp. 143-57.
41. James Moffatt, *An Introduction to the Literature of the New Testament*, pp. 197-202.
42. Butler, pp. 1-36; Leon-Dufour, pp. 280-81; Lewis A. Foster, "The 'Q' Myth in Synoptic Studies," *Bulletin of the Evangelical Theological Society*, 8(Fall, 1964): 111-19; Stewart Petrie, " 'Q' Is What You Make It," *Novum Testamentum*, 3(1959):28-33.
43. Raymond F. Surburg, *How Dependable Is the Bible?*, p. 142.
44. Reginald H. Fuller, *The New Testament in Current Study*, p. 74.

b. *Multiple-document theories.* Today it is commonly accepted that the two-document theory is inadequate to solve the problem of the sources of the synoptics. It is felt necessary to postulate further sources. If Q is defined as the non-Marcan material common to Matthew and Luke, the question naturally arises: What is the source of the verses (approximately 300) which are peculiar to Matthew? Likewise, what is the source of the approximately 580 verses which are peculiar to the third gospel? To include all of this material in Q would expand it to a work as long as a full gospel. The alternative suggestion that the material unique to Matthew and the material unique to Luke represent two recensions of Q is likewise unsatisfactory since it in reality makes two sources from Q.

In order to account for the material unique to Matthew and to Luke, Streeter has proposed "a four-document hypothesis."[45] The material peculiar to Matthew he attributes to a document, *M*, which originated in Jerusalem and was composed some time before the writing of the canonical Matthew. It contained primarily the sayings of Jesus. The material distinctive to Luke he designates *L* and advances the suggestion that Luke's gospel was composed in two editions. The first edition (Proto-Luke) consisted only of Q and *L*; after his preparation of Proto-Luke he came into possession of Mark's gospel and incorporated much of the Marcan material into his first edition to create our present gospel of Luke.

Streeter's theory has generally commended itself as more probable than the older two-document hypothesis. Continental scholars have been less inclined to follow Streeter than British scholars.[46] Harrison favorably evaluates the theory as follows: "It provides a broader base for the gospel tradition than the Two-Document Hypothesis afforded. Non-Markan material has thereby gained in status and is not so readily discarded as unreliable."[47] But the very existence of *M* and *L* as actual documents must remain conjectural. Streeter's theory of a Proto-Luke has won little acceptance.

In 1954 the French Catholic scholar Leon Vaganay in his *Le probleme synoptique* set forth a new and complex theory concerning the sources behind the synoptic gospels.[48] He maintains that the old-

45. Streeter, chap. 9.
46. Guthrie, p. 157 n. 1.
47. Everett F. Harrison, *Introduction to the New Testament*, p. 150.
48. See the convenient summary in Wikenhauser, pp. 235-39.

est real gospel was the Aramaic gospel of Matthew as attested by Papias; this he calls M. This original gospel, translated into Greek, designated Mg, is the source for the material common to all three synoptics. He holds that the material in Mg, exclusive of the passion narrative in it, was divided into five short books containing both narrative and discourse; this fivefold division is most clearly reflected in our canonical Matthew.

Vaganay holds that the material common to both Matthew and Luke was derived from a second source, which was originally in Aramaic but was also translated into Greek; this translated source he designates Sg. It consisted of sayings of Jesus; most of it was included in Luke's large insertion in 9:51—18:14. He holds that Matthew depended on Mg as his primary source, but used Sg as a secondary source.

The gospel of Mark, according to Vaganay, was the first of our present gospels. Mark derived his material partly from the catechetical teaching in Jerusalem as represented in Mg, but also drew directly from Peter's preaching at Rome. Mark, according to Vaganay, did not know Sg.

Vaganay holds that our gospel of Matthew is the best representative of M or Mg and therefore we are justified in calling it Matthew's gospel. But our gospel of Matthew made a number of transpositions in Mg and also used Mark as a secondary source. Luke, he holds, used Mark as his main source and also used Mg as a secondary source. He depended mainly upon Sg for his long insertion in 9:51—18:14. Luke did not use our Greek Matthew.

This theory has value in giving credence to the reliability of Papias' testimony concerning Matthew's Aramaic gospel. It recognizes the importance of this early gospel in the formation of the synoptic gospels. But Vaganay's theory is complicated and contains a number or suppositions which cannot be proved. Vaganay rejects the Q theory but his Sg is no more certain than the Q source which it replaces. This theory makes Mark a conflation of two oral sources. Wikenhauser observes, however, that "Mark is intelligible only as an original unit, not as a conflation of two sources."[49] Vaganay's theory

---

49. Wikenhauser, p. 238.

has not generally been accepted as a convincing solution of the synoptic problem.

Many Bible students feel that any theory of literary dependence which makes one canonical gospel dependent upon another constitutes an attack upon the integrity of the gospel writers. It is held to be inconsistent with a high view of inspiration. Schaff forcefully states this position as follows:

> The whole theory [dependence of one gospel on another] degrades the one or two Synoptists to the position of slavish and yet arbitrary compilers, not to say plagiarists; it assumes a strange mixture of dependence and affected originality; it weakens the independent value of their history, and it does not account for the omissions of most important matter, and for many differences in common matter. For the Synoptists often differ just where we would expect them to agree. . . . What should we think of a historian of our day who would plunder another historian of one-third or one-half of the contents of his book without a word of acknowledgment direct or indirect? Let us give the Evangelists at least the credit of common honesty, which is the basis of all morality.[50]

But other scholars, fully committed to the integrity of our gospels, reply that the objection is not as serious as it sounds. They point out that the copying was not slavish. The omissions, additions, and alterations point rather to individual freedom of expression in using common material. Nor should it be forgotten that in the Old Testament one biblical writer used the material of another. Harrison observes:

> Nearly one-fifth of the Old Testament consists of deuterographs or repetitions of identical or very similar material. The most prominent example is the relation of Kings and Chronicles. Yet among the Jews there was no bar to the acceptance of both as Scripture, and our Lord apparently acquiesced, for he accepted the Jewish canon. The church did the same. Therefore, if we are compelled on the basis of the evidence to accept a theory of literary dependence, it should not be felt that this impugns the doctrine of inspiration. Originality is not a necessary qualification for Scripture.[51]

50. Philip Schaff, *History of the Christian Church*, 1:598-99, 602.
51. Harrison, p. 153.

The prologue of Luke (Lk 1:1-4) makes it clear that Luke's use of sources in writing his gospel is consistent with the inspiration of his production. Gundry holds that where Matthew and Luke used material already recorded by Mark they did so "precisely because it was historically accurate and deserved a united testimony in its favor. Where they change Mark, they do so not in ways that falsify the record, but in ways that combat misinterpretation of Marcan information, add further details, omit others, and bring out different theological implications."[52] Theories advanced in the attempt to unravel the sources behind our gospels necessarily involve a large measure of conjecture and must always be recognized as tentative. Whatever conclusions the evidence may be held to establish, evangelical believers accept the integrity and authority of our gospels as we have them.

3. FORM CRITICISM

Since 1919 a new method of studying the gospel sources has been on the scene. The method was pioneered by Martin Dibelius with the publication of his book *Die Formgeschichte des Evangeliums,*[53] followed in 1921 by the independent study of Rudolf Bultmann in his *Die Geschichte der synoptischen Tradition.*[54] The German word *Formgeschichte* literally means "form-history" and indicates that the method is devoted to tracing and identifying the literary forms of the material composing our gospels. The approach had already been employed in the study of folklore in seeking to trace its structure and formation. Its application to the gospels was preceded by Hermann Gunkel's analysis of parts of the Old Testament literature, especially Genesis and the Psalms. The door to the application of this new method to the gospels was opened by K. L. Schmidt in 1919 in his book *Der Rahmen der Geschichte Jesu*[55] in which he sets forth his view that the greater part of Mark's gospel was composed of separate episodes or anecdotes artificially strung together by the editor, and that the connecting links supplied by the editor were devoid of historical value. In adopting this viewpoint the form critics felt freed from the historical framework stated in the gospels and at liberty to

52. Robert H. Gundry, *A Survey of the New Testament*, p. 69.
53. English translation, *From Tradition to Gospel*, 1935.
54. English translation, *The History of the Synoptic Tradition*, 1963.
55. K. L. Schmidt, *Der Rahmen der Geschichte Jesu.*

devote themselves to a study of the bits of tradition out of which they were constructed. Form criticism correctly states that there was a period during which the gospel was transmitted orally, before the production of our written gospels. It endeavors to get behind our gospels by studying the forms or patterns into which the various types of incidents or sayings attributed to Jesus were cast in the early oral stage. Form criticism postulates the existence of a large number of brief and independent sources behind our gospels.

a. *Literary forms.* In seeking to determine the nature and content of the oral tradition, form critics classify the material composing our gospels into various literary genres. The pioneers of the method did not agree on the designation and character of the different classes.‡ It is common today to use the more restrained classification given by V. Taylor.[56] The material is organized into five categories:

(1) Pronouncement stories.§ A pronouncement story consists of a narrative culminating in a saying of Jesus which expresses an ethical or religious precept. Frequently the subject is controversial. An illustration is the story concerning the payment of tribute to Caesar, ending in a notable pronouncement by Jesus (Mk 12:13-17). These stories were treasured as giving guidance to the Christian community and were used by preachers of the gospel to illustrate the message.

(2) Miracle stories. These accounts of healings and nature miracles center around the miracles. There are no sayings attached. They assume a common form: circumstances, miracle, effect. Dibelius calls them "tales." Bultmann compares these miracles with both Jewish and Hellenistic accounts and finds that they follow the same pattern.

(3) Stories about Jesus. These stories, which show considerable variety, center interest in Jesus Himself. They are edifying accounts which relate extraordinary things about Jesus. Form critics hold that it is difficult to distinguish between historical and legendary mate-

---

‡Dibelius distinguishes five main forms: paradigms, *Novellen* (tales), legends, parenesis (exhortations), myth (stories with a supernatural emphasis). Bultmann divides the materials into sayings and narratives, with subdivisions under each: (1) sayings, subdivided into apophthegms (sayings enshrined in a narrative: controversies, school discussions, biographical accounts), and sayings of the Lord (logia, prophetic or apocalyptic utterances, rules for the community, personal proclamations, parables); (2) narratives, subdivided into miracle accounts and biographical legends.

56. Vincent Taylor, *The Formation of the Gospel Tradition,* lectures 3-4.

§Corresponding to the paradigms of Dibelius and the apophthegms of Bultmann.

rial in many of these stories. A number of scholars assume that legendary elements were introduced to exalt the person of Jesus. The transfiguration story is regarded as revealing such mythical embellishment.

(4) Sayings of Jesus. The gospel texts reveal that the words of Jesus were of special interest to the writers. The sayings included in the accounts are of several types. Bultmann classifies them according to their content. *Proverbial* sayings reveal Jesus as a teacher of wisdom, in harmony with the celebrated wisdom teachers of the Orient. He holds that these sayings are the least authentic of the words of Jesus in the gospels and that many of them had been placed in the mouth of Jesus by the primitive church. *Prophetic* and *apocalyptic* sayings are those connected with the announced arrival of the Kingdom or with eschatological teaching. *Legislative* sayings relate to various pronouncements of law intended to regulate community life. *Personal proclamations* are sayings introduced by "I" in which Jesus speaks of Himself, His work, and His destiny. The *parables* form a well-defined group of sayings as one of the popular teaching instruments used by Jesus.

(5) Passion narratives. Neither Dibelius nor Bultmann includes these in his classification of literary forms. But form critics acknowledge that the passion narrative was the first part of the tradition to take definite and ordered form. But they do not agree as to whether the account first circulated as unconnected fragments later pieced together or was one closely-knit account.

b. *Basic principles.* In thus postulating a wide variety of brief and unconnected sources behind the synoptic gospels, the form critics operate according to certain well-defined principles and presuppositions.

(1) The "grand assumption" which makes form criticism both possible and necessary is that "Christian tradition circulated in the form of isolated units of material during the oral period."[57] It is assumed that prior to the written stage "the Christian community remained content to preserve its recollections of Jesus in the form of isolated stories that circulated independently."[58] The collection, selection,

57. R. C. Briggs, *Interpreting the Gospels*, p. 75.
58. Ibid.

and arrangement of this material in our gospels is the work of the gospel writers themselves.

(2) When the small units which were strung together in our gospels are detached from the framework into which they were placed, clear literary genres emerge. In an effort to understand the nature and structure of these different oral forms, the laws and patterns governing the development of folklore and tradition are applied to our gospel materials. Thus form criticism assumes that "the Synoptic Gospels belong to a type of literature that should be designated as folk literature, tales and sagas that enshrine stories of interest or value to certain people."[59]

(3) During the oral period these materials circulated in the early church as separate, circumstantial reports which were used for preaching and catechetical purposes. The individual pericope was valued because it met a need of the church in its task of instructing its members or preaching the gospel to non-Christians. Thus each literary unit originally functioned in a definite social setting (*Sitz im Leben*), and in order to interpret the true significance of the material it is necessary to try to see it in its community life setting. Thus the task of form criticism is that "of discovering the original units of the Synoptic tradition and of establishing the earlier history of the units."[60] Since these literary units at first circulated independently, the connecting links provided by the evangelists are of little value; attention rather must be given to their form and content.

(4) These literary forms developed because the Christian community needed and used them for specific purposes. The individual units thus basically reflect the life and faith of the early church. For the form critic there is little certainty that the material of our gospels actually goes back to historical events in the life of Jesus, as claimed. This determines one's view of the nature of the gospels. "The synoptic gospels are not biographies in the historical sense, but testimonies to the faith of primitive Christianity."[61] And the implication is that in its eagerness to use the original tradition to meet its needs, the church substantially altered the picture of Jesus presented in the gospels. These literary units must be evaluated as having been filtered through or created by the life of the church.

59. Harrison, p. 155.
60. Edgar V. McKnight, *What Is Form Criticism?*, p. 17.
61. Joachim Rohde, *Rediscovering the Teaching of the Evangelists*, p. 5.

c. *Assessment.* Form criticism has made an important contribution to gospel study in calling attention to the existence of recognizable literary forms in our gospels. But the evaluations made and the inferences drawn from these isolated forms are at least open to question. The variety of classifications made by the form critics indicates that the contents of our gospels do not yield completely to such a literary analysis and point to its subjective character. It is valuable to note that the miracle stories have definite pattern (circumstances, miracle, effect) and that there are parallels throughout the ancient world. But this need not be taken to prove that such stories in our gospels are due to folk development. In what other way could the historical event have been told? The skeptical evaluation of the historicity of these literary forms in the gospels is open to question. F. F. Bruce pertinently observes, "The classification of sayings of Jesus according to form can throw little light on their authenticity; much more depends on the individual critic's view of the person of Jesus."[62]

Form criticism has rendered service in calling attention to the importance of oral tradition. Bruce accepts as a positive contribution its demonstration of "the inadequacy of documentary hypotheses alone to account for the composition of the Gospel."[63] We can agree with the verdict of Hendriksen, "A really credible solution of the Synoptic Problem must leave room for both oral tradition and written sources."[64]

Form criticism renders service in reminding us that the materials embodied in our gospels had already shown their usefulness in the life of the church in furthering worship, instructing and guiding its members, or in reaching others with the message of the Redeemer. The material preserved had already demonstrated its living power in the daily life of the church. But form criticism fails to allow for the possibility that material about Jesus was preserved not merely for its current usefulness but because it was true. In the words of Kistemaker:

> The evangelical view is that the Gospels are a reliable account of the life, death, and resurrection of Jesus because these events are

62. Frederick Fyvie Bruce, "Form Criticism," in *Baker's Dictionary of Theology*, p. 227.
63. Ibid., p. 228.
64. William Hendriksen, *Bible Survey: A Treasury of Bible Information*, p. 394.

rooted in history. The form-critical view is that the Gospels are the
expression of the believer's faith in Jesus Christ. These expressions
of faith, composed by the early Christian church, are not used to
prove history; they are used to preach Jesus to the world.[65]

The basic assumption of form criticism that during the oral period
the gospel tradition was preserved only in isolated units is open to
question. To minister to the needs of its members and to refute the
attacks of its opponents the church needed a consistent picture of the
ministry, message, and significance of Jesus Christ. This need would
not be fully met by isolated units, which could not convey a coherent
account of His life and work. Form critics seem to have overlooked
the fact that the tradition treasured by the church originated in the
person of Jesus Christ who had a definite historical manifestation.
Form critics must admit that the early church, to meet the objection
that a crucified Jesus could not be the Messiah, must have presented
the facts pertaining to the death and resurrection of Jesus as a continuous story. Form critics may concede that the passion narrative
was an exception, but it is difficult to believe that the early Christians
lacked a sense of the importance of history. "Even though they centered attention upon interests of faith and practical life, they were
not devoid of a sense of what was true of Jesus in distinction from
what was true of themselves."[66] There is no warrant to simply dis-
miss the historical sequence of events reflected in the gospels as the
editorial invention of the evangelists. Acts reveals that the apostolic
preaching did not completely ignore historical sequence (cf. Ac
10:34-43).

Form criticism fails to give adequate recognition to the controlling
influence of Jesus' immediate followers upon the development of the
preaching of the early church. Not only did they take the lead in
proclaiming the message; they were also recognized as the authoritative source for the content of the message (Ac 2:41-42). Taylor
justly remarks, "If the Form-Critics are right, the disciples must have
been translated to heaven immediately after the Resurrection."[67]
Luke's preface (Lk 1:1-4) makes it clear that these "eyewitnesses
and ministers of the word" exerted a controlling influence over the

65. Simon Kistemaker, *The Gospels in Current Study*, pp. 45-46.
66. Floyd V. Filson, *Origins of the Gospels*, p. 108.
67. Taylor, p. 41.

gospel tradition which he recorded. At the time when our gospels were written there were many people in the church who "could still remember what Jesus had said and could have protested against the ascription to him of views which he had not expressed."[68] Both Christian and anti-Christian eyewitnesses would serve to keep the tradition true to the facts. "It is false," says Wikenhauser, "to ascribe the making of tradition to anonymous forces, to say that it was the community and the faith of the community which formed and handed on the tradition about Jesus. Creative power belongs not to a mass but only to individuals who tower over the mass."[69] The reverence of Jesus' disciples for their beloved Teacher and Lord would encourage them to remain true to His teachings and correctly proclaim the story of His words and deeds.

Filson notes that the inclusion of parables in the synoptic gospels shatters all attempts to make the church responsible for the creation of any considerable amount of the gospel tradition. The parable is a

> characteristic teaching form in the Synoptic Gospels. It is noticeably absent from the rest of the New Testament and from other early Christian literature. If the apostolic age had created these masterly mediums of teaching, other writings of that time would naturally have reflected the same method. But they do not. The primitive Church preserved a sense of the difference between Jesus' teaching method and their own ideas and methods.[70]

Evangelicals have been distressed by slashing attacks on the veracity of the gospels which have commonly followed the consistent application of the principles of form criticism. Not infrequently the authenticity of some pericope has been dissolved in the acid of radical form critical skepticism. It may be replied that such results do not necessarily follow from the method itself but occur when "form critics overstep the bounds of objectivity when analysis is exchanged for evaluation of the authenticity of the material."[71] Taylor in his cautious use of form criticism generally avoids these radical results. He says, "Form-Criticism seems to me to furnish constructive suggestions which in many ways confirm the historical

68. Bruce, p. 228.
69. Wikenhauser, p. 277.
70. Filson, p. 109.
71. Devon Wiens, "Biblical Criticism: Historical and Personal Reflections," *Directions* 1(October, 1972):109.

trustworthiness of the Gospel tradition."[72] But McKnight, in noting Taylor's claim, remarks, "It is obvious that Taylor has to modify the basic postulates and procedures of the earliest exponents of form criticism in order to come to his conservative results."[73]

4. REDACTION CRITICISM

The most recent self-conscious approach to synoptic studies is currently known as redaction criticism, although some would prefer to call it "composition criticism."[74] An offshoot of form criticism, it accepts form-critical techniques and conclusions but marks a shift of emphasis in gospel study. Form criticism centers its attention on identifying and theorizing about the individual units which compose our gospels; redaction criticism endeavors to view the gospel as a whole. Form criticism regards the writers of the synoptic gospels as little more than compilers of anonymous fragmentary materials; redaction criticism studies the writer in his own right. Form criticism concentrates on the varied forms of the traditional material common to the synoptics; redaction criticism directs attention to that which is distinctive in each gospel. Form criticism focuses attention on the theology of the church as reflected in the individual units; redaction criticism shifts the attention to the theology of the gospel writer himself.

a. *Approach.* A comparative study of the form critical materials found in each synoptic made it clear that each writer had molded and arranged his material to reflect his own views. This discovery naturally directed attention to the problem of the author's purpose in composing his gospel. It became clear that each writer was prompted by a theological motive. Thus redaction criticism centers its attention on the individual writer as theologian. It studies his use of the traditional material to determine his own theological contribution to the tradition. The essential concern of redaction criticism is not with the historical validity of the material which the writer used but rather with the theological motive underlying his use of the material. Redaction criticism assumes that "the Gospels are to be understood as the work of individual authors who interpreted the meaning of Jesus

72. Taylor, p. vi.
73. McKnight, pp. 47-48.
74. Rohde, p. 11.

with deliberate intention. Although they appropriated earlier fragmentary traditions, they structured and interpreted these traditions according to their own theological purposes."[75]

Robert H. Stein summarizes the approach of redaction criticism as follows:

> Redaktionsgeschichte seeks to discover the qualitative and quantitative uniqueness that distinguishes the evangelists from their sources, and, having ascertained these, it then seeks to ascertain the *Sitz im Leben* out of which each evangelist wrote and the particular purpose for which he wrote his gospel.[76]

Whereas form criticism concerns itself with the *Sitz im Leben* of the individual units of the gospel tradition, redaction criticism is concerned with the life-setting of the gospel in the theological purpose of the gospel writer himself. Marxsen clearly enunciates the approach of this new methodology by distinguishing three *Sitz im Leben*.[77] First, there is the setting in the life of Jesus and this concerns the relationship of the written record to the actual event. Second, there is the life-setting of the individual pericope in the life of the church. The third is the life-setting in the theological purpose of the writer and the theological climate of the Christian community where the gospel originated. This third stage is the development and special concern of redaction criticism. Recognition to all three stages must be given in the interpretation of the biblical text. Marxsen believes that the third stage can be reached only through the second, and not directly from the first. Although the second and third stages are closely related, redaction criticism goes beyond form criticism in its effort to emphasize the theology of the individual writer. The concern is to determine why he used his material as he did.

b. *Pioneers.* The application of this new approach to the synoptic gospels has come into prominence since the close of World War II. It has been spearheaded by three German theologians.[78] Hans Con-

75. Briggs, p. 107.
76. Robert H. Stein, "What is Redaktionsgeschichte?" *Journal of Biblical Literature,* 88(March, 1969):54.
77. Willi Marxsen, *Mark the Evangelist,* p. 23.
78. Hans Conzelmann, *The Theology of St. Luke;* Willi Marxsen, *Mark the Evangelist;* Günther Bornkamm, "End-expectation and Church in Matthew," in G. Bornkamm, G. Barth, and H. J. Held, *Tradition and Interpretation in Matthew,* rev. ed. For a study of various writers in this school see Joachim Rohde, *Rediscovering the Teaching of the Evangelists.*

zelmann applied this approach to the gospel of Luke, and concluded that Luke's gospel was motivated theologically rather than historically. Luke wrote as a theologian, not a historian. In his gospel he presents his understanding of salvation history. Willi Marxsen applied this method to the gospel of Mark and concluded that the gospel was formulated to present the writer's theological concerns for his own time. Günther Bornkamm studied the theological themes in the gospel of Matthew and concluded that Matthew imposed his own theological emphasis on the gospel tradition which he had collected and arranged. Although many redaction critics have a low evaluation of the historical accuracy of the contents of the synoptics, their professed concern is not with history but with the theology of the writer.

With these studies synoptic investigation received new direction. Rohde observes that this new method "is in principle applicable only to the synoptic gospels, including the Acts of the Apostles, and not to the Epistles."[80] He concedes that it may possibly be applied to the epistle of James.

c. *Assessment.* Redaction criticism renders valuable service in redirecting attention to the gospels in their entirety. It provides a needed corrective to the fragmenting tendency of form criticism. By centering attention on the individual writer redaction criticism helpfully brings back the element of personality into gospel criticism as over against the anonymity fostered by form criticism.

A valuable contribution of redaction criticism is the fact that it has stimulated fresh understanding of the theological themes of each gospel. The recognition that each gospel is not just a compilation of fragmentary materials, but is a piece of literature written with a special aim and a theological concern has renewed interest in the theological perspective of each gospel. There is a fresh willingness to accept each gospel as making its own distinctive contribution to our understanding of the person of Jesus Christ.[79]

The aim of redaction criticism, to view the evangelists as purposeful authors with their own theological convictions, has much in its favor. It must be recognized that they did not write impersonal

79. See I. Howard Marshall, *Luke: Historian and Theologian*; Ralph P. Martin, *Mark: Evangelist and Theologian*.
80. Rohde, p. 9.

biographies of Jesus; they used the historical material to bear witness to their faith in Christ Jesus. Each stressed certain theological themes and their productions do disclose variation in emphasis and purpose. In the words of Guthrie, "All the Evangelists were men who saw events as vehicles of truth regarding Jesus Christ, but there is no reason to suppose that the events were created in a theological interest."[81] They were reliable historians who interpreted the significance of the history which they recorded.

Reginald Fuller finds value in redaction criticism in that it has "diminished the formerly wide gap between the synoptics and the fourth gospel. The differences between them are still there, and they are very great. But both the synoptists and John use oral traditions, arranging them freely for their own kerygmatic purposes."[82]

The methodology of redaction criticism is liable to subjectivity in its efforts to ferret out the theological motives of the individual writers. Certain features may be arbitrarily categorized as expressions of the writer's theological purpose rather than historical events. Thus Marxsen holds that "Galilee" in Mark's gospel must not be understood merely as a historical reference; it is part of Mark's editorial work and has theological import. Mark wrote his gospel to warn the church in Judea to "go" to Galilee to await the *parousia* which he felt was imminent. According to Marxsen, the disciples were told to go to Galilee (Mk 16:7) to see not the resurrected Christ but His *parousia*.[83]

Since it is based on the views of form criticism, redaction criticism is subject to the same weaknesses. In adhering to the form-critical presupposition that the gospel tradition was developed by the church community, redaction criticism does not bring us any nearer to the events recorded in the gospels. The form critic, in fact, acknowledges that he is not concerned about the facts of history, rather, his interest is in the faith which the writers of the synoptics expressed in their writings. In centering attention upon the life-setting of the gospel in the faith of the author, redaction criticism pushes attention even farther away from the original events. One cannot escape the uneasy feeling that the ordinary Bible student, uninitiated in the

81. Guthrie, p. 219.
82. Fuller, p. 72.
83. Marxsen, pp. 111-16.

subtle insights of the redaction critics, can never hope to acquire a correct understanding of what the gospels intended to reveal about the teaching and work of Jesus Christ. Perrin justly observes, "Redaction criticism makes Life of Jesus research very much more difficult, it also raises fundamental questions with regard to the validity of a Life of Jesus theology."[84]

THE UNSOLVED SYNOPTIC PROBLEM

After three centuries of discussion and great expenditure of efforts, it cannot be said that a satisfactory solution to the synoptic problem has been found. Intensive efforts to find a solution have only heightened realization of its complexity. The painstaking efforts of scholars have surely resulted in a better understanding of numerous features and aspects of the gospels, but a fully satisfactory solution is not yet in sight. In 1912 D. A. Hayes remarked, "All of the solutions of the synoptic problem thus far offered are largely guesses in the dark. None of them is absolutely satisfactory. None of them may be more than partially right."[85] The verdict still stands.

The feeling that this complex problem has thus far eluded, and probably will continue to elude, a fully satisfactory solution is not new. About 150 years ago Johann Wolfgang von Goethe remarked that to embark on a historical and critical examination of the gospels was like trying to drink up the sea.[86] In 1893 J. A. Froude commented, "It might almost seem as if the explanation was laid purposely beyond our reach."[87] In 1909 Latimer Jackson was somewhat more optimistic:

> If some established results can be reckoned up, they are few in comparison with many open questions. . . . The present state of the Synoptic Problem has been described as chaotic. To a certain extent the description must be allowed. There is nevertheless some warrant for stating the position in more hopeful terms. The goal which for upwards of a century has been kept in view lies still ahead.[88]

In 1958 Wikenhauser concluded, "Up to the present no real solution

84. Norman Perrin, *What is Redaction Criticism?*, p. 69.
85. Doremus Almy Hayes, *The Synoptic Problem*, p. 11.
86. James Moffatt, *The Historical New Testament*, p. 262.
87. J. A. Froude, *Short Studies on Great Subjects* 1(1893): 276, as quoted in Harrison, p. 152.
88. *Cambridge Biblical Essays*, pp. 436, 454, as quoted in D. M. McIntyre, *Some Notes on the Gospels*, pp. 5-6.

has been found which explains the highly complex facts of the synoptic problem, nor is it likely that such a solution will be found."[89] And in 1971 Albright and Mann, in their commentary on Matthew, expressed the conviction that the synoptic problem "has become a veritable jungle of speculation."[90]

Hays appropriately calls the synoptic problem "the great enigma of the beginning of our New Testament canon."[91] The fact that our New Testament opens with three accounts of our Lord Jesus Christ which are so much alike and yet so strikingly different cannot fail to raise the question of their literary relationship. The fact that this very problem has defied solution by the most capable minds reminds us that the gospels are different from ordinary human documents. Something about these gospels places them beyond the reach of mere human explanation.

Evangelicals hold that it is impossible to explain the origins of the gospels apart from the activity of the Holy Spirit. The primary role of the Holy Spirit in the production of the gospels has been too commonly ignored or rejected in attempts to solve the problem. Guthrie rightly insists that "the operation of the Spirit in Gospel origins is a vital factor, indeed *the* vital factor, in the historical situation."[92] This is consistent with Jesus' promise to His disciples that the Holy Spirit would bring to their remembrance the things which He had taught, and would teach them the interpretation of His revelation (Jn 14:26; 16:12-14). It is unwarranted to reject the work of the Spirit in the production of the gospels because it does not fit into the normal categories of literary criticism. Literary and historical criticism may throw valuable light upon external circumstances and conditions connected with the writing of the gospels. But it cannot explain the inner guiding work of the Holy Spirit upon the authors. The Holy Spirit who controlled the formation and development of the gospel tradition also controlled the selection of the material by the different authors. As men voluntarily submitted to the guidance of the Spirit, He freely directed them in the selection of their material, whether from personal observation, eyewitnesses, or written sources. The preaching of the gospel was colored by individual emphases and

89. Wikenhauser, pp. 231-32.
90. W. F. Albright and C. S. Mann, "Matthew," in *The Anchor Bible*, p. CXCIV.
91. Hays, p. 11.
92. Guthrie, p. 232.

characteristic features which stemmed from the individual experiences and nature of the preachers. There was, however, a fundamental harmony in their message. The Holy Spirit, in superintending the composition of each gospel account, worked through the personality of the individual evangelist. Thus the account received a special emphasis and distinctive coloring appropriate to the writer's own purposes and the needs of his audience. "The Gospel writers were men of the Spirit whose purpose was to produce documents which would be spiritually useful in the ministry of the Church."[93] Their abiding vitality and unparalleled impact bear witness to the inspired character of their written accounts.

We may not be able to explain satisfactorily the literary origins of these inspired accounts as they have come down to us, but we gratefully accept every finding that contributes to a more adequate understanding of the gospels. But the Christian's chief concern is not the failure to find a fully satisfactory solution to the problem of literary origins. Rather, his primary concern is to faithfully study the gospels as the Spirit-provided means of growth in the grace and knowledge of our Lord Jesus Christ (2 Pe 3:18).

93. Ibid., p. 233.

8

THE GOSPEL ACCORDING TO JOHN

An Introduction to John

THE STUDENT who is familiar with the synoptic gospels is arrested by the distinctiveness of the fourth gospel. It belongs to the same unique genre of literature; it likewise proclaims the Good News of God's salvation in the person and work of Jesus Christ. Yet it possesses an independence of character and contents which have caused it to be called "the unique within the unique."[1] This uniqueness of the fourth gospel has always been recognized, causing it to be loved and esteemed as a priceless treasure of the Christian Church.

This gospel has evoked countless encomiums. Origen, the outstanding biblical scholar of the third century, characterized its value thus, "The Gospels are the first fruits of all the Scriptures, but of the Gospels that of John is the first fruits."[2] It was Luther's judgment that "the Gospel of John is unique in loveliness, and of a truth the principal gospel, far, far superior to the other three, and much to be preferred."[3] Alfred Plummer, a British scholar of the late nineteenth and early twentieth century, asserts that this gospel is "a book which stands alone in Christian literature, as its author stands alone among Christian teachers."[4] Hays quotes an unidentified writer as saying, "It is the chief of the Gospels and one can understand it only by reclining on the bosom of Jesus."[5] And Hendriksen, a contemporary scholar, asserts, "The Gospel according to John is the most amazing

1. Adam W. Miller, *An Introduction to the New Testament*, p. 306.
2. Origen *Commentary on John* 1. 6.
3. Martin Luther, preface to the New Testament of 1522, quoted in *Martin Luther, Selections from His Writings*, John Dillenberger, ed., p. 19.
4. Alfred Plummer, "The Gospel According to St. John," in *Cambridge Greek Testament for Schools and Colleges*, pp. xlviii-xlix.
5. Doremus Almy Hayes, *John and His Writings*, p. 77.

book that was ever written," because its author wholeheartedly believed the amazing claims of the One whose story he recorded.[6] The peculiar fascination that this gospel holds for the modern scholar is evident from the voluminous literature dealing with it.

It is ironic that a work of such tremendous spiritual dynamism, capable of evoking the highest eulogies, has also provoked fierce controversies. Modern critical scholars have encountered great difficulty in seeking to account for the origin and contents of this gospel. Selby remarks that it presents "some of the most difficult problems to be found in the New Testament."[7] Every feature of it has elicited diverse explanations. Baxter understandably observes, "The collision of pens, brains, theories and prejudices has so developed that one can scarcely be charged with erratic imaginativeness for suspecting in it a very stratagem of Satan to obscure by the dust of debate the outshining splendour of this most precious Gospel."[8]

The Authorship of the Fourth Gospel

Although an anonymous work, this gospel has traditionally been known as the gospel according to John. The comment in 21:24 makes it obvious that the original readers knew the identity of "the disciple that . . . wrote these things." Due to the controversy over authorship which has persisted since the nineteenth century, many modern scholars prefer to designate it "the fourth gospel" rather than "the gospel according to John."

1. EXTERNAL EVIDENCE

In A.D. 324 or 325 Eusebius in his noted *Ecclesiastical History* recorded the results of his investigations concerning the four gospels. He wrote about the apostle John, "His Gospel, which is known to all the churches under heaven, must be acknowledged as genuine."[9] In the same chapter he asserts, "But of the writings of John, not only his Gospel, but also the former of his epistles, have been accepted without dispute both now and in ancient times."[10] Thiessen declares, "The External evidence for the early date and Apostolic authorship

6. William Hendriksen, "Exposition of the Gospel According to John, Volume 1," in *New Testament Commentary*, p. 3.
7. Donald J. Selby, *Introduction to the New Testament*, p. 197.
8. J. Sidlow Baxter, *Explore the Book*, 5:301.
9. Eusebius *Ecclesiastical History* 3. 24. 1.
10. Ibid. 3. 24. 17.

of the Fourth Gospel is as great as that for any book in the New Testament."[11]

The principal witness for the apostolic authorship of this gospel is Irenaeus. In his work *Against Heresies,* written around A.D. 185, he explicitly names the apostle John as the author of this gospel. He asserts, "Afterwards [after the Synoptics were written], John, the disciple of the Lord, who also had leaned upon His breast, did himself publish a gospel during his residence at Ephesus in Asia."[12] This testimony concerning Johannine authorship is repeated several times,[13] with the additional information that John continued to live in Asia Minor or Ephesus until the time of Trajan (A.D. 98-117). Irenaeus wrote his work against the heretics while he was Bishop of Lyons in Gaul. As a youth he had lived in Asia Minor, where, according to his own testimony, he knew Polycarp, Bishop of Smyrna, who had been a personal disciple of the apostle John.[14] In a letter to Florinus, a boyhood friend, Irenaeus reminded him of their early mutual acquaintance with Polycarp and of Polycarp's reminiscences of his conversations with John and others who had seen the Lord.[15] Irenaeus insisted that he could recall the teachings of Polycarp, which he had heard as a youth, more clearly than events of recent years. In his letter to Florinus, who was about to break with the church and turn to Gnosticism, Irenaeus simply assumed that his friend accepted as factual the events which he recounted. Plummer points out that in *Against Heresies* it never occurs to Irenaeus "to maintain that the Fourth Gospel is the work of S. John; he treats it as a universally acknowledged fact."[16] Polycarp was martyred in A.D. 155, when he had been a Christian for eighty-six years. Only a generation separated Irenaeus and the apostolic age. Irenaeus also associated with Pothinus, his predecessor in Lyons, who knew the traditions of the early church in Gaul. He was an old man at the time of his martyrdom.

The history and position of Irenaeus give his testimony great weight. He had witnessed the martyrdom of Christian friends, which

---

11. Henry Clarence Thiessen, *Introduction to the New Testament,* p. 162.
12. Irenaeus *Against Heresies* 3. 1. 1.
13. Ibid. 3. 2. 2; 3. 3. 4; 3. 16. 5; 3. 22. 2; 5. 18. 2.
14. Ibid. 3. 3. 4.
15. Eusebius *Ecclesiastical History* 5. 20. 4-8.
16. Plummer, p. xxii.

must have caused him to take renewed interest in ascertaining the validity of the gospel documents, since they supported the beliefs for which men gave their lives. Because he was in close touch with the Roman and other churches, it is highly improbable that Irenaeus would so confidently assert the Johannine authorship of this gospel if other churches had rejected it. Hendriksen asserts, "Because of his many travels and intimate acquaintance with almost the entire church of his day, what Irenaeus says about the authorship of the Fourth Gospel must be considered of great significance."[17]

Confidence in Irenaeus' testimony is strengthened by the impressive supporting testimony of contemporary and subsequent writers. Theophilus of Antioch (c. 180) quotes John 1:1 and ascribes it to the apostle John.[18] Tertullian (c. 150-222) specifically ascribes this gospel to the apostle John.[19] Eusebius records that Clement of Alexandria (c. 155-216) in his *Hypotyposes*, in which he gave "the tradition of the earliest presbyters," placed this gospel as the last of the four gospels. Clement added that in view of the nature of the other gospels John, on the urging of his friends and with the illumination of the Spirit, composed "a spiritual Gospel."[20] Origen (c. 185-254), the pupil of Clement, indicates in his commentary on the fourth gospel that its author was John "who lay on Jesus' breast."[21]

This evidence establishes that the fourth gospel was accepted by the orthodox church as the work of the apostle John by the last quarter of the second century. Although John was not explicitly named as its author prior to A.D. 180, that position was accepted as the view of earlier times. Westcott makes the appropriate observation, "Christian theological literature practically begins for us with Irenaeus, Clement of Alexandria, and Tertullian, and these writers use the four Gospels as fully and decisively as any modern writer. . . . It is most significant that Eusebius, who had access to many works which are now lost, speaks without reserve of the Fourth Gospel as the unquestioned work of St. John."[22]

Earlier patristic writers did not make it a practice to quote verba-

17. Hendriksen, p. 22.
18. Theophilus of Antioch *To Autolycus* 2. 22.
19. Tertullian *Against Marcion* 4. 5.
20. Eusebius *Ecclesiastical History* 6. 14. 5-7.
21. Origen *Commentary on John* 1. 6.
22. Brooke Foss Westcott, *The Gospel According to St. John*, p. xxviii.

tim and specifically identify sources. But there is clear evidence that in the earlier part of the second century the fourth gospel was accepted as an authoritative work. There seem to be definite allusions to it in the writings of Justin Martyr (*c.* 100-165), Polycarp (*c.* 69-155), and Ignatius (martyred *c.* 116). When Tatian produced his *Diatessaron*, which may have been composed in Greek as early as A.D. 160, he viewed the fourth gospel as equal to the other three gospels in authority. Iverach points out that Tatian "was a pupil of Justin Martyr, and that fact alone renders it probable that the 'Memoirs of the Apostles', which Justin quotes so often, were those which his pupil afterward combined in the *Diatessaron*."[23] Scholars disagree over whether there is satisfactory proof that the gospel was used before A.D. 150. After an exhaustive reexamination of the evidence Braun concludes that there is ample evidence that this gospel was accepted in orthodox circles in Egypt, Rome, Syria, and Asia Minor, even from the early years of the second century.[24]

Morris concludes that a probable reading of the evidence shows that the heretic Marcion, who came to Rome in A.D. 110, accepted John's authorship of the gospel, but held that he was wrong in what he wrote.[25] The earliest known commentary on the fourth gospel was written by Ptolemaeus (*c.* 150), a follower of the Gnostic school of Valentinus, in which he refers to "John the disciple of the Lord" in support of his views.[26] Irenaeus makes it clear that the Valentinian heretics used John's gospel which they accepted as authoritative. Heracleon, a Gnostic commentator on John, who flourished during the middle of the second century, quoted from John 1:18 and attributed it to the disciple John, not John the Baptist.[27] Basilides, a Gnostic teacher in Alexandria during the reign of Hadrian (A.D. 117-138), quoted John 1:9 verbally.[28] The recently discovered "gospel of Thomas," Gnostic in orientation, is more akin to the synoptics than to John, but shows acquaintance with the fourth gospel. It identifies Thomas

23. James Iverach, "John, Gospel of," in *The International Standard Bible Encyclopaedia*, 3:1721.
24. Cited in Raymond E. Brown, "The Gospel According to John (i-xii)," in *The Anchor Bible*, p. lxxxi.
25. Leon Morris, "The Gospel According to John," in *New International Commentary on the New Testament*, p. 26.
26. Irenaeus *Against Heresies* 1. 8. 5.
27. J. H. Bernard, "A Critical and Exegetical Commentary on the Gospel According to St. John," in *International Critical Commentary*, 1:lxxiii.
28. Clement of Alexandria *The Stromata* 7. 17. 22.

as "the Twin" (Jn 11:16; 20:24; 21:2), an identification found only in the fourth gospel. Only this gospel records individual incidents concerning Thomas. The gospel of Thomas is generally dated at A.D. 140-150. Bernard comments, "The acceptance of the Fourth Gospel by many Gnostics as well as Catholics creates a strong presumption that it had been given to the public as an authoritative work at a time before controversy had arisen between Christian heretic and Christian orthodox."[29] This clearly pushes the origin of this gospel back into the earliest part of the second century. Since the Gnostics freely referred to the fourth gospel, members of the orthodox church may well have been hesitant to use it.

Recently discovered papyri bear unequivocal evidence that the gospel of John was used in Egypt at the beginning of the second century. The oldest known fragment of a New Testament manuscript, Papyrus 52, known as the Rylands Papyrus, is dated on paleological grounds between A.D. 125 and 150, presumably nearer the beginning of that period. This fragment of a codex of John contains only portions of John 18:31-33, 37-38, but it is conclusive evidence that the gospel must have been used in Egypt at the very beginning of the second century. The Egerton Papyrus 2, dated before A.D. 150, preserves part of an apocryphal gospel which depended on the fourth gospel.[30] This discovery confirms that the fourth gospel existed and was accepted as an authoritative work at the beginning of the second century. Allowing sufficient time for the gospel to reach Egypt, this papyrus evidence strongly supports the traditional view that the gospel was written by the apostle John during the latter part of the first century.

But opponents of the traditional view insist that there is external evidence which invalidates the view that the fourth gospel was written by John the son of Zebedee. The attack is made along several lines.

It is held that evidence for the early martyrdom of James and John, the sons of Zebedee, makes the traditional view impossible. In the history of Philip of Side (c. A.D. 430) the statement is made, "Papias in the second book says that John the theologian and James his

---

29. Bernard, 1:lxxiii.
30. H. I. Bell and T. C. Skeat, eds., *Fragments of an Unknown Gospel*; C. H. Dodd, *New Testament Studies*, pp. 12-52.

brother were killed by the Jews."[31] A similar assertion appears in the Chronicle of George the Sinner (9th century).* That this purported statement of Papias is not an accurate reproduction of his remark is clear from its inaccuracies. At the time of Papias the expression "the theologian" was not yet applied to John, nor was James killed "by the Jews," for Acts 12:2 shows that he was executed by order of Herod Agrippa I. Neither writer was known for his accuracy as a historian. While admitting these inaccuracies, Moffatt asserts, "It is indubitable that the work of Papias must have contained some statement of this nature about the two sons of Zebedee."[32] But neither Irenaeus nor Eusebius, who knew the complete work of Papias, adopted the view that John was martyred. This fact leads Barrett to observe, "If they read there the tradition that Philip and George record they must have suppressed it in the interests of their own opinion. In fact, we are almost compelled to choose between the veracity of Irenaeus and Eusebius on the one hand and the intelligence and accuracy of Philip and George on the other. It is a comparison which does credit to the earlier writers."[33]

The claim that John was martyred apparently was motivated by the prophecy of Jesus to the sons of Zebedee that they would drink His cup (Mk 10:39). Moffatt maintains that unless we admit that the words of Jesus were not fufilled, "we must admit that he foretold a martyr-death for the two men, and also that this had come to pass by the time Mark's gospel was published."[34] But such a conclusion is unwarranted. The words of Jesus do not demand the view that they would be physically martyred. Luke records the martyrdom of James (Acts 12:2) but he apparently knew nothing of the martyrdom of John. Galatians 2:9 proves that John was not martyred during James' lifetime. The silence of the entire New Testament concerning John's martyrdom, as well as the consistent tradition that John died at an advanced age in Ephesus, offers serious difficulty to any

31. Quoted from Alfred Wikenhauser, *New Testament Introduction*, p. 288. For a bibliography of sources for the fragments of Philip's history, see F. L. Cross, ed., *The Oxford Dictionary of the Christian Church*, pp. 1063-64.

*"Thirty copies of this Chronicle are now known; only one contains Papias' remarks about John's martyrdom." A. Feuillet, "The Johannine Writings," in A. Robert and A. Feuillett, *Introduction to the New Testament*, p. 640.

32. James Moffatt, *An Introduction to the Literature of the New Testament*, p. 604.
33. C. K. Barrett, *The Gospel According to St. John*, p. 87.
34. Moffatt, pp. 602-3.

claim that John was early martyred. The words of Jesus to James and John require no more than a prediction of serious suffering for them. In the common Greek the word "martyr" meant a "witness" and certainly John's experiences of persecution amply fulfilled the prediction of Jesus that he would drink the "cup."

Attempts are also made to establish the martyrdom of John by an appeal to ancient church calendars. A Syrian martyrology of A.D. 411 commemorates John and James on December 27 and calls them "apostles in Jerusalem."[35] This would suggest Jerusalem as the place of their martyrdom. But the martyrology of Carthage for the same date gives "St John the Baptist and James the Apostle killed by Herod."[36] This is clearly a case of confusion since John the Baptist is also commemorated on June 24th. These martyrologies can hardly stand as independent witnesses. The assumed martyrology celebrating the two brothers on the same date offers no valid evidence to prove that John was early martyred in Jerusalem. Influenced by Jesus' prophecy to the two brothers, the inclusion of John among the martyrs was probably motivated by the feeling that martyrdom was more honorable for an apostle than a natural death. While rejecting the traditional view, Kümmel admits that the claim for John's early martyrdom "cannot speak decisively against the composition of John by John, the son of Zebedee."[37]

Another line of attack against the traditional view is drawn from the silence of Ignatius. Ignatius in his letter to the Ephesians (c. A.D. 116) mentions Paul and his relation to the Ephesian church but says nothing about John. The letter was written while Ignatius was on his way to Rome to martyrdom, and, as Harrison observes, "a man bound for martyrdom would naturally be more interested in Paul the martyr than in one who died a natural death."[38] But an argument from silence is precarious and has weight only if it can be shown that the author should have informed us on the point. In illustration, Guthrie points to the remarkable fact that "Theophilus of Antioch, who does not mention the names of any Gospel writers except John and does not even mention the name of Christ," could not have been ignorant of these facts but for some reason chose not

35. Cf. H. Lietzmann, *Die drei ältesten Martyrologien*, Kleine Texte 2, pp. 7f.
36. Ibid., pp. 5f.
37. Werner Georg Kümmel, *Introduction to the New Testament*, p. 174.
38. Everett F. Harrison, *Introduction to the New Testament*, p. 219.

to mention them.[39] Bernard notices at least twenty verses in the fourth gospel that have parallels in the writings of Ignatius. He recognizes that this does not prove "any conscious literary obligation to the Fourth Gospel, although this is possible. But it is in accordance with all probabilities, that Ignatius had read this famous book which had been produced with the imprimatur of the Church at Ephesus a quarter of a century before he wrote to the Christians in that place."[40]

Opponents of the traditional view, which associates this gospel with the apostle John at Ephesus, assert that it is based on a case of mistaken identity.[41] It is claimed that Irenaeus was mistaken in his assertion that Polycarp had known John the apostle personally. The point is made that there is no mention of such close relations with the apostle John in the surviving letters of Polycarp, nor is the connection mentioned in the ancient account of his martyrdom. The youthful memory of Irenaeus, it is concluded, erroneously equated the apostle John with another influential leader at Ephesus known as John "the Elder" whom Polycarp knew. Support for this second John is found in the words of Papias:

> I shall not hesitate also to put down for you along with my interpretations whatsoever things I have at any time learned carefully from the elders and carefully remembered, guaranteeing their truth. For I did not, like the multitude, take pleasure in those that speak much, but in those that teach the truth; not in those that relate strange commandments, but in those that deliver the commandments given by the Lord to faith, and springing from the truth itself. If, then, any one came, who had been a follower of the elders, I questioned him in regard to the words of the elders,—what Andrew or what Peter said (*eipen*), or what was said by Philip, or by Thomas, or by James, or by John, or by Matthew, or by any other of the disciples of the Lord, and what things Aristion and the presbyter John, the disciples of the Lord, say (*legousin*). For I did not think that what was to be gotten from the books would profit me as much as what came from the living and abiding voice.[42]

39. Donald Guthrie, *New Testament Introduction*, p. 261, n. 1.
40. Bernard, 1:lxxi.
41. Kümmel, pp. 168-73; Moffatt, p. 610.
42. Eusebius *Ecclesiastical History* 3. 39. 3-4.

Eusebius made the following comment on these words from Papias:

> It is worth while observing here that the name John is twice enumerated by him. The first one he mentions in connection with Peter and James and Matthew and the rest of the apostles, clearly meaning the evangelist; but the other John he mentions after an interval, and places him among others outside the number of the apostles, putting Aristion before him, and he distinctly calls him a presbyter. This shows that the statement of those is true, who say that there were two persons in Asia that bore the same name, and that there were two tombs in Ephesus, each of which, even to the present day, is called John's.[43]

It is obvious that the interpretation which Eusebius drew from Papias' quotation was theologically motivated. The view that there were two men named John in Ephesus provided him with a welcome opportunity to get rid of the apostolic authorship of the book of Revelation since he strongly disliked the chiliasm which Papias promoted. He found sanction for this view in the opinion of Dionysius of Alexandria who held that the Apocalypse and the gospel of John had different authors.[44]

Admittedly Papias expressed himself poorly and his statement allows two different interpretations. The interpretation accepted by Eusebius holds that Papias mentioned two different men named John; the other view is that both references apply to the apostle John. The problem is still debated today and scholarly opinion is sharply divided. Eusebius accepted the apostolic authorship of the fourth gospel but rejected apostolic authorship for the Apocalypse. Modern negative criticism follows Eusebius in insisting on two different men but generally reverses his position, attributing the authorship of the Revelation to the apostle John but assigning the gospel of John to John the Elder.

Eusebius does not seem to be quite fair in his interpretation of Papias when he says that Papias called the second John "*a* presbyter." Papias called him "the presbyter," and that may be a different thing. He also overlooks the fact that the John mentioned in the second clause, like the John in the first clause, is called one of "the presby-

43. Ibid. 3. 39. 5-6.
44. Ibid. 7. 25. 6-7, 14-16.

ters" and one of "the disciples of the Lord." The expression "the disciples of the Lord" seems to mean personal followers of Jesus. While Aristion is never mentioned in the New Testament, it is possible that he was a personal follower of Jesus who survived until the end of the first century.

Papias clearly mentions two sources of information. The first source was the information gleaned from the followers of the deceased apostles; the other source was the information he received from Aristion and John himself. Eusebius ignores the significance of the change in tense from "said" (*eipen*) to "say" (*legousin*). Papias' reference to the value which he placed on "the living and abiding voice" is more significant if the second source was information received from personal disciples of Jesus. His reference to "the books" implies that he was acquainted with written accounts, among which must have been at least Matthew and Mark, since he elsewhere commented on their authorship.

According to the interpretation adopted by Eusebius, Papias received his information from the followers of the apostle John, not from the apostle John himself, thus forming three links in Papias' chain of information. Eusebius' critical interests thus led him to discredit the testimony of Irenaeus that Papias "was a hearer of John."[45] In order to establish the existence of two men named John at Ephesus Eusebius concluded that the second John mentioned by Papias could not have been the apostle John. But Farrar points out:

> In his History he reasons himself into the belief that Papias was only the pupil of 'the Presbyter;' but he had all the writings of Papias in his hand when he wrote the *Chronicon*, and there he says, without any hesitation, that Papias was a pupil of the Apostle. 'John the Presbyter' is a creation of Eusebius' later criticism.[46]

Irenaeus, who likewise knew all the writings of Papias, evidently did not read Papias as did Eusebius in his History. Eusebius did not profess to have any information about this "John the Elder" at Ephesus; he simply allowed his theological bias to adopt the guess of Dionysius of Alexandria that there must have been two men named John. That there were two tombs at Ephesus does not prove the

45. Ibid. 3. 39. 1.
46. F. W. Farrar, *The Early Days of Christianity*, p. 623.

existence of two different Johns; they probably represented rival claims to being the burial place of the apostle John. The distinction between the apostle John and John the Elder is based solely on the passage Eusebius quoted from Papias and his interpretation of it. That two men named John lived in Ephesus is commonly accepted by modern commentators. Whole chapters have been written about this shadowy "John the Elder."[47] His existence seems first to have been discovered by Eusebius. Zahn states his conviction that "the 'Presbyter John' is a product of the critical and exegetical weakness of Eusebius."[48] D. Moody evaluates the evidence for distinguishing two Johns with the remark that "it hangs on the precipice of prejudice created by the antichiliastic attitude of Origen and Eusebius."[49] Eusebius himself accepted the apostolic authorship of this gospel; the distinction which he discovered can only be used against the traditional view by reversing his views concerning the authorship of the gospel and the Apocalypse.

Guthrie observes that even if the existence of John the Elder were granted on the basis of Papias' ambiguous evidence, "there is no reason to believe that his pen could have produced the Fourth Gospel."[50] Papias certainly gave no hint that this Elder John possessed the needed literary prowess to produce this unique gospel. The only point in favor of this "confusion theory" is that he bore the name traditionally associated with this gospel.

Opponents of the traditional view point to the fact that certain individuals and groups in the early church rejected the fourth gospel. Marcion's rejection of it was theologically motivated. He rejected it because it contained doctrines which were objectionable to him (cf. p. 195), not because he held critical doubts concerning its authorship. Irenaeus mentioned that in his day certain people openly rejected "John's Gospel, in which the Lord promised that He would send the Paraclete."[51] It seems obvious that those who opposed the fourth gospel were anti-Montanists who overreacted against the heresy of Montanus and his stress on the new gift of the Spirit.

The Johannine writings were rejected by a small heretical sect

47. Cf. Burnett Hillman Streeter, *The Four Gospels: A Study of Origins*, chap. 16.
48. Theodor Zahn, "John the Apostle," in *The New Schaff-Herzog Encyclopedia of Religious Knowledge*, 6:205b.
49. Dale Moody, *The Letters of John*, p. 118.
50. Guthrie, p. 268.
51. Irenaeus *Against Heresies* 3. 11. 9.

(A.D. 170) whom Epiphanius of Salamis (*c.* 315-403) later contemptuously called the *Alogi,* thus cleverly indicating that the members of this sect were without the teaching of the Logos as well as devoid of reason. Whether or not this sect was related to the people mentioned by Irenaeus is not certain.

The rejection of the fourth gospel in the early centuries of the church by some heretical groups is of little importance. Their efforts to discredit the fourth gospel proved ineffectual, and any appeal today to their futile efforts to discredit the traditional view may be regarded as grasping at straws.

Apostolic authorship of the fourth gospel was universally accepted in the Christian church from the beginning of the third century until the nineteenth century.

2. INTERNAL EVIDENCE

B. F. Westcott's masterly presentation of the internal evidence, first published in 1880 as part of the "Speaker's Commentary," is still the classic formulation of the evidence drawn from the gospel itself.[52] Westcott holds that the gospel contains indirect as well as direct evidence concerning its authorship. He concludes that both lines of evidence firmly support the external testimony to its apostolic origin.

Westcott's formulation of the indirect evidence consists of the following chain: 1) the author was a Jew; 2) the author was a Jew of Palestine; 3) the author was an eyewitness of what he describes; 4) the author was an apostle; 5) the author was the apostle John. He supports each link in the chain with a full presentation of evidence found in the gospel itself. He established the last point through the expression "the disciple whom Jesus loved," as confirmed by the picture in the synoptics.

Westcott finds direct evidence in the gospel itself in 1:14; 19:35; 21:24 as confirming the writer's identity. The pronoun "we" in 1:14, "we beheld his glory," is a direct reference to the writer himself. While the "we" is not to be limited to the apostles, it certainly did not exclude them. Since the point of the verse is "that the Incarnation was historical, and the sight of the Incarnate Word was histori-

---

52. Brooke Foss Westcott, "St. John," in *The Speaker's Commentary, New Testament,* vol 2.

cal," the writer's use of the first person demands the view that he himself had been an eyewitness of Christ's ministry.[53]

Westcott next points to 19:35, "And he that hath seen hath borne witness, and his witness is true: and he knoweth that he saith true, that ye also may believe," an assertion introduced parenthetically. It likewise identifies the apostle John as the author of this book. Westcott points out that the use of the perfect tenses "he that hath seen hath borne witness," rather than the aorist, leaves no room to doubt "that the words taken in their context assert that the eyewitness was still living when the record was written."[54] He recognizes that "he knoweth" (*ekeinos oiden*) might either mean that the writer was making "an appeal to an eyewitness separate from himself," or that he was making "an appeal to his own actual experience, now solemnly recorded for the instruction of his readers."[55] Those who oppose the traditional view concerning authorship claim that *ekeinos*, "that one," must mean that the writer was referring to a third party. Westcott counters this by pointing out examples from classical authors as well as John's own use of this pronoun (1:18; 5:39; 9:37) which establish that a speaker can use this pronoun to refer to himself. Its use here reflects John's personal attitude. Having already established his own presence at the crucifixion scene as the disciple whom Jesus loved (19:26-27), he now uses it to "separate himself as the witness from his immediate position as a writer."[56] In this mental attitude the writer of the gospel "looks from without upon himself (*ekeinos*) as affected at that memorable moment by the fact which he records, in order that it may create in others the present faith (*pisteuēte*) which it had created in his own soul. The comment from this point is therefore perfectly compatible with the identification of the witness and the author."[57] The writer's identification of himself as the disciple "whom he [Jesus] loved" (19:26), also found in 13:23; 20:2; 21:7, 20,† viewed in the light of the privileged position of Peter, James, and John as revealed in the

---

53. Westcott, p. xxv.
54. Ibid., p. xxvii.
55. Ibid., p. xxvi.
56. Ibid.
57. Ibid.

†In each instance the imperfect tense, denoting linear action, is used. In 20:2 alone the verb *phileō* rather than *agapaō* is used, but the meaning is the same.

synoptics, can only be understood as the apostle John's modest self-identification.

Westcott holds that 21:1-23, although by nature an appendix to the gospel, was written by John himself and was part of the gospel when it was published. But he holds that verse 24, "This is the disciple that beareth witness of these things, and wrote these things: and we know that his witness is true," was the confirmatory testimony of the Christian community where the gospel was written. It asserts that this witness was present in their midst, and that he was the individual who "wrote these things." Westcott concludes, "The fourth Gospel claims to be written by an eyewitness, and this claim is attested by those who put the work in circulation."[58]

Conservative scholars in general have found Westcott's analysis of the internal evidence convincing and satisfactory. But modern liberal scholars, while generally agreeing with Westcott's chain of evidence, have balked at his conclusion that the writer was the apostle John. They generally agree that an eyewitness source lies behind this gospel but refuse to accept that eyewitness as the writer of our gospel. Morris observes, "Westcott has not so much been confuted as bypassed. Nobody seems to have dealt adequately with his massive argument. But scholars today evaluate the evidence differently."[59]

Various objections to the traditional view, which identifies the apostle John as the author, have been raised on the basis of the gospel itself.

It is maintained that the Christology of the fourth gospel is so high that "it is almost impossible to believe that a personal disciple could thus have merged the actual figure of Jesus in the conception of a divine being."[60] Hendriksen retorts, "It is a bold assertion when proof is wholly lacking."[61] He raises the counter question, "Is the Christology of Paul any lower?" and points to Colossians 2:9; Philippians 2:6; Romans 9:5. He also notes that Matthew 11:27-28 embodies a Christology that is the very essence of the Johannine Christology. There is no essential difference between the Christ of the fourth gospel and the Christ of the synoptics.

Hunter cites as an objection that it is "psychologically unlikely

58. Ibid., p. xxviii.
59. Morris, p. 9.
60. Ernest Findlay Scott, *The Literature of the New Testament*, p. 242.
61. Hendriksen, p. 10.

that the Apostle John would have styled himself 'the disciple whom Jesus loved'."[62] Such a designation of himself, it is asserted, would have been egotism on his part. If the designation was intended to assert that Jesus expressed preferential love for the writer, it would admittedly involve a difficulty. The synoptic gospels show that Peter, James, and John did indeed stand in a position of special privilege and intimacy with Jesus (Lk 8:51; Mk 9:2; 14:33). And this disciple's position at the Last Supper clearly indicates his intimacy with Jesus (Jn 13:23). So does the fact that while on the cross Jesus committed His mother to the care of this disciple (Jn 19:26-27). Westcott well observes, "The words express the grateful and devout acknowledgment of something received, and contain no assumption of a distinction above others. Christ loved all (xiii. 1, 34, xv. 9); St. John felt, and confesses, that Christ loved him, and shewed His love in this signal manner."[63] The designation is fully consistent with the traditional view that it was the writer's modest expression of personal gratitude for the love which Jesus bestowed on him, love which was in no way exclusively bestowed on him. This view finds support from the fact that the names of James and John, in contrast to the synoptics, never occur in this gospel, although they are mentioned once as "the sons of Zebedee" (21:2). Yet this writer is always careful to identify by name any disciple brought into the story (1:40, 44; 6:71; 11:16; 14:22). In this gospel John the Baptist is always called simply John, without any further qualification. The synoptic writers felt it necessary to distinguish between John the Baptist and John the apostle. Since John the disciple wrote this gospel, however, it never occurred to him that the two Johns needed to be distinguished. It is difficult to see why any other writer would have failed to observe the distinction between the two men. Guthrie further points out that the patristic writers without question accepted the designation "the beloved disciple," as a reference to the apostle John.[64]

Recently suggested identifications of this beloved disciple are highly improbable. One suggestion is that this beloved disciple was John Mark.[65] But this novel theory encounters serious difficulties.

62. A. M. Hunter, Introducing the New Testament, p. 50.
63. Westcott, p. xxiv.
64. Guthrie, p. 246 n. 1.
65. Pierson Parker, "John and John Mark," Journal of Biblical Literature 70(June 1960):97-110.

It demands that Mark was present at the Last Supper, but the synoptics indicate that only the Twelve were present. Who then wrote the second gospel? Harrison notes, "Confidence in tradition would be seriously shaken on this new hypothesis.[66] The rich young ruler has been nominated for this honor because Mark 10:21 states that Jesus loved him.[67] But there is no evidence that he became a believer or ever had the implied close connections with Jesus as His disciple. More probable is the suggestion that this beloved disciple was Lazarus whose sisters referred to him in their appeal to Jesus as "he whom thou lovest" (Jn 11:3).[68] But this view would demand that Lazarus was present at the Last Supper, improbable in light of the synoptics. All of these suggestions are harder to reconcile with the facts concerning this beloved disciple than the traditional view that he was John the disciple.

In a different category is the view advanced by Loisy that the beloved disciple is symbolical and non-historical and must be regarded as a type of the ideal believer.[69] This view makes nonsense of the historical references connected with this disciple. Guthrie pointedly remarks, "It is a fair principle of criticism that if a figure can reasonably be regarded as historical it should not be turned into a symbol which can mean anything the interpreter cares to read into it."[70]

In rejecting the traditional ascription of authorship Scott insists that this gospel could not be the work of John, a Galilean Jew, because of the Hellenistic character of its theological concepts.[71] He regards the gospel as a particular expression of Hellenistic Christianity molded and shaped by Greek speculation and Hellenistic piety. He feels that John, as one of the "pillars" of Jewish Christianity (Gal 2:9), in his later years could not have made "the complete change in his whole mental attitude"[72] which the traditional view demands. But we may reply with Richardson:

66. Harrison, p. 225.
67. Guthrie, p. 248.
68. Floyd V. Filson, "Who Was the Beloved Disciple?" *Journal of Biblical Literature* 68(June 1949): 83-88; "The Gospel of Life," in *Current Issues in New Testament Interpretation*, ed. William Klassen and Graydon F. Snyder, pp. 119-22.
69. A. Loisy, *Le Quatrieme Evangile* (Paris, 1903), cited in A. Robert and A. Feuillet, *Introduction to the New Testament*, p. 606. For other advocates and variant views see Guthrie, pp. 248-49 and notes.
70. Guthrie, p. 249.
71. Scott, p. 242.
72. Ibid.

To say that a Galilean fisherman could never have written such a book begs the question about what kind of a book it is; the assertion is justified only if we agree (as in fact we do not) that it is the masterpiece of a philosophical genius, steeped in the reasonings of the Platonists and Stoics, who was attempting to divest the essential gospel of its Jewish wrappings in order to make it acceptable to the "higher paganism" of the Hellenistic world.[73]

Discoveries since the time Scott advanced his claim (1932) have largely negated his argument. Sanders points out that the Dead Sea Scrolls prove that "now it is no longer necessary to look beyond Palestine and the first century A.D. for the environment in which these ideas, so characteristic of John, could have originated. John can no longer be regarded as a Hellenistic document pure and simple."[74] It is now evident that the theological views of the fourth gospel could have arisen in the moral and religious climate of first century Palestine. In thought and vocabulary it is essentially Palestinian. The Aramaic background behind the fourth gospel is now receiving ready recognition. Marshall states, "There are signs that an Aramaic sayings source lies behind John—Aramaic being, of course, the mother tongue of Jesus. . . . All the indications are that the linguistic background of John is Aramaic, although the theory that it was originally written in Aramaic is unconvincing."[75] This recognition is in full agreement with the traditional view that it was written by a disciple of Jesus.

Opponents of apostolic authorship maintain that the portrayal of Jesus' Messiahship in the fourth gospel disagrees with that in the synoptics. The synoptics only gradually apprehend Jesus' Messiahship, while the fourth gospel boldly declares it from the very beginning. This alleged contradiction does not do full justice to the facts. The fourth gospel relates that the Messiahship of Jesus was openly acknowledged by the disciples from the beginning (Jn 1:19-51), and the synoptics state that he was recognized early by John the Baptist (Mk 1:7-8) and by the demons (Mk 1:24, 34; 3:11). That Peter confessed Jesus' Messiahship at Caesarea-Philippi (Mk 8:29; Mt 16: 16-20; Lk 9:20) does not prove that the disciples had not previously

73. Alan Richardson, "The Gospel According to Saint John," in *Torch Bible Commentary*, p. 17.
74. J. N. Sanders, "John, Gospel of," in *The Interpreter's Dictionary of the Bible*, 2:943.
75. I. H. Marshall, "John, Gospel of," in *The New Bible Dictionary*, p. 649.

regarded Him as the Messiah. Viewed in the light of the fourth gospel it was a judgment of long standing, but unfavorable developments among the people and the Jewish leaders toward His Messianic identity made it essential for Jesus to elicit a firm confession from His disciples. The fourth gospel presents the disciples as confessing Jesus as Messiah from their first contacts with Him, but it also makes it clear that the disciples' Messianic conception developed during their association with Jesus. This is the obvious significance of the statement in 2:11 that "his disciples believed on him." The miracle recorded in 2:1-10 gave them an enlarged conception of His Messianic character. Likewise Peter's confession in 6:68 implies that Jesus' shattering of their hopes that He would rule as King over Israel led to a new perception of the kind of Messiah He was. The disciples' confession in 16:30 indicates a further development in their understanding of His true nature. The words of Jesus in 16:12-13 make it clear that the disciples' fullest understanding of the person and work of Christ awaited Pentecost. Thus it is not possible to establish that the Messianic self-disclosure found in the fourth gospel is contradictory to the gradual disclosure of His Messianic identity presented in the synoptics.

The strongest objection to the apostolic origin of the fourth gospel is based on the striking difference between the discourses of Jesus in the fourth gospel and those in the synoptics. Thus Moody Smith asserts, "If Jesus actually spoke as he speaks in the various strands of the Synoptic tradition, I find it impossible to believe that he also spoke as does the Johannine Christ."[76] This assumes that the discourses in the fourth gospel are the invention of a later writer. But the one who claims that these discourses were invented by a later writer must answer the question, What writer was capable of inventing material with such majestic grandeur and unmistakable impact of reality? The distinctiveness of the discourses in the fourth gospel is patent. But that distinctiveness would discredit the apostolic authorship of the gospel only if it misrepresented the Christ of the synoptics. It has not been established that the fourth gospel actually conveys such a misrepresentation. R. H. Lightfoot observes, "The Church has never been aware of any fundamental incompatibility

76. D. Moody Smith, Jr., "A Major New Commentary on John" [book review], *Interpretation* 21(October 1967):475.

between the portrait of the Lord in this gospel and that in the other three. This question has long ago been settled by the religious consciousness of Christendom."[77] The differences may be partially accounted for by the fact that they were addressed to different audiences. A student of rabbinic literature, Israel Abrahams, asserts, "Most remarkable of all has been the cumulative strength of the arguments adduced by Jewish writers favourable to the authenticity of the discourses in the Fourth Gospel, especially in relation to the circumstances under which they are reported to have been spoken."[78] It is also possible that the differences arose in part from the fact that John paraphrased the teaching of Jesus in the light of his later meditations, but this suggestion must be used with caution. The fourth gospel contains many sayings which are similar in form and content to those found in the synoptics.[79] That the Jesus of the synoptics did at times speak in the style set forth in the fourth gospel is demonstrated by the two remarkable passages in Matthew 11:25-27 and Luke 10:21-22. Morris reminds us that "in history Jesus has proved a gigantic figure" and that it is entirely possible "that He is the Sitter behind both Gospel portraits, that the Synoptics depict Him from one aspect, John from another."[80] He suggests that our inability "to put the two pictures together satisfactorily may mean no more than that we are not big enough to comprehend the whole Christ."[81]

It is our conclusion that the critical attempt to disprove the traditional ascription of authorship on the basis of internal evidence has failed.

3. CONCLUSION

Both the external and the internal evidence firmly connect John, the son of Zebedee, with the origin of the fourth gospel. Archbishop Temple declared, "I regard as self-condemned any theory about the origin of the Gospel which fails to find a very close connection between it and John the son of Zebedee."[82] We agree with this dictum, but it leaves open three possible views concerning its actual author-

77. R. H. Lightfoot, *St. John's Gospel: A Commentary*, p. 1.
78. As quoted in Harrison, p. 223.
79. See the list in Hendriksen, pp. 14-16.
80. Morris, pp. 19-20.
81. Ibid., p. 20.
82. William Temple, *Readings in St. John's Gospel*, p. x.

ship. First, John may have composed it himself, probably with the aid of an amanuensis. Second, a disciple of John may have written it, using the memoirs of John or the authentic traditions concerning John's teaching. A third view is that the gospel is the product of a Johannine "school," possibly closely connected with southern Palestine. That school was responsible for the development of the Johannine theology and its members produced the Johannine literature.

The second and third suggestions are compromise views. The third is speculative. Therefore, little decisive evidence can be established for or against it. It rejects the strong external evidence and is of no real value in solving the problem of the gospel's authorship. The second view, adopted by some moderately conservative scholars, is a mediating position between the traditional view and the liberal rejection of apostolic authorship.[83] We agree with Harrison, "It is doubtful that the facts in the case demand even this measure of concession."[84] It does not accept the external evidence at face value, and there seems to be no decisive internal evidence which demands this concession. It draws support from the claim that 19:35 appeals to an eyewitness other than the writer. But this is not a necessary interpretation of the verse (see p. 204). Its contents do not hint that it records a testimony that is second hand.

The traditional view that this gospel was written by the apostle John is strongly supported by both the external and the internal evidence. R. H. Lightfoot fairly remarks, "This traditional ascription still receives support, and has never been shown to be impossible."[85] Sanders states its probability thus, "A man who was a youth at the time of the Crucifixion could well have published the gospel in the nineties when he was himself, as the tradition asserts, an old man, perhaps the last survivor of those who had seen the Lord."[86] All the evidence, both external and internal, combine to make this the most probable view. Kistemaker well concludes, "The traditional view, because of archaeology and recent literature discoveries simply cannot be dismissed as was done in the past. This view has merits of its own."[87] With that verdict we fully agree.

83. Hunter, *Introducing the New Testament,* p. 50; R. V. G. Tasker, "The Gospel According to St. John," in *Tyndale New Testament Commentaries,* pp. 11-17.
84. Harrison, p. 225.
85. Lightfoot, p. 2.
86. Sanders, 2:945.
87. Simon Kistemaker, *The Gospels in Current Study,* p. 124.

THE AUTHOR OF THE FOURTH GOSPEL

James and John, "the two sons of Zebedee" (Mt 26:37; Mk 10:35), were natives of Galilee. Before they became disciples of Jesus, they followed their father's trade as fishermen on the sea of Galilee (Mk 1:19-20). Their mother's name was Salome (Mk 15:40 in conjunction with Mt 27:61). On the basis of John 19:25, compared with Matthew 27:56; 27:61 and Mark 15:40, 47, it is generally agreed that Salome was the sister of Mary the mother of Jesus. This relationship harmonizes well with the glimpses in the gospels of the close relationship of this family to Jesus. The family seems to have been well-to-do, since the father had "hired servants" (Mk 1:20), and Salome was one of the women who followed Jesus and ministered to Him of their substance (Lk 8:3 compared with Mt 27:55-56; Mk 15:40-41). Her active association with Jesus during His Galilean itineraries probably came after the death of her husband; Zebedee is not mentioned again in the gospels after Jesus called his two sons to discipleship (Mk 1:20).

The opening story of John's gospel makes it clear that John was among a group of Galileans who attended the preaching ministry of John the Baptist and became his disciples; upon meeting Jesus they became His first followers (Jn 1:19-51), and for a brief time stayed with Him as His disciples (2:12; 3:22; 4:2). After initially associating with Jesus, John and these other disciples returned to their former employment. At the beginning of His great Galilean ministry Jesus called John and his brother to full-time discipleship (Mt 4:21-22; Mk 1:19-20; Lk 5:7-11). Later John was included among the select group of twelve apostles (Mk 3:13-19; Lk 6:12-16). The names in the lists of the Twelve always appear in three groups of four each; John is always among the first four (Mt 10:2-4; Mk 3:16-19; Lk 6:14-16; Ac 1:13-14). On three occasions during Jesus' ministry, John, with Peter and James, received special privileges of intimacy (Mk 5:37; 9:2; 14:33). He and Peter were sent by Jesus to prepare for the last Passover (Lk 22:8). During the Last Supper he occupied a position next to Jesus which enabled him to lean upon Jesus' bosom (Jn 13:23). After Jesus was arrested, John followed Him into the court of the high priest's house. His acquaintance with the maid who kept the door enabled him to bring in Peter also (Jn 18:15-18). During the crucifixion he took his place beside the cross, and Jesus committed His mother into his care (Jn 19:26-27). On the resurrection morning he and Peter ran to the empty tomb, and that evening he was among the group who saw the risen Lord (Jn 20:2-10, 19-23). He was among the seven to whom the risen Lord appeared at the Sea of Galilee (Jn 21:2).

Jesus called James and John *Boanērges,* "Sons of thunder" (Mk 3:17), apparently because of their zealous and impetuous temperament, evidenced in their angry reaction at the refusal of a Samaritan village to offer Jesus lodging (Lk 9:54). John's misguided zeal caused him to rebuke a man who was casting out demons in the name of Jesus (Lk 9:49). The selfish ambition of the two brothers led them to ask Jesus for the places of honor in His coming kingdom (Mk 10: 35-40). The fact that John came to be known as the apostle of love bears eloquent witness to the transforming power of Jesus upon him. The wild, rushing torrent of his impetuous nature was brought under control, but the Johannine literature reveals that John, while mellowed by divine love, never lost his fiery attitude toward sin.

In the first chapters of Acts John appears on three different occasions, always in close association with Peter: the healing of the cripple at the gate of the temple (3:1); their boldness before the Sanhedrin (4:13); their ministry to the Samaritan converts of Philip (8:14-17). When Paul and Barnabas returned to Jerusalem after their first missionary journey, John was recognized as one of the "pillars" of the Jerusalem church (Ac 15:6; Gal 2:9). How long John remained in Jerusalem is not known.

Tradition solidly maintains that John spent the closing years of his life in Ephesus. He continued to live there until the end of the first century, long after the other disciples had passed away. This harmonizes with the conservative view concerning his authorship of the Johannine epistles and the Apocalypse. "He lived a life of quiet usefulness, bringing forth fruit in old age. Of that fruit, so rich and ripe, the fourth gospel forms no meager part."[88]

THE PURPOSE AND READERS OF THE FOURTH GOSPEL

Matters concerning the purpose and the intended readers of the fourth gospel are closely related and may be considered together. This is the only gospel which contains a full and precise statement

88. Herbert L. Willett and James M. Campbell, *The Teachings of the Books,* p. 73.

of the author's purpose. In seeking to understand any book it is always wise to consider it in the light of the author's declared purpose. "Many other signs therefore did Jesus in the presence of the disciples, which are not written in this book: but these are written, that ye may believe that Jesus is the Christ, the Son of God; and that believing ye may have life in his name" (20:30-31). The structure and contents of this gospel agree with the author's declared purpose.

The author was purposefully selective in the use of his material. Of all the material available to him, he used only that which best fulfilled his purpose. The abundance of available material is strikingly indicated by the concluding comment in 21:25. The reference to his work as "this book" implies that he knew of other books dealing with this material; the most natural suggestion is that he is referring to the synoptic gospels.

His central theme is the person and work of Jesus. The author's twofold purpose in presenting His story is connected with the faith of his readers. "That ye may believe that Jesus is the Christ, the Son of God" (20:31) relates to the intellectual conviction of his readers, the doctrinal core of their faith. "That believing ye may have life in his name" states the resultant spiritual experience of his readers. Both are essential to a full-orbed presentation of the Christian faith. He is writing a gospel, not merely a biography of Jesus.

Textual evidence is divided on the question whether the words "that ye may believe" should be read as the present tense (*hina pisteuēte*) or the aorist tense (*hina pisteusēte*).‡ The former would mean that John's purpose is to encourage and confirm the existing faith of believers, which was under strong attack from false teachers; the latter would mean that the work was addressed to non-Christians and was designed to be an evangelistic instrument. The present tense seems preferable, but history and experience confirm that this gospel has effectively promoted both functions.

John wrote to establish and confirm the historical reality concern-

---

‡The critical editors are divided. Westcott and Hort and Nestle use the present tense. Souter and the first edition of the United Bible Societies text use the aorist; the third edition of the Bible Societies text puts the sigma of the aorist tense in brackets to mark the doubtful character of the text. The Textus Receptus uses the aorist.

ing the nature of the man "Jesus."§ While John constantly kept before his readers the fact of Jesus' humanity, his purpose was to show
that He was more than human, that in truth He "is the Christ, the
Son of God." His historical account of Jesus was intentionally interpretative of His true nature. He portrays Jesus as "the Christ," the
Messiah, the personal fulfillment of the Old Testament messianic
promises.|| John's gospel stresses Jesus' Messianic identity through-
out, from its very commencement (1:19-51), to its close, as seen in
His Palm Sunday entry into Jerusalem (12:12-19), His discussions
with Pilate (18:33-37), and Pilate's refusal to modify the wording
over the cross (19:19-22). This is the only gospel which records
that the people wanted to make Jesus king. He refused (6:14-15),
doubtless because of their inadequate conception of His kingship.
This emphasis upon Jesus' identity as Messiah establishes that the
true fulfillment of the Old Testament promises and the hopes of the
Jewish people lie in Him.

This gospel, more strongly than the synoptics, stresses the uniqueness of the person of Jesus as "the Son of God." This revelation concerning His divine nature is embodied in the opening prologue (1:
1-18), is repeatedly demonstrated by the signs of Jesus which called
attention to His divine power, and finds prominent expression in
His discourses. His claims to deity especially stirred the fierce anger
of the Jewish leaders (cf. 5:16-18; 8:57-59; 10:30-33; 19:7), causing
them to denounce Him as a blasphemer. This gospel constantly reveals the challenge that the person and message posed for His hearers. As "the Son of God" He was indeed "the fulfiller of the destiny
of mankind."[89] The gospel gives a large place to the events connected with His death and resurrection. It underlines the universal
scope of His redemptive work (3:16-17; 6:40). His unique nature
as the Son of God gave universal efficacy to His atoning work.

This irrefutable evidence concerning Jesus' Messiahship and deity
in this gospel was recorded for the further purpose "that believing

§In the Revised Version we find that Mark calls our Lord "Jesus" only thirteen
times. Luke calls Him "Jesus" eighty-eight times. Matthew calls Him "Jesus" one
hundred and fifty-one times. John calls Him "Jesus" two hundred and forty-seven
times." G. Campbell Morgan, *The Gospel According to John*, pp. 13-14.

||Only in this gospel is the term "Messiah" preserved in its transliterated form
(1:41; 4:25).

89. Westcott, p. 297.

ye may have life in his name." John's ultimate purpose for his readers is that they may experience eternal life through faith in the One portrayed. Faith in Him is the essential condition. Throughout his gospel John shows the development of faith and unbelief in relation to Him. Men either "commit themselves to Christ in faith and so enter life or they refuse to commit themselves and remain in darkness and the condition of lostness."[90] Thus ultimately this gospel, which has a message for all mankind, becomes very personal, "What must I do?"

John's statement of purpose need not exclude other, subordinate aims, which have been suggested. These suggested purposes for the fourth gospel must be evaluated in the light of its contents and John's own stated aim.

An early suggestion was that John wrote to supplement the synoptics. This is suggested in the statement of Clement of Alexandria, "Last of all, John, perceiving that the external facts had been made plain in the Gospel [i.e., the synoptics], being urged by his friends, and inspired by the Spirit, composed a spiritual Gospel."[91] The other gospels had set forth the external facts; John wrote to provide the deeper spiritual background for those facts. Eusebius himself advanced the idea that John wrote to supply an account of Jesus' activity before John the Baptist was imprisoned.[92] Both assertions indicate that John wrote later than the synoptists and imply that he had read their works, or at least was familiar with their contents. But modern scholars are not agreed as to what extent, if at all, John used the synoptics in composing his own gospel.[93] Views range all the way from the position that John was entirely independent of the synoptics to the assumption that he drew material from all three of them. As we see it, John was familiar with the *contents* of the synoptics but, as an eyewitness, was not dependent upon them for his material. We agree with Guthrie's view, "If the evidence is insufficient to prove literary dependence on the Synoptics, there are enough indications to show that the author assumed that his readers would be acquainted with the contents of the other Gospels. Only under such a hypothesis can his choice of material be intelligently understood."[94]

90. Morris, p. 40.
91. Eusebius *Ecclesiastical History* 6. 14. 7.
92. Ibid. 3. 24. 7-12.
93. Cf. Brown, pp. xliv-xlvii; Kümmel, pp. 143-48.
94. Guthrie, p. 274.

Hendriksen notes that certain passages in John's gospel "seem to indicate that John presupposed that the readers had read the Synoptics" and cites 3:24, 11:2, and 18:13 as instances.[95] But this need not imply that John regarded the synoptics as inadequate, or that he deliberately aimed to correct them. The large amount of new didactic material which he introduced suggests that his gospel aimed at bringing into greater prominence the spiritual aspects of the Christian message as seen in the light of the fuller experience of the Christian church. Yet, in the words of Richardson, "This does not mean that St. John is any less an historian than are the Synoptic Evangelists, for all history-writing is concerned with the interpretation of facts."[96] It is obvious that the fourth gospel does supplement the material of the synoptics, but such a supplemental function was a natural result of his selecting material to achieve his stated aim.

Others have suggested that this gospel was a polemic against unbelieving Jews.[97] That the gospel does contain sharp attacks upon the unbelief of "the Jews" regarding Jesus' Messianic identity is clear (5:16-18, 37-47; 7:1, 19; 8:22-24, 37-59; 10:31-39; 19:7). But this attitude of hostility is portrayed in the other gospels also. Since John's stated aim was to show that Jesus was the Messiah expected by the Jewish nation, his gospel naturally recorded the hostile reaction of the Jews to Jesus' claim. The gospel records the actual controversies between Jesus and the Jewish leaders, but it is probable that these controversies were preserved in such a way as to meet the needs of the church in answering similar arguments during John's day. There is no warrant to claim that this polemic against the Jews was a principal aim of the gospel.

It has been suggested that one purpose of the gospel was to correct a zealous veneration of John the Baptist.[98] Acts 19:1-7 reveals that there was a John the Baptist movement in Ephesus during the days of Paul. But this passage offers meager evidence for the view that John wrote to rebuke the sectarians of John the Baptist. The statements in this gospel which show the inferiority of the Baptist to Jesus arise quite naturally out of John's aim to portray the uniqueness of

95. Hendriksen, p. 32.
96. Richardson, p. 26.
97. See Kümmel, pp. 162-63; R. M. Grant, "The Origin of the Fourth Gospel," *Journal of Biblical Literature* 69(December 1950):305-22.
98. See Kümmel, p. 162 for advocates of this view.

Jesus who, as "the Christ, the Son of God," was uniquely superior to the Baptist. If such a John the Baptist movement did plague the church when John wrote, the execution of his stated aim would naturally counteract the movement. It certainly cannot have been a major purpose behind the writing of this gospel.

Many hold that John wrote his gospel for the purpose of combatting Gnosticism. At that time, erroneous teaching was being promulgated which claimed to be Christian. An early and persistent tradition claims that John wrote to refute the errors of Cerinthus, a Gnostic teacher who was a contemporary of John at Ephesus near the end of the first century. Irenaeus indicates that this was a purpose of the fourth gospel.[99] Jerome in the preface to his *Commentary on Matthew* says that John wrote "at the time when the seeds of heresy were springing up (I refer to Cerinthus, Ebion, and the rest who say that Christ has not come in the flesh, whom he in his own epistle calls Anti-Christs)."[100] In light of the first and second epistles of John, it is very probable that John was combatting a false teaching known as Docetism, which denied the incarnation, insisting that Jesus only appeared to have a human body. But the claim that the gospel was written as a polemic against Gnosticism, whether of the Cerinthian or the Docetic type, is not as self-evident as is sometimes thought. No doubt John was aware of the danger of Gnosticism when he wrote, and his gospel indeed proved to be a useful instrument in combatting that false teaching. But if this was a motive in writing, it had no great prominence. This negative function could at most have been only secondary to the fulfillment of the supreme purpose set forth in 20:30-31.

A popular modern view is that the aim of the fourth gospel was to present a kind of "Hellenized" Christianity. Christianity rapidly moved beyond Judaism and came to identify itself with the Gentile world. Therefore there was a need to assimilate the ideas of Greek philosophy in order to make the message of Christianity more intelligible to the devout and thoughtful persons of a large Hellenistic city like Ephesus.[101] But it is no longer so evident that the gospel

99. Irenaeus *Against Heresies* 3. 3. 4; 3. 11. 1.
100. Jerome *Commentary on Matthew*, Preface.
101. Scott, pp. 249-50.

must be interpreted against the thought background of Hellenistic readers. Guthrie observes that "certain parallels in the Qumran literature with the Johannine literature suggest that some of the terms which were previously confidently regarded as of Greek origin were in fact found in a Jewish milieu just prior to and contemporary with the rise of Christianity."[102] Morris feels that "it cannot be said that the view that the Gospel is a manifesto of Hellenistic Christianity has very much to commend it." This is due to the fact that recent evidence makes it increasingly clear that this Gospel "is a product of Jewish and not Hellenistic ways of thinking."[103] This realization has led to the more probable suggestion of Van Unnik that the main purpose of this gospel was to provide a missionary handbook to win the Jews in the Diaspora to faith in Jesus.[104] Brown, however, suggests, "If the language of the Johannine argument against the Jews serves as a guide, the purpose must have been one of countering Jewish propaganda rather than of persuading the Jews with a hope of mass conversion."[105] He holds it more probable that if the gospel was directed at Jewish readers it was aimed at that small group who believed in Jesus but had not yet severed their relations with the synagogue.[106]

The thrust and message of this gospel is best understood, in keeping with its declared purpose, as the Johannine witness to the divine revelation in the unique person and work of Jesus "the Christ, the Son of God." In his book *Witness and Revelation in the Gospel of John* Boice shows the focal significance of this witness.[107] The universal note sounded in this Gospel (3:16; 10:16; 12:32) makes it evident that its intended scope should not be restricted to a narrow circle of readers. It was written to present the true nature of the supreme revelation in Christ as confessed by the Church, and to make an appeal to the world at large which was the object of God's redemptive love in Christ Jesus.

102. Guthrie, p. 278.
103. Morris, p. 39.
104. W. C. van Unnik, "The Purpose of St. John's Gospel," in *Studia Evangelica*, p. 410.
105. Brown, pp. lxxiii-lxxiv.
106. Ibid., pp. lxxiv-lxxv.
107. James Montgomery Boice, *Witness and Revelation in the Gospel of John.*

THE PLACE AND DATE OF THE FOURTH GOSPEL

1. PLACE

The gospel of John gives no indication as to the place where it was written, and scholarly surmises disagree on the point.

The almost unanimous voice of ancient tradition points to Ephesus as the place of origin. This is the explicit testimony of Irenaeus, "John, the disciple of the Lord, who also leaned upon His breast, did himself publish a Gospel during his residence at Ephesus in Asia."[108] Polycrates, bishop of Ephesus, wrote that "John, who was both a witness and a teacher, who reclined upon the bosom of the Lord, . . . also sleeps at Ephesus."[109] Brown observes, "The anti-synagogue motif in the gospel makes sense in the Ephesus region, for Rev ii 9 and iii 9 attest bitter anti-synagogue polemics in this area of Asia Minor."[110] In support of this tradition Morris notes that "Ephesus is not far from Phrygia, the centre of the Montanist movement, and the Montanists made early use of this Gospel."[111] If there is a polemic against the disciples of John the Baptist in this gospel, Ephesus would be the probable place. The Ephesian origin of the gospel is in full accord with the traditional view concerning the origin of the Johannine epistles. An Ephesian origin is demanded by the book of Revelation. The contents of the fourth gospel are consistent with this tradition. In support of the traditional view Westcott asserts, "No valid objection has been brought against the belief which was preserved on the spot by a continuous succession of Christian teachers."[112]

Two other places have been advocated by scholars who discount the force of tradition. Antioch of Syria has been advocated. Ephraem the Syrian (d. 373) is the only Church Father to connect this gospel with Antioch. According to a Syriac fragment appended to the Armenian translation of his commentary on Tatian's *Diatessaron*, he remarks, "John wrote that [gospel] in Greek at Antioch, for he remained in the country until the time of Trajan." Ephraem's source for this information is not known. In support of a Syrian origin Kümmel points to "marked parallels in subject matter with the 'Odes

108. Irenaeus *Against Heresies* 3. 1. 1.
109. Eusebius *Ecclesiastical History* 3. 31. 3.
110. Brown, p. ciii.
111. Morris, p. 59.
112. Westcott, p. xl.

of Solomon,' which supposedly belong to Syria, and with Ignatius of Antioch, who apparently is the oldest user of John. Furthermore, the conceptual world shows relationship with the Gnosticizing circles on the edge of Judaism."[113] Morris recognizes this view as "the most popular alternative suggestion."[114] Yet the evidence is not strong. Brown asserts, "There is really nothing here that would convince us that the Gospel was written in Syria."[115] This view does not account for the strong external testimony in support of Ephesus.

Alexandria has also been nominated as the place of origin. Favorable evidence is the fact that the earliest known manuscript of this gospel (Papyrus 52) came from Egypt. But the force of this argument is undermined by the fact that it was due to the climate of Egypt that papyrus documents were preserved; it cannot be proved that there were no papyrus manuscripts of a comparable date in existence elsewhere. Appeal is also made to the fact that this gospel was used by the Egyptian Gnostics, since Egypt was an early center of Gnosticism. Lake and Lake support this view with the claim that "the gospel is extremely Philonic."[116] Brownlee, while accepting Alexandria as the probable place of origin, recognizes that this claim by Lake and Lake is "greatly exaggerated."[117] Support has also been sought from the supposed affinity between the fourth gospel and the hermetic writings.[118] Brownlee further points to the mixed population of Alexandria and the fanatical character of its citizens as probably offering "all the requirements for a milieu in which the preaching of John would be especially appropriate."[119] But there is no tradition which connects John and his preaching with Alexandria.

The scholars who reject the Ephesian tradition have not established their own views with more convincing evidence. We accept Ephesus as the most probable place of composition. It is strongly supported by external evidence and inferences based on the internal evidence have not been proved to be inconsistent with it.

113. Kümmel, p. 175.
114. Morris, p. 59.
115. Brown, p. ciii.
116. Kirsopp Lake and Silva Lake, *An Introduction to the New Testament*, p. 53.
117. William H. Brownlee, "Whence the Gospel According to John?" in *John and Qumran*, p. 189, n. 84.
118. See J. N. Sanders, *The Fourth Gospel in the Early Church*, pp. 40-42.
119. Brownlee, pp. 189-90.

2. DATE

No precise date for the writing of the fourth gospel can be established. The old view of the radical scholars that the gospel arose during the middle or end of the second century has been effectively silenced by the papyrus discoveries in Egypt (cf. p. 221). The latest possible date for the composition of the gospel is A.D. 98, for according to the testimony of Irenaeus John continued to live at Ephesus until the time of Trajan (A.D. 98-117). Eusebius, in summing up the earlier tradition concerning the gospels' order of appearance asserts that John knew of the synoptics and that he finally wrote down what he had been proclaiming orally.[120] (Cf. pp. 179-80.) In accepting the view that John wrote last, the earliest date for the gospel of John may be determined by the date accepted for the last synoptic. Our view is that the synoptics were written between A.D. 64 and 68. But since the fall of Jerusalem is not mentioned in John, it was most probably written some time after A.D. 70. This would suggest a date somewhere between A.D. 80 and 98. Some, like Lenski, prefer a date "somewhere near 80 or 85" because "the three Epistles of John were most likely written after the Gospel, and the Revelation last of all."[121] But because of the roughness of the language in the Revelation many scholars hold that it is more probable that Revelation was written first and the gospel last of all. There is, however, another possible explanation for the language in Revelation: John wrote it on Patmos where he had no assistance with the language. He wrote the gospel at Ephesus with the aid of an amanuensis. No one has been able to resolve the problem with certainty. That John could have written the gospel last of all, as late as A.D. 95, cannot be summarily denied by reason of his advanced age. Clement of Alexandria relates that even after John's return from Patmos he carried on an active ministry as overseer of the churches in Ephesus and the surrounding districts.[122] It is clear that John must have continued to be physically strong and mentally vigorous into old age. Kümmel says, "Today it is almost common opinion that John was written in the last decade of the first century."[123] We hold that chapter 21 was written by John and was

120. Eusebius *Ecclesiastical History* 3. 24. 7.
121. R. C. H. Lenski, p. 20.
122. Eusebius *Ecclesiastical History* 3. 23. 1-19.
123. Kümmel, p. 171.

part of the gospel at the time of its publication; verses 21-23 clearly imply that John had reached old age at the time.

In recent years there has been support for a date before A.D. 70. This is largely due to the recognition that the intellectual milieu behind the fourth gospel can be reconciled with the general atmosphere prevailing in Palestine before A.D. 70. This view receives impetus from the generally accepted Aramaic element behind this gospel as well as the thought climate revealed by the Dead Sea Scrolls. The view of Gardner-Smith that the fourth gospel is independent of the synoptics also supports an early date.[124] The present tense in John 5:2, "Now there *is* in Jerusalem by the sheep gate," is pointed out as internal evidence that it was written before A.D. 70, since the writer otherwise would have used "was." But Westcott holds that the present tense simply proves that the author was personally acquainted with Jerusalem before its destruction and by using the present tense "he recalls a familiar scene" and thus "lives again in the past, and forgets the desolation which had fallen upon the place which rises before his eyes."[125] In 11:18 the writer uses the past tense, "Bethany *was* near to Jerusalem." Kistemaker thinks this implies that "the Roman armies had obliterated the little village so that it could no longer be found, yet by giving the exact distance in relation to Jerusalem, John tells the reader where he may find Bethany."[126] Turner and Mantey hold that the picture of the conflict between Judaism and Christianity, with Christianity on the defensive, is more appropriate to a date before A.D. 70, since with the collapse of the Jewish state and the rise of Christianity the situation was altered.[127] But it may be replied that the conflict as described is due to the author's faithful depiction of the scene as it existed at the time of his story, although he wrote later.

While a date before A.D. 70 is appealing, it faces the difficulty of being forced to reject the established tradition of the church that the gospel of John was written sometime in the last quarter of the first century. We hold that the most satisfactory date falls between A.D. 80 and 95.

124. P. Gardner-Smith, *Saint John and the Synoptic Gospels.*
125. Westcott, p. xii.
126. Kistemaker, p. 122.
127. George Allen Turner and Julius R. Mantey, *The Gospel According to John*, p. 18.

THE TEXTUAL PROBLEMS IN THE FOURTH GOSPEL

There are two passages in the received text of the gospel of John which manuscript evidence reveals in all probability do not belong to the original text. The words in 5:3b-4, containing the explanation for the moving of the water in the pool, are, as Lenski observes, "textually so doubtful that they must be cancelled."[128] The noted passage concerning the woman taken in adultery, 7:53—8:11, is also, according to the manuscript evidence, a later addition. It is absent from every Greek manuscript earlier than the eighth century, except Codex D, and is not found in most early versions. Feuillet observes that "Greek writers do not refer to it until the eleventh century."[129] Those manuscripts that do contain the passage reveal an extraordinary number of variants; some mark it as doubtful, while others insert it after John 7:36 or 21:24; some manuscripts insert it after Luke 21:38.[130] Thiessen says, "Practically all scholars today accept it as a true incident in the life of Jesus, but not as a genuine part of John's Gospel."[131] So conservative a commentator as Lenski says, "Since John did not write this section, we give no exposition of it."[132]

Chapter 21 presents a problem of a different nature. Scholars generally agree that it is not a part of the original structure of the gospel. It seems to be a supplement to the gospel, in which some of the apostles are dealt with personally. Although it contains important information concerning Jesus' reinstatement of Peter, it probably was added to correct a rumored misinterpretation of Jesus' words concerning the beloved disciple. But manuscript evidence proves that it was a part of the fourth gospel when published. No copies without the last chapter have ever been found. That the apostle John stands behind its contents is obvious. No convincing evidence of a different hand in this chapter can be demonstrated. Lenski observes, "The so-called linguistic evidence, the fund of words and the general style, is in favor of John as being the writer also of chapter 21."[133] Since 21:24 is the comment of a different hand, many scholars hold that the entire chapter was added by another. We hold it as probable that

128. Lenski, p. 362.
129. A. Feuillet, in *Introduction to the New Testament*, p. 627.
130. For the manuscript evidence see the critical apparatus in the United Bible Societies text.
131. Thiessen, p. 176. See also the discussion in Hendriksen, 2:33-35.
132. Lenski, p. 592.
133. Ibid., p. 1400.

John wrote the chapter himself, except the comment in verse 24, perhaps also verse 25. Others hold that the chapter was added by someone close to John and with John's approval. Thus Lenski says, "The reproduction of John's oral narrative by the Ephesian presbytery, one of whom did the writing, John himself accepting the result, removes all difficulties as to the inspiration of chapter 21."[134] The problem cannot be resolved.

It has often been postulated that there are dislocations in the present arrangement of the text. The thought supposedly falters and the sequence would be greatly improved by a rearrangement of the material. Thus it is held that 3:31-36 fits better after 3:21 than in its present location, since it is held to be intelligible neither in the mouth of John the Baptist nor as a reflection of the author. Chapters 5 and 6 should be interchanged, since 6:1 follows naturally after 4:43-54 but does not follow well after chapter 5. The words in 7:15-24 are a continuation of the discourse in chapter 5:19-34. For the sake of sequence 10:19-29 should be transposed to the close of chapter 9. The original position of 12:44-50 was in the middle of 12:36. Since 14:31 marks the departure from the upper room, chapters 15 and 16 should be restored to the middle of 14:31. In chapter 18 verses 14-23 originally stood between verses 14 and 15.[135]

Commentators like Bernard,[136] MacGregor,[137] and Bultmann[138] organized their commentaries around their respective reconstructions. The most elaborate attempt at rearrangement is that of Hoare,[139] whose results are quite different from those of previous efforts at rearrangement.# The efforts at restoring the text of John have not produced agreement. These proposed rearrangements are subjective in nature and reflect the interpreter's own preconceptions.

134. Ibid., p. 1401.
135. See James Moffatt, *The New Testament: A New Translation*, and the transpositions made in John.
136. Bernard, "The Gospel According to John," in *International Critical Commentary*.
137. G. H. C. Macgregor, "The Gospel of John," in *The Moffatt New Testament Commentary*.
138. Rudolf Bultmann, *Das Evangelium des Johannes*.
139. F. R. Hoare, *The Original Order and Chapters of St. John's Gospel*.

#Hoare's rearrangement results in the following sequence of segments: (a) 1:1-51; (b) 4:3b-43; (c) 2:1—4:3a; (d) 4:44—5:47; (e) 7:15-24; (f) 6:1—7:14; (g) 7:25-52; (h) 8:12-28a; (i) 12:34-50; (j) 8:28b—9:41; (k) 10:19—11:33; (l) 12:23b-33; (m) 11:34—12:23a; (n) 10:1-18: [(o) 7:53—8:11]; (p) 13:1-19; (q) 15:17—16:4a; (r) 13:20—14:14; (s) 16:15b-23; (t) 14:15-24a; (u) 16:4b-15a; (v) 14:24b—15:16; (w) 16:24—21:25. Hoare, *The Original Order and Chapters of St. John's Gospel*, pp. 109-44.

Such rearrangements of the text find no support from the existing manuscripts.** The recently discovered papyrus, Bodmer II, dated about A.D. 200, gives no support for any of the proposed transpositions. Selby points out that these proposed rearrangements do not really solve the problem since the material can be transposed in different directions.[140] While they may solve one felt difficulty, they create others. The results are quite unconvincing.

Teeple asserts, "No one yet has demonstrated convincingly that the gospel has been disarranged."[141] Morris observes that if there is disorder in the present text it is difficult to give a convincing explanation of how the present text came into existence.[142] Proposed explanations have not gained general acceptance. Because of the difficulty of providing satisfactory rearrangements of the text, modern commentators like Dodd,[143] Barrett,[144] and Brown[145] prefer not to resort to rearrangement. Morris well observes, "It is always better to try and make sense of the manuscript as it stands than to try our hand at varying the order."[146] The course of wisdom is to take the text as it stands and seek to understand the mind of the writer behind this gospel.

THE CHARACTERISTICS OF THE FOURTH GOSPEL

1. SIMPLICITY AND PROFUNDITY

The fourth gospel has aptly been compared to "a pool in which a child can wade and an elephant can swim."[147] It is characterized by an amazing clarity which makes it attractive and intelligible to any beginner in the Christian faith, yet there are depths in it which even the most accomplished scholar after years of study feels he is unable to plummet. Philip Schaff remarks, "It is as simple as a child and sublime as a seraph, gentle as a lamb and bold as an eagle, deep

----

**The rearrangement in John 18:13-27 found in the Palestinian Syrian version and in Cyril are clearly of secondary origin. See the evidence in the United Bible Societies text.

140. Selby, p. 216.
141. H. M. Temple, "Methodology in Source Analysis of the Fourth Gospel," *Journal of Biblical Literature* 81(September 1962):286.
142. Morris, pp. 54-55.
143. C. H. Dodd, *The Interpretation of the Fourth Gospel*, p. 290.
144. Barrett, p. 20.
145. Brown, pp. xxvi-xxviii.
146. Morris, p. 56.
147. Ibid., p. 7.

as the sea and high as the heavens."[148] This striking double character is something which the simplest reader is conscious of, yet the ablest scholar cannot fully explain.

2. STYLE AND VOCABULARY

The style is very simple. There are none of the long and involved sentences which characterize the letters of Paul. Its clauses and sentences are generally connected by simple conjunctions. The author makes frequent use of parallelism, giving his style something of a rhythmical character reminiscent of Hebrew poetry. He frequently expresses his thought both negatively and positively. The arrangement at times is somewhat loose and repetition is employed for the sake of connection and emphasis. Feuillet remarks, "Literary effect was not his aim and yet this is what he achieved: he is a *highly effective artist.*"[149]

The vocabulary is comparatively limited. Scroggie notes that the author "uses fewer words than any of the Synoptics, but while these are poor in number, they are profound in meaning."[150] Favorite words are "know," "abide," "true, truth," "life, to live," "his hour," "darkness," "light," "witness, testimony," "believe in" (the noun "faith" is never used), "the world," "receive," "send," and others. This is the only gospel which uses the double "amen" in introducing important utterances of Jesus. Some notable phrases are "cometh into the world," "born of God, born again," "came down from heaven," "the last day," "walk in the night, walk in darkness," "the prince of this world," "love me, love one another," "answered and said."

3. SIGNS AND DISCOURSES

This gospel describes eight miracles, seven of which Jesus performed before His resurrection and one after. Six of the miracles are peculiar to this gospel: 1) turning water into wine (2:1-11); 2) healing of a nobleman's son (4:46-54); 3) healing of an impotent man at the pool of Bethesda (5:1-9); 4) giving sight to a man born blind (9:1-7); 5) raising of Lazarus who had been dead four days (11:17-

---

148. Philip Schaff, *History of the Christian Church*, p. 688.
149. A. Feuillet, "The Fourth Gospel," in *Introduction to the New Testament*, p. 610.
150. W. Graham Scroggie, *A Guide to the Gospels*, p. 414.

228 An Introduction to the New Testament

44); 6) draught of fishes (21:1-14). The two miracles in common with the synoptics are the feeding of the 5,000 (6:1-14; Mk 6; Mt 14; Lk 9) and Jesus walking on the sea (6:16-21; Mk 6; Mt 14). Other miracles are mentioned, but are not described in detail (2:23; 6:2; 20:30). In John these miracles are always designated as "signs," for they point to the deeper truth concerning Jesus as Messiah and Son of God. But there is no good reason to limit the "signs" in this gospel to miracles. The cleansing of the Temple was not a miracle but it definitely had sign value (2:13-22). The signs were intended to reveal the true nature of the person of Jesus and to awaken faith in Him. But the signs did not automatically produce conviction. "For those open to truth the signs become valid guides into faith, for those perversely set against the truth remain unbelieving (12:37)."[151]

In John these signs are at times the occasion for a discourse by Jesus giving the interpretation or application of the sign, as in the discourse following the feeding of the 5,000 (chap. 6). At other times the discourses are in the nature of a controversy occasioned by the sign, as in the controversy following the healing of the blind man on the Sabbath (chaps. 9-10). Some of these discourses might better be termed dialogues (4:7-27). The discourses served as a further revelation of Jesus' nature and formed another level of appeal for faith in Him (14:10-11). One feature of Jesus' discourses peculiar to this gospel is the presentation of the seven great "I am" sayings of Jesus (6:35; 8:12; 10:9, 11; 11:25; 14:6; 15:5).†† Distinctive to this gospel are the profound discourses delivered to the Twelve alone as recorded in John 13-17.

The space devoted to the words of Jesus in the fourth gospel is larger than that in any synoptic. John contains none of the parables so familiar from the synoptics; the story-parable gives way to a few complex allegories (cf. chap. 10, the Good Shepherd, and chap. 15, the vine and the branches). In John the words of Jesus are not simply individual *logia* or collections of sayings, but discourses that center around and develop a specific theme.

151. Selby, p. 222.

††G. Campbell Morgan, *The Gospel According to John*, p. 161, includes John 8:58, "Verily, verily, I say unto you, before Abraham was born, I am" among these "I am" sayings, thus making eight in all.

4. CONTRAST TO SYNOPTIC NARRATIVE

The narrative of the fourth gospel is highly selective (20:30). Before Passion Week it records only two incidents in common with the synoptics—the feeding of the 5,000 (6:1-13), and the walking on the sea (6:16-21). Much of what it relates about Passion Week is not found in the synoptics (the discourses to the disciples, 13-17; the details of the trial before Pilate, 18:28—19:16; the post-resurrection appearances, 20:11-18; 21:1-23). While this gospel observes the same broad chronological sequence of the story found in the synoptics, for the most part it strikes out along lines of its own.

The history of Jesus' activities contained in this gospel is obviously quite incomplete. Thiessen remarks that the historical events here recorded make up "at the utmost an account of but 20 days of our Lord's ministry."[52] It does not mention Jesus' nativity or boyhood, does not describe His baptism or temptation, and is silent about the transfiguration. While in the synoptic gospels the ministry of Jesus took place almost wholly in Galilee before Passion Week, John's gospel tells little of the great Galilean ministry. It records an earlier ministry in Judea, Samaria, and Galilee (1:19—4:54) not mentioned in the synoptics. Most frequently in John's gospel the scene of Jesus' ministry is in Jerusalem, usually at the time of a Jewish feast (2:13; 5:1; 6:4; 7:2; 10:22; 11:55). This gospel dwells at great length on events and discourses which took place during a twenty-four hour period during Passion Week (chaps. 13-19), but leaves unrecorded the institution of the Lord's Supper or the Lord's agony in Gethsemane.

The fourth gospel is characterized by its specificity regarding the exact time and place of events which are recorded. The chronological indications of Jesus' ministry are more complicated than those in the synoptics. From the presentation in the synoptics it might be concluded that Jesus' ministry lasted slightly longer than one year, but John's gospel mentions at least three Passovers (2:13; 6:4; 12:1).‡‡ The synoptics record only the Passion Week journey to Jerusalem, while the fourth gospel speaks of four different journeys to Jerusalem

152. Thiessen, p. 176.

‡‡It is possible that the feast in 5:1 also was a Passover, but there is no scholarly agreement on the point.

(2:13; 5:1; 7:10; 12:12). Events during these visits were crucial for the development of the work of Jesus.

While the story of Jesus in John's gospel is obviously fragmentary, it has a more compact structure than the synoptics. Unlike the synoptics which often rather loosely string together a series of events or sayings without clear indications of time or place, this gospel consists of a comparatively "small number of graphic narratives which are broadly and dramatically presented and form a coherent unity."[153] The events of this gospel are selected and arranged in harmony with the author's purpose to portray Jesus as the promised Messiah and Son of God.

5. UNIQUE PROLOGUE

The profound and majestic prologue (1:1-18) is unique to the gospels. While the opening statement of Luke's gospel is historically oriented, this prologue is theologically oriented. Gossip says:

> No book in literature has so breath-taking an opening as these stupendous findings on the life and character about to be described, flung down so confidently as the only possible explanation of them, given us as a kind of thesis, of which all the facts that are to follow are the proof.[154]

The portrayal of Christ as the *logos* or Word in this prologue does not occur in any other passage in John's gospel or in the synoptics.

6. CHARACTER PORTRAYAL

This gospel gives a remarkably vivid and lifelike portrayal of various individuals. They appear as distinct types of personal faith or unbelief when brought into personal confrontation with Christ. "In this Gospel," says Scroggie, "34 individuals are brought to our notice; 23 of them are named, and 11 are unnamed."[155] They present an interesting variety: Peter the impulsive; Thomas the cautious; Judas the traitor; Nicodemus the seeker; Pilate the unstable worldling; Caiaphas the unscrupulous; the sinful Samaritan woman open to Christ's revelation; the blind man healed who became a bold witness;

153. Alfred Wikenhauser, *New Testament Introduction*, p. 294.
154. Wilbert F. Howard and Arthur John Gossip, "The Gospel According to John," in *The Interpreter's Bible*, 8:463.
155. Scroggie, p. 449.

the helpless paralytic at the pool; the nobleman who acted upon a simple word of Jesus.

This gospel also sketches various groups of people with vividness and precision. Among them are the jealous disciples of John the Baptist; Jesus' disciples as a group failing to understand Him yet adhering to Him; the inhabitants of Sychar so ready to believe in Jesus; the brothers of Jesus in their unbelief presuming to advise Jesus; the Greeks who desired to get an interview with Jesus during Passion Week; the chief priests who out of hatred for Jesus at once claimed and denied their national independence.

Truly the pages of this gospel are crowded with vivid portraits of living and distinct individuals and groups. Plummer observes, "If these groups and individuals are creations of the imagination, it is no exaggeration to say that the author of the Fourth Gospel is a genius superior to Shakespeare."[156]

7. SYMBOLISM

Plummer asserts, "The whole Gospel from end to end is penetrated with the spirit of symbolical representation."[157] This symbolism is obvious in the allegorical words of Christ concerning the sheepfold and the Good Shepherd (10:1-18), or the vine and the branches (15:1-7). That symbolic significance is attached to the miracles is evident from the fact that they are called "signs." Thus the miracle of the feeding of the 5,000 carried a deeper meaning which Jesus explained the following day in His discourse on the bread of life (chap. 6). The healing of the man born blind received its fuller significance in the profound discussion which followed that miracle (9:35–10:21). But this symbolic meaning attached to the events does not compromise their historicity. In the words of Sanders, "There is no reason to doubt that the author believed that the events he narrates actually happened. The fact that he finds them full of symbolical significance is no argument to the contrary. He chose those which best suited his purpose."[158] The ordinary events of history are full of deeper meaning for those who have eyes to see.

156. Plummer, p. xliii.
157. Ibid., p. xliii.
158. Sanders, 2:946.

8. ESCHATOLOGY

Unlike the synoptics, John's gospel contains no long eschatological discourse portraying the Son of Man returning in glory to judge the world. Jesus is presented as the Saviour of the world (4:42), and men who accept Him pass from death unto life (5:24), while those who reject Him remain under the wrath of God (3:36). Eternal life is presented as a present reality for the believer (5:24; 6:40, 47; 8:51; 11:26), but there is also recognition of the futuristic aspect of salvation (12:25). The coming resurrection will lead to life or to judgment (5:28-29). Christ will come to receive His own unto Himself to consummate their salvation (14:3; 21:22). The eschatology of this gospel has both present and future aspects. It may best be described as "inaugurated eschatology."

9. FATHER-SON RELATIONSHIP

Central in John's portrayal of the person of Jesus Christ is His unique relationship to the Father. God is Spirit (4:24) and He sent the preexistent Son into the world to reveal Him and give life to the world. The Son is the perfect revelation of the Father (14:8-11). The Holy Spirit, sent by the Father (14:26) and the Son (15:26), is the Agent who interprets and quickens this revelation to the believer (16:14-15).

10. AUTHOR'S COMMENTS

A prominent feature of this gospel is John's practice of adding interpretative comments and explanations. The synoptics generally let the facts speak for themselves; this gospel not infrequently inserts the author's personal comments. Scroggie finds no less than twenty-two such comments.[159] This feature is consistent with the interpretative character of the gospel. Yet in at least two passages this feature creates questions of interpretation. It is not certain whether the words in 3:16-21 are a continued quotation from Jesus or are the author's own summary comment. There is a question whether the words in 3:31-36 are those of John the Baptist or of the author. In the other places it is clear that the author is adding his own explanation or comment.

159. Scroggie, p. 453.

AN OUTLINE OF JOHN

The theme of the gospel of John is "Jesus, the Christ, the Son of God" (20:31). It portrays both faith and unbelief which were evidenced in response to the self-revelation of Jesus. Faith grows with the disclosure of His true nature, while unbelief becomes increasingly hostile. Unbelief culminates in Jesus' crucifixion, while faith is vindicated in the resurrection.

I. Prologue, 1:1-18
   A. The Word: His essential and eternal relations, vv. 1-5
   B. The Word: His revelation to men and their response, vv. 6-13
   C. The Word: His incarnate manifestation, vv. 14-18

II. Manifestation of Jesus to the World, 1:19—12:50
   A. Opening events in His manifestation, 1:19—2:11
      1. Testimonies of John the Baptist, 1:19-34
         a) Testimony to the committee from the Jews, vv. 19-28
         b) Testimony identifying Christ to his disciples, vv. 29-34
      2. Testimonies of the first disciples of Jesus, 1:35-51
         a) Testimony of the first group, vv. 35-42
         b) Testimony of the second group, vv. 43-51
      3. Testimony of His first sign, 2:1-11
   B. Public manifestations of Jesus, 2:12—4:54
      1. Manifestations in Judea, 2:12—3:36
         a) In the Temple, 2:12-22
         b) In the city of Jerusalem, 2:23—3:21
            (1) The ministry to the crowd, 2:23-25
            (2) Ministry to Nicodemus, 3:1-21
         c) In the land of Judea, 3:22-36
            (1) Parallel ministry with John, vv. 22-24
            (2) Testimony of John to Jesus, vv. 25-30
            (3) Testimony from above, vv. 31-36
      2. The manifestation in Samaria, 4:1-42
         a) Departure for Galilee, vv. 1-4
         b) Self-revelation at Jacob's well, vv. 5-38
            (1) Conversation with the Samaritan woman, vv. 5-26
            (2) Conversation with the disciples, vv. 27-38
         c) Testimony of the Samaritans of that town, vv. 39-42

 3. Manifestation in Galilee, 4:43-54
  a) Welcome received in Galilee, vv. 43-45
  b) Sign wrought at Cana of Galilee, vv. 46-54

C. Fuller self-revelation and the developing conflict, 5:1—11:54
 1. Beginning of open conflict in Jerusalem, 5:1-47
  a) Sign of healing at the pool, vv. 1-9*a*
  b) Immediate controversy because of the healing, vv. 9*b*-18
  c) Resultant discourse of Jesus to the Jews, vv. 19-47
   (1) Nature and authority of the Son, vv. 19-30
   (2) Witnesses to the Son and the ground of unbelief, vv. 31-47
    (*a*) Nature of the witnesses to the Son, vv. 31-40
    (*b*) Grounds of the Jews' unbelief, vv. 41-47
 2. Crisis for faith and unbelief in Galilee, 6:1-71
  a) Sign in the feeding of the 5,000, vv. 1-15
  b) Sign to the disciples on the sea, vv. 16-21
  c) Discourse in the synagogue at Capernaum, vv. 22-59
   (1) Gathering of the seeking multitude, vv. 22-25
   (2) Discussion with the multitude about the search for life, vv. 26-40
   (3) Replies to the difficulties of the Jews, vv. 41-59
    (*a*) Difficulty concerning His Person, vv. 41-51
    (*b*) Difficulty concerning His method, vv. 52-59
   (4) Effects of the discourses on His disciples, vv. 60-71
    (*a*) Effect upon many of His professed disciples, vv. 60-66
    (*b*) Effect upon the twelve, vv. 67-71
 3. Further revelation of faith and unbelief in Jerusalem, 7:1—10:42
  a) Revelations connected with the Feast of Tabernacles, 7:1—8:59
   (1) Expressions of opposition before the feast, 7:1-13
    (*a*) Hostile intention of the Jews in Judea, v. 1
    (*b*) Unbelieving advice of His brothers, vv. 2-9
    (*c*) Tension among the multitudes at Jerusalem, vv. 10-13

(2) Revelations during the midst of the feast, 7:14-36
    (*a*) Divine teaching and the Jews' murderous intention, vv. 14-24
    (*b*) Divided reaction of the people in Jerusalem, vv. 25-31
    (*c*) Hostile reaction of the Jewish leaders, vv. 32-36

(3) Discussions on the last day of the feast, 7:37-52
    (*a*) Great proclamation to the crowd, vv. 37-39
    (*b*) Reactions of the crowd to the proclamation, vv. 40-44
    (*c*) Reaction of the leaders upon failure to arrest Jesus, vv. 45-52

(4) Discussions after the feast, 7:53—8:59
    [The woman taken in adultery, 7:53—8:11]
    (*a*) Self-revelation as the light of the world, 8:12-20
    (*b*) Consequences of unbelief in Him, 8:21-30
    (*c*) Claims of Christ and antagonism of unbelief, 8:31-59

b) Revelation upon healing a blind man on the Sabbath, 9:1—10:21
(1) Sign of healing and the immediate reaction, 9:1-12
(2) Judgment upon the sign by the Jews, 9:13-34
    (*a*) First examination of the healed man, vv. 13-17
    (*b*) Examination of the parents of the healed man, vv. 18-23
    (*c*) Reexamination and expulsion of the healed man, vv. 24-34
(3) Beginning and nature of Christ's new flock, 9:35—10:21
    (*a*) Entry of a believer into the flock, 9:35-38
    (*b*) Judgment upon the unbelieving, 9:39-41
    (*c*) Discourses concerning the new flock, 10:1-18
        i) Portrayal of the fold and the flock, vv. 1-6
        ii) Self-identification as the Good Shepherd, vv. 7-18
    (*d*) Division because of the revelation, 10:19-21

       c) Rejection of the revelation at the feast of Dedication, 10:22-39

       d) Interval of retirement from Jerusalem, 10:40-42

    4. Final sign and the conspiracy of the rulers, 11:1-54

       a) Events preparatory to the sign, vv. 1-16

       b) Scene upon the arrival at Bethany, vv. 17-37

       c) Raising of Lazarus dead four days, vv. 38-44

       d) Reactions of faith and unbelief, vv. 45-53

       e) Retirement to the city of Ephraim, v. 54

  D. Closing events of His public ministry, 11:55—12:50

    1. Tension over Jesus at Jerusalem before the Passover, 11:55-57

    2. Manifestations of faith and unbelief at the Passover, 12:1-36

       a) Anointing during the supper at Bethany, vv. 1-8

       b) Reactions to the presence of Jesus, vv. 9-11

       c) Public entry of Jesus into Jerusalem, vv. 12-19

       d) Last public ministry in Jerusalem, vv. 20-36

         (1) Request of some Greeks to meet Jesus, vv. 20-22

         (2) Reflections of Jesus in response, vv. 23-33

         (3) Last warning of Jesus to the multitude, vv. 34-36

    3. Solemn fact of Jewish unbelief, 12:37-50

       a) Unbelief in the light of prophecy, vv. 37-43

       b) Summary of the message of Jesus, vv. 44-50

III. Farewell Manifestation of Jesus to His Disciples, 13:1—17:26

  A. Two events in self-manifestation, 13:1-30

    1. Love-prompted act of foot washing, vv. 1-20

       a) Performance of the action, vv. 1-11

       b) Commentary on the action, vv. 12-20

    2. Elimination of the betrayer, vv. 21-30

  B. Final revelations to His disciples, 13:31—16:33

    1. Discourse in the upper room, 13:31—14:31

       a) Announcement of His impending departure, 13:31-35

       b) Answers to the problems of the disciples, 13:36—14:24

         (1) Revelation in response to Peter's question, 13:36—14:4

           (*a*) Inability of Peter to follow Him now, 13:36-38

           (*b*) Goal and purpose of His going away, 14:1-4

         (2) Revelation in reply to Thomas' question, 14:5-7

   D. Crucifixion and death of Jesus, 19:17-37
      1. Crucifixion and superscription over the cross, vv. 17-22
      2. Scene around the cross of Jesus, vv. 23-27
      3. Completion of His redemptive work, vv. 28-30
      4. Piercing of Jesus' side after His death, vv. 31-37
   E. Burial of Jesus by two noted Jews, 19:38-42

 V. Vindication of Faith in the Resurrection, 20:1-29
   A. Empty tomb of Jesus, vv. 1-10
   B. Appearances of the risen Christ, vv. 11-29
      1. Appearing to Mary at the tomb, vv. 11-18
      2. First appearance of Jesus to His disciples, vv. 19-23
      3. Second appearance of Jesus to His disciples, vv. 24-29
   C. Purpose of this Gospel, 20:30-31

VI. Supplement, 21:1-25
      1. Risen Lord and the group of seven disciples, vv. 1-14
      2. Risen Lord and two individual disciples, vv. 15-23
      3. Authentication of the gospel, vv. 24-25

A BOOK LIST ON JOHN

Barclay, William. "The Gospel of John." In *The Daily Study Bible*. 2 vols.
2d ed. Philadelphia: Westminster, 1956.
    Prints the author's own translation. A series of popular studies well
adapted to the lay reader. Barclay is strongest in his study of word
meanings. Contains good illustrative material.
Barrett, C. K. *The Gospel According to St. John*. London: S.P.C.K., 1960.
    Greek text. A 120-page introduction deals fully with critical problems.
This commentary, the work of a noted British scholar, provides much
help for the advanced student of the gospel of John.
Bernard, J. H. "A Critical and Exegetical Commentary on the Gospel
According to St. John." In *International Critical Commentary*. *Edited*
by A. H. McNeile. 2 vols. 1928. Reprint. Edinburgh: T. & T. Clark,
1958.
    Greek text. A 180-page introduction, in which the author rejects the
traditional view of authorship, deals fully with the critical problems.
The commentary is based on the author's rearrangement of the text of
the gospel. Valuable for the discerning advanced student.
Brown, Raymond E. *The Gospel According to John*. The Anchor Bible.
2 vols. Garden City, N.Y.: Doubleday, 1966.
    This massive 1,200-page work by a Roman Catholic scholar is fully

abreast of the latest theological trends. In his lengthy introduction Brown holds that the material of this gospel was moulded by the preaching of John the apostle but was put into its present shape by a later redactor who probably added a considerable amount of material. The author's translation, appearing section by section, is followed by notes on the text, general comments, and detailed comments. Each section concludes with an important bibliography, including works in various languages. Brown accepts the prologue as an early Christian hymn, adapted to serve as an overture to the writer's narrative. Important for detailed critical study of the fourth gospel.

Bultmann, Rudolf. *The Gospel of John: A Commentary.* Translated by G. R. Beasley-Murray, general editor; R. W. N. Hoare; and J. K. Riches. Philadelphia: Westminster, 1971.

A massive (nearly 750 pages) and outstanding work of scholarship by a noted radical German New Testament scholar. A short introduction for this English edition was written by Walter Schmithals. The text is accompanied by extensive footnotes, most of which deal with technical matters. Due to extensive rearrangement of the gospel text, a listing of the sections of the gospel and the corresponding pages in the commentary text is appropriately added. Of great value for the advanced, discerning student.

Gaebelein, Arno Clemens. *The Gospel of John.* New York: Pubn. Office "Our Hope," 1936.

A paragraph-by-paragraph interpretation of John by a noted evangelical Bible teacher and writer of the past generation. Contains many fine spiritual insights into the truths of this gospel.

Godet, F. *Commentary on the Gospel of St. John, with a Critical Introduction.* Translated from the second French edition by Frances Crombie and M. D. Cusin. Vol. 1. Edinburgh: T. & T. Clark, 1876; Vols. 2-3, 1877.

An older commentary by a noted conservative French scholar of the past century. Still outstanding as an evangelical interpretation of the fourth gospel, even if unaware of recent critical trends.

Hendriksen, William. "Exposition of the Gospel According to John." In *New Testament Commentary,* vol. 1. Grand Rapids: Baker, 1953.

An important study of the fourth gospel by a noted contemporary evangelical scholar. It offers a new translation, a study of introductory problems, an analysis of the text, and a brief synthesis at the close of each section. An up-to-date, readable exposition.

Hovey, Alvah. "Commentary on the Gospel of John." In *An American Commentary on the New Testament.* Philadelphia: 1885. Reprint. Amer. Bapt. Pubn. Soc., n.d.

A full verse-by-verse exposition of John by an accomplished conservative Baptist scholar of the past century. Still valuable for its unfolding of the meaning of the text.

Howard, Wilbert F., and Gossip, Arthur John. "The Gospel According to St. John." In *The Interpreter's Bible,* vol. 8. New York: Abingdon, 1952.

The informative introduction and the brief exegetical notes are by Howard. The exposition by Gossip is full and offers much interpretative and homiletical material. The theological viewpoint is liberal.

Kelly, William. *An Exposition of the Gospel of John.* Reprint. Denver, Col.: Wilson Foundation, 1966.

The mature product of a noted Plymouth Brethren scholar of the last century. A thoroughly conservative interpretation of the fourth gospel.

Lange, John Peter. "The Gospel According to John." In Lange's *Commentary on the Holy Scriptures.* Translated and edited by Philip Schaff. Reprint. Grand Rapids: Zondervan, n.d.

The material in this volume of 650 two-column pages is divided into four parts under each section of the gospel: textual and grammatical; exegetical and critical; doctrinal and ethical; homiletical and practical. While much of the material is dated, it contains an abundance of riches for those willing to dig into its contents.

Lenski, R. C. H. *The Interpretation of St. John's Gospel.* Columbus, Ohio: Lutheran Book Concern, 1942.

This massive volume of nearly 1,500 pages is the work of a noted conservative Lutheran scholar. Prints the author's own literal translation. The interpretation is based on a careful and thorough study of the original text and offers a richly rewarding guide for a detailed study of John.

Lightfoot, R. H. *St. John's Gospel: A Commentary.* Edited by C. F. Evans. Oxford: Clarendon, 1956.

Lightfoot's primary concern is to exegete the text of the gospel. The text is divided into large units which are followed by a careful exposition. There are also notes on the text dealing with textual, critical, and interpretative matters. The introduction, reworked by the editor, adds to the value of the volume.

Luthi, Walter. *St. John's Gospel: An Exposition.* Translated by Kurt Schoenenberger. Richmond, Va.: Knox, 1960.

This volume consists of a series of sermons first preached in Switzerland in 1932-42. Luthi is closely associated with the theological views of Karl Barth. A stimulating, provocative series of sermons.

Macgregor, G. H. C. "The Gospel of John." In *The Moffatt New Testament Commentary.* New York: Harper, n.d.

An important volume in this noted liberal New Testament Commentary series. Prints the Moffatt version and follows the textual rearrangement of John found in Moffatt's translation.

Meyer, Heinrich August Wilhelm. *Critical and Exegetical Hand-Book to the Gospel of John.* Translated from the German. American edition edited by A. C. Kendrick. New York: Funk & Wagnalls, 1884.

Greek text. A full verse-by-verse treatment of John's gospel. Rich in references to other works on the gospel current during the past century. Fully acquainted with critical scholarship up to the time of its production.

Morgan, G. Campbell. *The Gospel According to John.* New York: Revell, n.d.

A series of expository sermons by this noted expository Bible teacher. Valuable for the many insights into this gospel.

Morris, Leon. "The Gospel According to John." In *New International Commentary on the New Testament.* Grand Rapids: Eerdmans, 1971.

A massive commentary by a noted conservative biblical scholar. The introduction offers sensible conservative views on various critical questions. The bulk of the commentary is devoted to exegesis of the text, printing the American Standard Version. Contains a number of notes on specific subjects. A volume of abiding importance for the student.

Pink, Arthur W. *Exposition of the Gospel of John.* 4 vols. Swengel, Pa.: Bible Truth Depot, 1945.

A full treatment of John's gospel by a Calvinistic Bible teacher who was also a voluminous author. It seeks to unfold the meaning of the text and apply it to the daily life of the believer. Rich in spiritual content. Avoids the technical and aims at the practical.

Plummer, A. "The Gospel According to St. John." In *Cambridge Greek Testament for Schools and Colleges.* 1882. Reprint. Cambridge: Cambridge U., 1905.

Greek text. Valuable introduction espouses the conservative view regarding introductory problems. The notes on the Greek text set forth its meaning concisely.

Reith, George. *The Gospel According to St. John.* Handbooks for Bible Classes and Private Students. 2 vols. 1889. Reprint. Edinburgh: T. & T. Clark, 1948.

These handy, closely-packed volumes provide a good interpretation of John by a conservative minister of the past century. Remarkably rich in spiritual insights.

Richardson, Alan. *The Gospel According to Saint John.* Torch Bible Commentary. New York: Collier, 1962.

A brief commentary, well adapted to the lay reader, based on the English Revised Version. The work of a contemporary British scholar.

Sanders, J. N. *A Commentary on the Gospel According to St. John.* Black's New Testament Commentaries. London: Adam & Charles Black, 1968.

Offers a fresh translation of the fourth gospel, and provides scholarly comments on the text; technical matters are discussed in the footnotes. Sanders suggests that John Mark wrote the fourth gospel and that chapter 21 was added by a different author.

Tasker, R. V. G. "The Gospel According to St. John." In *The Tyndale New Testament Commentaries.* Grand Rapids: Eerdmans, 1960.

Well suited for the ordinary Bible reader. Gives a running commentary section by section, rather than verse by verse. Additional notes following the running commentary give attention to exegesis, translations, and historical points. Tasker holds that the gospel was written by an unknown individual close to the apostle John.

Turner, George Allen, and Mantey, Julius R. "The Gospel According to John." In *The Evangelical Commentary.* Grand Rapids: Eerdmans, 1964.

An important volume in a series of conservative commentaries that was never completed. The 44-page introduction gives a modern treatment of critical problems. The commentary is in two parts. The exegesis gives a careful unfolding of the text on the basis of the original, and the exposition offers a larger interpretation of the passage under study. While thoroughly conversant with the latest critical scholarship, the position of the author is consistently conservative and evangelical.

Vine, W. E. *John: His Record of Christ.* 1948. Reprint. Grand Rapids: Zondervan, 1957.

Does not deal with introductory problems, but accepts as unquestioned the apostolic authorship and full authority of the gospel. The work of an accomplished Greek scholar, the volume combines scholarly insights with simplicity of diction and spiritual warmth.

Westcott, B. F. *The Gospel According to St. John: The Authorized Version with Introduction and Notes.* 1880. Reprint. Grand Rapids: Eerdmans, 1950.

One of the classical commentaries on John. Still richly rewarding in spite of its age. An admirable presentation of the conservative position.

Whitelaw, Thomas. *The Gospel of St. John: An Exposition Exegetical and Homiletical.* Reprint. Fincastle, Va.: Scripture Truth Book Co., n.d.

Following a sixty-page introduction, which espouses the traditional view, the material is presented in two parts, an exposition and homiletical suggestions. Comparable to the Pulpit Commentary.

Part 2

THE ACTS

9

THE ACTS OF THE APOSTLES

As a part of sacred Scripture, the Acts of the Apostles demands and richly rewards prolonged and serious study. Since Acts has no companion work in the New Testament, it requires independent study and naturally lends itself to the book method of Bible study. All that was said concerning the book method of study in connection with the gospels (see pp. 36-37) will apply here. Because of the crucial importance of Acts for the remainder of the New Testament, a mastery of its contents is essential for the Bible student. A thorough mastery of Acts is acquired through repeated reading and diligent consecutive study of its contents. It is the part of wisdom to gain a thorough knowledge of its contents before delving into critical questions connected with it. It is the indispensable basis for such critical study.

As you study Acts, remember that it is the second volume of a two-volume work. The realization that Luke intended this book to be the sequel to his gospel will add interest and increased significance to its character and contents.

Although we will follow the book method for our basic study of Acts, we cannot help but notice that it invites a comparative study with the New Testament epistles. Such a comparative study is in effect limited to the Pauline epistles, although the epistle of James clearly seems to fall within the period covered by Acts. The pastoral epistles (1-2 Timothy and Titus), however, are thought to have been written after the time covered by Acts (most conservative scholars agree with this). You will find it a challenging and rewarding study to discover and correlate information in the Pauline epistles which is parallel to the Acts account.* The problem of the relationship of Acts to the Pauline epistles has occasioned much scholarly discussion. The self-revelation contained in the epistles provides much information about Paul that is not found in Acts, but Acts also provides information about which the epistles are completely silent. The two sources of information make their own distinctive contribution to our picture of Paul, but it must be admitted that they are not readily harmonized. Some critical scholars, indeed, insist that they cannot be reconciled and have accordingly questioned the accuracy of one or the other source. But the greater part of the information derived from the Pauline epistles magnificently confirms the picture of Paul presented in Acts. While not minimizing the difficulties that do exist, evangelical scholars hold that both Acts and the Pauline epistles can be accepted as authentic sources of information. In making such a study seek to find your own reconciliation in the light of your understanding of both sources.

AN INTRODUCTION TO ACTS

The Acts of the Apostles is unique among the books of the New Testament. The gospels present four accounts of the story of Jesus, but Acts provides the only account of the beginning and early expansion of the Christian church. It is our chief source of information concerning that period. Without Acts we would be in almost total darkness concerning the early church. This book forms the connecting link between the fourfold record of the ministry of Jesus and the other documents of the New Testament, which interpret the significance and results of His life and work to the world at large. Acts has well been called "one of the most important and influential books of all time."[1]

The book of Acts is the sequel to the third gospel (Ac 1:1). It is the second part of a two-volume work which forms somewhat more than one-fourth of the entire New Testament. The two parts are sufficiently complete and independent to circulate separately, yet in

---

*A valuable aid for such a study is Frank J. Goodwin, *A Harmony of the Life of St. Paul,* which endeavors to blend Acts and the Pauline epistles to form one continuous story of the life of Paul, employing the language of the Scriptures themselves. Much supplemental information is appended.

1. E. M. Blaiklock, "The Acts of the Apostles," in *Tyndale New Testament Commentaries,* p. 11.

the author's plan and purpose they belong together. The two documents are best understood when viewed as parts of a larger whole. Together they form a comprehensive study on the beginnings of Christianity. Like Paul, Luke conceived of the gospel as consisting in two parts. In Galatians 4:4 Paul writes, "When the fulness of the time came, God *sent forth his Son*" (emphasis added). That was the first part of the gospel story. But he continues, "God *sent forth the Spirit* of his Son" (4:6, emphasis added), and that introduces the second part of the story of redemption. Luke has the same twofold view of the gospel of God. Accordingly, he wrote his story in two parts. In the gospel of Luke he traces the story of God sending His Son, that God became incarnate in Jesus Christ. In the book of Acts he traces the story of the sending of the Holy Spirit, how God is forming the mystical body of Christ, the Church. The work of the Holy Spirit is central to both phases of this redemptive activity.

THE TITLE OF THE BOOK

It is possible, even probable, that this second volume of Luke's work originally had no separate title. Without exception it is designated *Acts* (*Praxeis*), or some expansion thereof, in all Greek manuscripts, the versions, and the Church Fathers. The Greek manuscripts have the title in various forms, "Acts" or "The Acts," "Acts of Apostles, or "Acts of the Apostles," and even "Acts of the Holy Apostles." Irenaeus refers to it paraphrastically as the "true testimony of the acts and teachings of the Apostles"[2] or "Discourses and Acts of the Apostles."[3] The Muratorian Canon uses the exaggerated title "The Acts of all the Apostles," which probably represented a conscious attempt to exclude spurious "Acts" which clamored for acceptance. It is clear that no single title commanded general acceptance, implying that an authentic title was lacking. But there is agreement on the designation of the book as "Acts." This was a common designation in the Hellenistic Age for a description of the deeds of an outstanding individual, as, for example, "The Acts of Alexander" or "The Acts of Hannibal." The identifying genitive "of apostles" or "the apostles" naturally served to indicate more specifically the nature of the book.

2. Irenaeus *Against Heresies* 3. 15. 1.
3. Ibid. 3. 12. 1.

It is not strictly accurate to call this book "The Acts of the Apostles." Although the apostles are named in chapter 1 and are afterwards collectively referred to some twenty times (chaps. 2-15), only three of the original twelve are named in the remainder of the story. Only Peter is a prominent figure, and that in only the first half of the book. Nor is Luke's account confined to the "acts" of those mentioned; he also gives large place to their thoughts as set forth in their discourses. Without the definite article, "apostles" may be viewed as designating the representative workers who had a definite part in the spread of Christianity.

THE AUTHORSHIP OF ACTS

The book of Acts, like the third gospel, is anonymous, and not even its title indicates authorship. Yet in the prologue of both works the author refers to himself by the first person pronoun, and it is obvious that Theophilus, the recipient of both volumes (Lk 1:4; Ac 1:1), knew his identity.

1. EXTERNAL EVIDENCE

The uniform tradition of the early church ascribes this work to Luke, and no alternative suggestions are mentioned. The earliest explicit testimony to the Lucan authorship of Acts is the so-called *Anti-Marcionite Prologue* to Luke (c. A.D. 150-180), which in discussing the third gospel adds, "And afterwards this same Luke wrote the Acts of the Apostles."[4] The fragmentary *Muratorian Canon* (c. 160-200) says:

> But the Acts of all the Apostles were written in one volume. Luke compiled for "most excellent Theophilus" what things were done in detail in his presence, as he plainly shows by omitting both the death of Peter and also the departure of Paul from the city, when he departed for Spain.[5]

The preserved text is uncertain but its general drift is clear. The writer means to say that Luke intended to relate only what he him-

---

4. For the Greek sentence, see F. F. Bruce, *The Acts of the Apostles*, p. 1. For an English translation of this prologue, see E. Earle Ellis, *The Gospel of Luke*, p. 41.
5. For the Latin text, see F. F. Bruce, *The Acts of the Apostles*, p. 1. For a bibliography on the Muratorian Canon, see F. L. Cross, ed., *The Oxford Dictionary of the Christian Church*, p. 934.

self had witnessed. The writer accepts the Lucan authorship as an unquestioned fact, although he is prone to make some unfounded inferences of his own from the book.

Literature dating from the end of the second century, among the oldest of surviving Christian writings, shows uniform acceptance of the Lucan authorship of Acts. Irenaeus in his *Against Heresies* (A.D. 185) in citing or discussing the book of Acts takes it for granted that Luke was the author.[6] Clement of Alexandria (*c*. 155-215) in his writings frequently quoted from Acts and in *Stromata* he remarks, "As Luke in the Acts of the Apostles relates that Paul said, 'Men of Athens, I perceive that in all things ye are too superstitious.'" Tertullian (*c*. 150-220) frequently quotes from or alludes to Acts. In his work *On Fasting* he says, "In the self-same commentary of Luke the third hour is demonstrated as an hour of prayer, about which hour it was that they who received the initiatory gift of the Holy Spirit were held for drunkards."[8] Eusebius, who knew the testimony of the earlier witnesses, in his *Ecclesiastical History*, published in A.D. 324 or 325, explicitly asserts that Luke wrote two books, the gospel and the Acts,[9] and remarks that "Luke also in the Acts speaks of his [Paul's] friends and mentions them by name."[10] Zahn summarizes the evidence with the observation:

> The fact that the book is seldom ascribed explicitly to Luke, even by those who mention its rejection by Marcion, and that it is constantly cited simply as *The Acts* with or without *of the Apostles*, shows that no other opinion concerning its authorship had been expressed in any quarter.[11]

Salmon concludes that the evidence available by the end of the second century "shows the authority of the Acts as well established as that of the Gospels."[12]

2. INTERNAL EVIDENCE

The internal evidence concerning the authorship of Acts is en-

6. Irenaeus *Against Heresies* 3. 13. 3; 3. 14. 1; 3. 15. 1.
7. Clement of Alexandria *The Stromata* 5. 12.
8. Tertullian *On Fasting*, chap. 10.
9. Eusebius *Ecclesiastical History* 3. 4. 7.
10. Ibid. 3. 4. 5.
11. Theodor Zahn, *Introduction to the New Testament*, 3:3.
12. George Salmon, *An Historical Introduction to the Study of the Books of the New Testament*, p. 294.

twined with that of the third gospel, and was dealt with above (see pp. 118-24). It is our conclusion that the internal evidence is consistent with the uniform external testimony to Lucan authorship.

3. MODERN REACTIONS

In the introduction to his commentary on *The Acts of the Apostles*, published in 1916, W. O. Carver writes:

> Twenty-five years ago one held to the "traditional view" of Luke's personal authorship on peril of his standing as a respectable scholar. Fortunately those who have never found sufficient reason for serious doubt that Luke wrote Acts now find themselves in the distinguished company of Harnack, Ramsay, Moulton and many another whose careful learning commands fullest respect.[13]

Today some liberal scholars, like Kümmel and Haenchen,[14] reject the traditional view, but there is a growing tendency among scholars of widely divergent viewpoints to accept the traditional Lucan authorship of Acts as the most probable view. R. R. Williams notes that Acts "is still ascribed by most modern scholars to the author to which it was ascribed by second-century Christian writers," and, while declining to be dogmatic, concedes that this view "is certainly the most probable hypothesis."[15] Macgregor in *The Interpreter's Bible*, after surveying the evidence, gives "a somewhat cautious 'Yes'" to the traditional view of authorship.[16] E. M. Blaiklock, a classical scholar with firm conservative convictions, asserts, "It would be difficult to find a book in the whole range of ancient literature concerning which a stronger case can be made in support of a traditional authorship."[17] And Marshall, a conservative British scholar, mildly states his view with the remark, "The conclusion that the author of Luke-Acts stood close to Paul and that he was in fact Luke the physician still remains the most likely historical explanation of the phenomena."[18]

13. William Owen Carver, *The Acts of the Apostles*, p. 5.
14. Werner Georg Kümmel, *Introduction to the New Testament*, pp. 123-32; Ernst Haenchen, *The Acts of the Apostles: A Commentary*, pp. 112-16.
15. R. R. Williams, "The Acts of the Apostles," in *Torch Bible Commentaries*, pp. 15, 19.
16. G. H. C. Macgregor and Theodore P. Ferris, "The Acts of the Apostles," in *The Interpreter's Bible*, 9:20.
17. Blaiklock, p. 14.
18. I. Howard Marshall, *Luke: Historian and Theologian*, p. 220.

THE SOURCES BEHIND ACTS

Luke says nothing in Acts concerning his sources for his history, but it may safely be assumed that the careful research which he invested in his gospel (Lk 1:1-3) also characterized his second volume. Since its reliability as a historical account depends upon the reliability of the sources drawn upon, scholarly investigation has devoted much attention to the sources behind this book. The liberal critics have left no stone unturned in their efforts to ferret out the assumed sources employed in its composition. But as Wikenhauser points out, their hypothetical reconstructions of the sources "have reached no satisfactory or universally accepted conclusions."[19]

Acceptance of the Lucan authorship does not deny Luke's need for sources of information in writing his history. Since Luke himself was not present at the events related in the first fifteen chapters, and did not witness all the things recorded in the remainder of the book, he had to depend on sources, whether oral or written, for much of his material. An acceptance of Lucan authorship does, however, render the problem of sources less speculative and less complicated.

For a good part of the second half of his volume Luke has the advantage of personal experience. In the "we-sections" (Ac 16:10-17; 20:5–21:18; 27:1–28:16), and possibly some others, as for example the events connected with Paul's arrest in Jerusalem (Ac 21:19–24:21), Luke writes as an eyewitness. These we-sections are similar to a travel diary; Luke may well have kept such a diary when traveling with Paul. That he used it when writing his book is a natural assumption. This is supported by the fact that these sections are noticeably vivid and exact concerning time and place. The first half of the book is much less graphic and has few specific dates.

For his account of Paul's missionary activities in which he did not participate, Luke might readily turn to Paul himself. While Luke was collecting the material for his history, it is but natural that Paul would communicate to him an account of his work and experiences in the cities of Thessalonica, Athens, Corinth, and Ephesus. Furthermore, as Blaiklock points out, communications and emigration were well established, and thus Luke, who was in Philippi, could keep in touch with Paul's work in other cities.[20] Luke also had ample oppor-

19. Alfred Wikenhauser, *New Testament Introduction*, p. 327.
20. Blaiklock, p. 17.

tunity to glean information from the members of Paul's missionary party, such as Silas, Timothy, and Aristarchus. On the trip to Jerusalem during the third missionary journey Luke would have been able to acquire information about the earlier years of the church from Philip the Evangelist and Mnason, an early disciple, in whose homes he stayed (Ac 21:8, 16).

During Paul's two-year imprisonment at Caesarea (Ac 24:27), Luke would have had time to travel throughout Palestine and interview various individuals for information concerning the events recorded in the first half of his book. At Jerusalem he might have interviewed people such as Peter, Barnabas, and James, who would be able to inform him about the beginning and early days of the church there. Those three, as well as Paul, might have given him information concerning the martyrdom of Stephen and the persecution which followed. Mark could have related the events in chapter 12, while Cornelius the centurion (Ac 10:1) could have given him the information for the major part of chapters 10-11. And information concerning the development of the church at Syrian Antioch may have been gained from Barnabas and Paul, as well as other members of that church.

It is obvious that Luke diligently gathered reminiscences preserved in the church at Jerusalem, but it has not been established whether the sources he drew upon were wholly oral or were both oral and written. The latter possibility is commonly accepted. Blaiklock remarks, "The episodic nature of chapters i-v suggests that Luke may have drawn upon such written records for the earlier incidents of his history."[21] Harrison holds it probable that these sources were in Aramaic, judging from some awkward constructions which occur, and cites Acts 3:16 as a prime example.[22] Bruce concludes that because of textual difficulties in these early chapters of Acts "we may postulate an underlying Aramaic document there with more confidence than anywhere else in Acts."[23] But others are not so sure that Luke used documentary sources. Wikenhauser remarks, "In the last few decades the view has gradually gained ground that it is quite impossible to prove that written sources were used for the first half

21. Ibid., p. 19.
22. Everett F. Harrison, *Introduction to the New Testament*, p. 242.
23. F. F. Bruce, *The Acts of the Apostles*, p. 22.

of Acts."[24] The various attempts to establish written sources for the first part of Acts have not proved convincing. Such efforts are very largely a matter of guesswork. Grosheide concludes that Luke had ample oral information so that "the contents of his book do not demand anything more."[25] The Aramaic features in the first part of Acts do not prove that Luke used written sources; they may simply prove that he faithfully preserved the flavor of his original informants. C. S. C. Williams thinks it probable that "Luke wove together these oral traditions so skillfully that it is impossible now to tell what his sources were."[26]

There remains the matter of the speeches in Acts. They are not to be regarded as "dictophonic reports" of what was said on the occasion. Nor should it be maintained that the accounts of these speeches are wholly free of Luke's own peculiarities of style. But it is unwarranted to stamp them as Luke's free compositions, setting forth what he thought should have been said on the occasion. The speeches are presented as real reports of what took place and they have the marks of authenticity. Rackham notes that "they are all exactly suitable to the occasion and are distinctly coloured by the particular and local circumstances."[27] Further, these speeches reflect the characteristics of the individual speakers; for example, the speeches of Peter can be readily distinguished from those of Paul. In confirmation of the authenticity of the speeches, Bruce points out that the style of the speeches, especially those in the earlier part of Acts, is inferior to Luke's own narratives. Bruce takes this to demonstrate that Luke presented these speeches with considerable literalness from an Aramaic source.[28] The theological content of the early speeches in Acts is quite harmonious with the primitive theology of the early church.

Luke may well have derived his account of the speeches in the early part of Acts from a "Jerusalem source." But the nature or identity of such a source can only be conjectured. Robertson suggests, "The oral tradition was probably active in preserving the early

---

24. Wikenhauser, p. 327.
25. F. W. Grosheide, "Acts of the Apostles, The," in *The Encyclopedia of Christianity,* 1:51.
26. C. S. C. Williams, "A Commentary on the Acts of the Apostles," in *Harper's New Testament Commentaries,* p. 11.
27. Richard Belward Rackham, "The Acts of the Apostles," in *Westminster Commentaries,* p. xliii.
28. Bruce, p. 18.

speeches of Peter and even of Stephen."[29] Paul himself heard Stephen's speech and it made a deep impression on his mind; he would have been able to recall its essence for Luke in later years. Since the ancients knew how to take shorthand notes[30] it is not impossible that an eyewitness recorded the gist of the speeches of Peter and Stephen.

It is certain that Luke heard Paul's speech to the Ephesian elders at Miletus (Ac 20); it is practically certain that he also heard Paul's address to the mob from the steps of the Tower of Antonia (Ac 22). In all probability Luke personally heard Paul's speeches before Felix (chap. 24) and Festus (chap. 25), as well as the defense before Agrippa II (chap. 26). He heard what Paul said to those on the ship the night before it was shipwrecked (chap. 27), as well as the address Paul made to the assembled Jews in Rome (chap. 28). Luke was not present when Paul delivered the sermon in the synagogue at Antioch of Pisidia (chap. 13), the address to the would-be worshipers at Lystra (chap. 14), or the speech to the Athenian court (chap. 17). Yet all of these speeches are so characteristically Pauline and so admirably adapted to the situation that their authenticity cannot be doubted. Paul himself may have carefully recalled for Luke what was said on those occasions. The suggestion of Blaiklock that "Paul probably had his speeches in manuscript" seems improbable.[31] Even the minor speeches in Acts, as for example, those of Gamaliel (5:35-39), the Ephesian town clerk (19:35-41), and Tertullus (24:2-8), are natural and in keeping with the circumstances and the character of the speaker and are best viewed as giving the gist of what was actually said. Whatever the actual sources for the speeches in Acts, it is undeniable that they are masterpieces which add greatly to our understanding of the life and thought of the early church.

THE PURPOSE OF ACTS

Acts itself contains no indication of its author's purpose. But its close connection with the third gospel (Lk 1:1-4; Ac 1:1-5) leaves

29. A. T. Robertson, "Acts of the Apostles," in *The International Standard Bible Encyclopaedia*, 1:43.
30. See W. Harold Mare, "The Role of the Note-taking Historian and His Emphasis on the Person and Work of Christ," *Journal of the Evangelical Theological Society* 15(Spring 1972):107-21 and the bibliography cited.
31. Blaiklock, p. 17.

no room for doubt that in this second volume Luke was likewise guided by a practical and historical aim. Acts was written that Theophilus might know "the certainty concerning the things" (Lk 1:4) relating to the origin and history of the church.

With the rapid spread and growth of the Christian church there developed a definite need for an authoritative account of its origin and history. New converts needed and desired authoritative information concerning the nature of the movement they had joined, the activities of its leaders, and their experiences in the furtherance of the gospel. Luke intends to give his readers a coherent account of the historical origin and early development of the Church of Jesus Christ. His personal experience of the salvation proclaimed by the church, and his participation in the spread of that message had deeply impressed him with the importance of the story. He desired that others too should be informed and gripped with assurance concerning the wonderful message of the gospel of Christ.

But it needs to be observed that in presenting his historical account, Luke did not aim at writing a history of the whole church. Many events in the history of the apostolic church are passed over in complete silence. The activities of most of the original twelve apostles are left completely unmentioned. Luke does not give a systematic account of the geographical spread of the gospel. He does not record how the gospel was first brought to Galilee, or to Damascus, Egypt, Cyrene, or Rome. While he traces geographical expansions, he does not always record them in the order in which they occurred. Certain apparently minor incidents in the history are enlarged upon, while many others needed for a rounded history of the church are left out. These features lead Hadjiantoniou to remark, "We conclude that just as it was not the purpose of the evangelists to give a full biography of Jesus Christ, in the same way it is not the purpose of the author of the Book of the Acts to give a complete chronicle of the Apostolic Church."[32] But what Luke did record serves to give an admirable picture of the supernatural origin and expansion of Christianity under the empowerment and leadership of the Holy Spirit.

An apologetic aim may well be postulated as a secondary purpose

32. George A. Hadjiantoniou, *New Testament Introduction*, p. 157.

of Acts. This apologetic thrust seems to look in two directions, to meet the charges of the Jews against Christianity and to present Christianity in a favorable light to the Roman world.

Acts makes clear the close connection between Christianity and Judaism. Christianity is seen as the heir of Judaism, yet distinct from it. Christianity had come under suspicion in part because of the charges levelled against it by the Jews. In reply Luke places Christians over against Jews and shows, by recounting the historical facts, that Christianity is not a politically dangerous movement. Its history proves that the attacks upon Christianity were generally inspired by Jews.† Those attacks began in Jerusalem, when Christianity was still closely identified with Judaism. Jewish hostility continued as Christianity spread beyond Palestine. Christians were openly persecuted and accused before the Roman authorities of disturbing the peace and of fostering disloyalty to the emperor (Ac 17:7; 18:13). Luke's account demonstrates, however, that the Roman authorities found these charges to be groundless and perceived that the Jews were the real aggressors. On various occasions the Christian movement came to the notice of the Roman governmental leaders who uniformly found that Christianity was not treasonable, as its Jewish opponents charged.

The rapid spread of Christianity, and the violent attacks that were often made upon it, brought Christianity to the attention of Graeco-Roman intellects, of whom Theophilus was a worthy representative. Their interest gave Luke the opportunity to provide them with a clear and accurate account of the rise and development of Christianity. It was a religious movement which justly merited their attention and support.

The contents of Acts suggest that Luke was also motivated by a missionary concern. His thrilling account of the spread of the gospel makes it self-evident that he did not write his story as a detached, impersonal historian. He was a Christian worker committed to the furtherance of the gospel (Ac 16:10-14) and produced his historical account of the origin and development of the Christian church. with a missionary motive. His basic hope was that his story might

---

†Acts records two instances in which a violent attack upon Christianity had a Gentile origin (16:19-40; 19:23-41), and in each instance it was due to the fact that individuals felt that financial interests were being threatened.

lead many readers to accept the Christ whom the church proclaimed as its Saviour and Lord. Acts 1:8 is commonly accepted as the key verse of the book. Setting forth its basic stress and structure, it clearly establishes Luke's missionary interest. Writing this book was his contribution toward fulfilling Christ's command to bear witness of Him, empowered by the Spirit, everywhere.

We would suggest that Luke's abrupt ending of the book of Acts is connected with his missionary interest. Luke brings his story to an unexpected close with the comment that Paul remained a prisoner in Rome for two years, preaching and teaching without hindrance (Ac 28:30-31). His mentioning the two-year period indicates that he knew the duration of Paul's imprisonment, but he says nothing about the outcome of that imprisonment. The abrupt ending naturally leaves the reader with a sense of incompleteness. Varied suggestions have been advanced to explain this abrupt ending. Most natural seems the view that Luke intended to remind his readers that the story which he had told was indeed incomplete. His story of the triumphant spread of the gospel in the face of persistent opposition proclaimed the heartening truth, "Nothing can stop the gospel."[33] But its victorious career has not yet been consummated. Therefore let all those who are committed to this victorious message courageously join in fulfilling their Lord's commission to carry the gospel "unto the uttermost part of the earth" (Ac 1:8). It is a task to which every believer in Christ is called.

Luke's narrative of the development of the Christian church also served a theological purpose. It effectively traces the spiritual development of the Church as the Body of Christ under the leadership of the Holy Spirit. It shows how Christianity, which arose out of Judaism, was led step by step to recognize God's purpose that it be an intrinsically universal body. As the spiritual Body of Christ the Church is composed of all true believers, who, irrespective of race or national origin, are united in one spiritual organism with a common Christ-centered life. In Ephesians 2:13-18 Paul paints a glorious picture of what God is now doing on the basis of Christ's work of reconciliation. He is now forming a new humanity composed of both Jews and Gentiles, united on a basis of equality by virtue of their

33. R. R. Williams, p. 27.

transforming faith-union with Christ. Acts demonstrates the out-working of this divine purpose in the expanding realization of the nature and scope of the church. Under the guidance of the Spirit the transition was made by slow steps. In the initial stage the church was composed of Jewish believers. Then Samaritans, who stood half-way between Jews and Gentiles, were brought into the church (8:4-24); then Gentiles who had come under the proselytizing influence of Judaism were reached (10:1–11:18); and then Gentile believers were accepted into the church directly from paganism (11:20-26). This transition was not achieved without serious doctrinal problems for those involved, and Acts records some of the struggles which believers experienced during this transition period. Acts demonstrates that Christianity is an intrinsically universal faith.

THE DATE AND PLACE OF ACTS

1. DATE

There is no clear or uniform tradition from the early church concerning the date of Acts. The center of interest focused rather upon the book's authorship. Irenaeus is silent concerning the date of Acts, but he asserts that Mark was written after the death of Paul.[34] If the priority of Mark is accepted (see pp. 168-73), then Irenaeus' assertion carries with it the assumption that Luke also wrote his gospel, and by implication Acts, after the death of Paul. The imperfectly preserved *Muratorian Canon* seems to say that Luke was silent about Peter's death and Paul's journey to Spain because he had not personally witnessed either. This scant evidence points to a date after the death of Paul for Acts.

With the fourth century another view found expression. Eusebius in his *Ecclesiastical History*[35] implies that Luke finished Acts while Paul was a prisoner in Rome (Ac 28:30-31). Yet Eusebius does not explicitly state that Luke then finished Acts, only that he brought his story to a close with Paul's two-year imprisonment and that he continued "his history down to the time that he was with Paul." The view of Eusebius is an inference drawn from the close of Acts. Wikenhauser thinks that Eusebius "was perhaps the first to put this forward,

34. Irenaeus *Against Heresies* 3. 1. 1.
35. Eusebius *Ecclesiastical History* 2. 22.

and subsequent sources for this dating seem to depend on him."[36] In his *Lives of Illustrious Men* (chap. 7) Jerome expressly claims that Acts was written immediately after the two-year Roman imprisonment; apparently he drew his conclusion from the remark of Eusebius. There is thus no firm early tradition to offer guidance concerning the dating of Acts.

Conclusions concerning the dating of Acts must be based on such evidence as can be gleaned from the book itself. However, any purported evidence for a precise date based on the contents of Acts is largely inferential.

The earliest possible date for the completion of Acts is two years after Paul's arrival in Rome as a prisoner (Ac 28:30-31). The exact time of that arrival is uncertain, but it was probably the spring of A.D. 61; thus A.D. 63 would be the earliest possible date for Acts. Acts must have been composed later than the third gospel, since the reference in Acts 1:1 to "the former treatise" is a natural reference to that gospel. Thus the date of Acts is naturally connected with the date accepted for Luke. C. S. C. Williams, however, has advanced the suggestion that "the former treatise" refers to an earlier draft of Luke's gospel which he sent to Theophilus and that our present Luke was written later than Acts, after Luke received a copy of Mark's gospel.[37] This novel suggestion would free Acts from the dating accepted for the third gospel and permit an early dating for Acts. It is an interesting hypothesis that lacks historical verification.

A second century date for Acts has been advocated by radical critics. Such a late date was popularized by the Tübingen school of critics on the basis of their proposed reconstruction of church history. They postulate that Acts was written to conciliate the clash between the Pauline and the Petrine elements in the church, hence a considerable time interval had to be allowed for this development to take place. But their subjective reconstruction of the early history of the church has been rightly abandoned and with it has come a general tendency to abandon a second century dating for Acts. (The findings of modern historical Greek grammar make a mid-second century dating for Acts highly improbable.) An exception is John Knox who thinks that "Luke-Acts as a finished work belongs to the middle of

36. Wikenhauser, *New Testament Introduction*, p. 342.
37. C. S. C. Williams, *Acts*, pp. 12-13.

the second century."[38] Knox holds that our present gospel of Luke must be an enlargement of a gospel used by Marcion in A.D. 140 as part of his canon. Since it is obvious that Marcion could not have accepted Luke without a knowledge of Acts, Knox concludes that our canonical Acts had not yet been written. He postulates that "the very skilful author" who was responsible for our canonical Luke "was also responsible for its association with Acts (and, of course, for *its* final form also) and that he did his work not far from A.D. 150."[39] But such a reading of the situation seems highly unlikely. Cadbury well remarks, "It seems extremely unlikely that the Gospel of Luke would ever have been canonized had it not been generally known before the time of Marcion. In other words, Marcion more probably took the Gospel from the Church than did the Church from Marcion."[40] Knox's explanation for the omission of Acts from Marcion's canon is much less probable than the view that Marcion arbitrarily rejected Acts for the same reason that he rejected the three gospels.

A date after A.D. 93 has been advocated on the ground that the writer of Acts was dependent upon the *Antiquities of the Jews* by Josephus, the Jewish historian. The claim for dependence is based on the fact that both Acts 5:36 and Josephus[41] refer to an uprising under a Jew named Theudas. There is, however, a discrepancy in the two accounts. According to Josephus, Theudas led his revolt some time after A.D. 44. Thus the address of Gamaliel recorded by Luke would be dated earlier than that revolt. But it has been pointed out that according to Josephus, the insurrection of Theudas took place during the procuratorship of Fadus. A little later the sons of Judas, the leader of the revolt in A.D. 6, were executed by the successor of Fadus. Critics claim that this accounts for Luke's order, Theudas . . . Judas in Acts 5:36-37. But this charges Luke with a very careless reading of Josephus. Bruce well remarks, "It is strange that a discrepancy should be taken to prove dependence."[42] Harrison points out that it is "hardly logical to hold that Luke depends on Josephus and yet be obligated to admit that Luke shows wide divergence from him in relating events that are supposedly the same."[43] The claim

38. John Knox, *Marcion and the New Testament*, p. 121.
39. Ibid., p. 123.
40. H. J. Cadbury, "Subsidiary Points," in *The Beginnings of Christianity*, 2:358.
41. Josephus *Antiquities of the Jews* 20. 5. 1.
42. Bruce, p. 24.
43. Harrison, p. 240.

that Luke was dependent on Josephus is not taken seriously by modern scholars.

Many scholars place Acts some time after A.D. 70. Zahn, a conservative scholar, asserts, "It may be assumed with practical certainty that Luke wrote his work about the year 75."[44] The major reason for this dating is the prevailing view that Luke used Mark in writing his gospel. Since Mark is commonly dated around A.D. 66-68, the third gospel must be later than that, and Acts still later. The length of the interval between Luke and Acts is not known, but several years have been postulated. This would place Acts some time after A.D. 70. Support for such a date for Acts has also been inferred from the claim that the formulation of Jesus' eschatological discourse in Luke 21 shows that it was written after A.D. 70. But this claim arises from a subjective interpretation of the phenomena in Luke and cannot be accepted as unquestioned (see p. 137). Goodspeed enumerates a number of reasons for dating Acts well after A.D. 70.‡ As assumed evidence of a late date, Goodspeed mentions the literary features of Acts, its infancy interest, resurrection interest, doctrine of the Holy Spirit, interest in punitive miracle, the passing of the Jewish controversy, interest in Christian psalmody, church organization, speaking in tongues, the inference from Acts 20:25, 38 that Paul was dead, Paul's elevation to the stature of a hero, the emergence of the sects, nonacquaintance with Paul's collected letters, and the assumed background of a wide-ranging Gentile mission.[45] But Goodspeed's reasons for a late date for Acts are mainly inferences from its contents, and different interpretations can be drawn. Guthrie holds that none of the reasons advanced by Goodspeed demand a date later than the early sixties.[46] For those who accept Lucan authorship the latest possible date would be the death of Luke, which is generally held to be around A.D. 85.

A strong case can be made for a date at the end of the two-year imprisonment mentioned in 28:30, probably A.D. 63. Bruce advances the following arguments in favor of this early dating: 1) It best explains the abrupt ending of Acts. 2) The favorable attitude of the

44. Zahn, 3:159.

‡Goodspeed dates Acts about A.D. 90, but he does accept Lucan authorship and suggests that Luke had gathered much of his material long before publication.
45. Edgar J. Goodspeed, *An Introduction to the New Testament*, pp. 191-95.
46. Donald Guthrie, *New Testament Introduction*, p. 346.

Roman officials toward Christianity would be hard to explain if the
Neronian persecution of A.D. 64 had already begun. 3) Silence about
the fall of Jerusalem in A.D. 70 would be hard to explain if that crucial
event had already occurred. 4) Luke betrays little acquaintance with
the Pauline epistles. 5) Acts contains no hint of Paul's death. 6) The
theological concepts and terminology in Acts are very primitive.[47]

These arguments, pointing to a date of A.D. 63 for Acts, are attractive. But such an early date can be received *only* if the commonly
accepted view that Luke used Mark is rejected, or if a date in the
fifties is postulated for Mark. Either condition presents problems.
The first must boldly reject one of the common conclusions of synoptic criticism; the second must set aside the patristic evidence concerning the date of Mark's gospel. (See the introduction to Mark.)

The inference that the abrupt ending of Acts points to the time of
its publication is attractive, but does not establish the point. Others
have drawn a different inference. Wikenhauser objects to the view
that the ending of Acts is connected with the time of publication,
because it "raises the question why Luke did not wait for the end of
the trial, which must have been near at hand."[48] Ramsay suggests
that the ending is abrupt because Luke intended to write a third
volume.[49] Bruce replies that this view has little to commend it, and
observes that "even if this was his [Luke's] intention, this is a curious
place to break off the second volume; the first volume has a more
appropriate ending."[50] Another view is that the ending of Acts was
intended to mark the church's breaking through religious, racial, and
national limitations to an unhindered preaching of the gospel.[51] Still
others think that Luke closed as he did because he had achieved his
purpose of describing the gospel's victorious course to the capital of
the Roman Empire.[52] Hanson holds that "Luke did not describe
Paul's acquittal, and his subsequent career, because he knew that the
people for whom he was writing were acquainted with these facts
already."[53] Clearly not all scholars are agreed that the abrupt ending

47. Bruce, pp. 11-13.
48. Wikenhauser, p. 343.
49. W. M. Ramsay, *St. Paul the Traveller and the Roman Citizen*, pp. 27-28.
50. Bruce, p. 11.
51. Frank Stagg, *The Book of Acts: The Early Struggle for an Unhindered Gospel*, pp. 1-4, 266.
52. Wikenhauser, pp. 343-44.
53. R. P. C. Hanson, "The Acts in the Revised Standard Version," in *The New Clarendon Bible*, p. 34.

of Acts indicates the date of its publication. The uniform favorable attitude of the Roman officials toward Christianity which Luke describes has led to the presumption that Paul would be acquitted. He had established that Christianity was not dangerous to the Roman state, and he did not feel it essential to carry the point further.

The apologetic element discernible in Acts would not seem to have any clear justification if Acts had been written when the attitude of the Roman government was definitely favorable toward Christianity. But changed circumstances soon made such a defense of Christianity pertinent. Manson holds that "the most obvious occasion for such a public defense of Christianity comes with the savage attack on the Church made by Nero in A.D. 64 and the Jewish war of A.D. 66-70."[54] This is upheld by Williams, who points out that Christians "were implicated, at least according to popular opinion, to a greater or lesser degree in the Jewish war."[55] But Luke's story effectively refutes the charge that the Christian church was involved in the Jewish war by showing that Christianity, while the true heir of Judaism, was yet distinct from it. In fact, the Jews themselves viewed Christianity as an opponent of Judaism. After A.D. 70, when the Jewish rebellion was crushed and Judaism was discredited in the eyes of the Roman world, such a defense would lose much of its significance. Hanson suggests that by stopping his story where he did Luke "may even have meant to make the point that in natural circumstances, when angry tyrants do not interfere with the course of justice, Christianity expects, and receives, fair treatment at the hands of the Roman Government."[56] These considerations would suggest a date shortly before A.D. 70 for the publication of Acts.

If Luke did use Mark's gospel in writing his own account of the story of Jesus, then the third gospel, consistent with our dating of Mark, may be dated in A.D. 66 or early 67. The length of the interval which elapsed between the publication of the third gospel and Acts can only be conjectured. Luke must certainly have been gathering material for his second volume while making his investigations for the gospel. It would seem that he could have completed Acts within a year after the publication of his gospel. Thus we suggest A.D. 67

54. T. W. Manson, *Studies in the Gospels and Epistles*, p. 56.
55. C. S. C. Williams, p. 13.
56. Hanson, p. 33.

or 68 as the probable date of Acts. This would place it shortly after the death of Paul, who was martyred under Nero in A.D. 65 or possibly the early part of 66. Wikenhauser, who accepts a date after Paul's death, points out that this is in harmony with the oldest tradition concerning Acts.[57]

2. PLACE

Where Luke was when he completed "the Acts" is not known. The book itself provides no certain evidence on the point. The view that Luke was in Rome is based on the assumption that he published his book at the time of the close of his story. He may have written some or most of it while he was in Rome with Paul. But that would not prove that he was still in Rome when it was published. Tradition is almost completely silent concerning the place where Acts was written. A Coptic inscription of the sixth or seventh century connects Acts with Achaia, but little weight can be given to this late tradition. Modern scholars have nothing positive to suggest concerning the place of writing.

THE CHARACTERISTICS OF ACTS

1. MISSIONARY DOCUMENT

Acts is fundamentally a missionary document. It is an account of the missionary expansion of the church during the first thirty years of its existence. The Great Commission in Acts 1:8 provides the key to its contents. Acts tells the story of the founding and early days of the church in Jerusalem, its spread to Judea, Samaria, and parts beyond Palestine: Syria, Asia Minor, Macedonia, Greece, and Rome. There are hints that the missionary work of the early church also reached into other areas, such as Ethiopia and North Africa. This missionary account embodies basic principles that are relevant for the missionary task of the church during all ages.

2. SPIRIT'S POWER

Acts is the record of the Spirit-empowered witness of the early church to its risen Lord. It records the Pentecostal coming of the Holy Spirit and the Spirit's leadership in the development of the

57. Wikenhauser, p. 343.

church. The Spirit specifically directed each successive step in the expanding scope of the church. The Holy Spirit, mentioned fifty-six times, is the central person in Acts. The thrust of the message of Acts may be summarized in the decree issued by the Jerusalem Conference, "It seemed good to the Holy Spirit, and to us" (Ac 15:28). The Spirit's empowering of the church's witness is the key to its amazing success.

3. FRAGMENTARY ACCOUNT

Luke's account of the early history of the Christian church is of necessity fragmentary. The first part of the book is characterized by an "episode–summary" method of presentation: a significant single event is described, and a summary statement is given which sets forth the results achieved during that particular period (2:42-47; 4:32-35; 5:12-16; 5:42; 6:7; 9:31; 12:24). The statement in 9:31 is revealing in that it mentions the church in Galilee, although the narrative has not previously mentioned that a church was planted there. The fragmentary nature of the account is also clear from the fact that, excluding chapter 1, only three of the twelve apostles—Peter, John, and James—are mentioned by name in the story. While Peter is the prominent character in the first half of the book, important facts about his life, related elsewhere, (Gal 2:11-21; 1 Co 9:5) are not mentioned. Paul, who is obviously Luke's hero, is the central figure in the second half of the story, but important events in Paul's life, mentioned in other passages, are passed over in silence (2 Co 11:24-26; Gal 1:17). Even the narrative in the second half of the book, devoted to the story of Paul, is uneven. Some parts are highly condensed (cf. 18:22; 19:1), while other parts are recorded in considerable detail (cf. the trip to Jerusalem, 20:7–21:16, or the journey to Rome, 27:1–28:16). Luke was selective in writing his history. He could not tell the full story in the space he had allotted to himself, nor was it demanded by his purpose.

4. BIOGRAPHICAL INTEREST

Luke's deep interest in people is evident from the large number of individuals he brings into the picture. More than one hundred people appear. Scroggie observes, "Some of the characters are portrayed at length, but the most of them, briefly; Jews and Gentiles,

Christians and Pagans, rulers and subjects, philosophers and artisans are here."[58]

5. SPEECHES

Speeches constitute a prominent part of the contents of Acts. No less than twenty-four addresses or excerpts of addresses are included: nine by Peter (1:16-22; 2:14*b*-36; 3:12*b*-26; 4:8*b*-12; 5:29*b*-32; 8:20-25; 10:34*b*-43; 11:5-17; 15:7-11); nine by Paul (13:16*b*-41; 14:15-17; 17:22*b*-31; 20:18*b*-35; 22:1-21; 24:10*b*-21; 26:2-23; 27:21-26; 28:17-20); one each by Gamaliel (5:35*b*-39); Stephen (7:2-53), James (15:13*b*-21), Demetrius (19:25*b*-27), the Ephesian town clerk (19:35*b*-40), and Festus (25:24-27). They vary as to content and purpose, but each makes an invaluable contribution toward the total picture.

6. HISTORICAL FACTS

As a historical work, Acts is characterized by its reference to a wide variety of historical facts. It contains some eighty geographical references. Provinces, areas, cities, and local sites are mentioned. Various official titles are used: procurator, consul, praetor, politarch, Asiarch, and others. Historical events and the individuals connected with them, as well as cultural and religious affairs, are introduced. Luke uses historical data as part of his effort to relate the story of the Christian movement to the contemporary historical scene. For this reason he also refers to various individuals who were familiar figures on the scene of world affairs.

Luke's inclusion of historical data has made him subject to searching critical investigation concerning his historical accuracy. Acts has stood up triumphantly under meticulous investigation.[59] Archaeological discoveries have in a remarkable way confirmed Luke's accuracy. An example is his accuracy regarding various provincial or local governmental titles. It has been found that he uses them with precision, although the fluctuating political status of provinces and

58. W. Graham Scroggie, *Know Your Bible: A Brief Introduction to the Scriptures,* 2:73.
59. W. M. Ramsay, *The Bearing of Recent Discovery on the Trustworthiness of the New Testament;* W. M. Ramsay, *St. Paul the Traveller and the Roman Citizen;* A. T. Robertson, *Luke the Historian in the Light of Research;* I. Howard Marshall, *Luke: Historian and Theologian,* chap. 3; W. W. Gasque, "The Historical Value of the Book of Acts," *The Evangelical Quarterly* 41 (April-June, 1969): 68-88.

communities would predispose an uninformed writer to inaccuracy. In dealing with the question of historicity, Sherwin-White remarks, "For Acts the confirmation of historicity is overwhelming. . . . Any attempt to reject its basic historicity even in matters of detail must now appear absurd. Roman historians have long taken it for granted."[60]

Although there are a number of references to historical events in Acts, most are indefinite and provide few fixed points for the establishment of a firm chronology. It is known that the death of Agrippa I (Ac 12:20-23) occurred in A.D. 44, and the coming of Gallio to Corinth as proconsul (Ac 18:12) probably should be dated at May, 52. Festus probably became procurator of Judea in A.D. 60 (Ac 25:1), but there is no general agreement about that date.[61] Consequently, efforts to construct a chronology for the events in Acts have resulted in a diversity of suggested datings.[62]

7. DOCTRINAL IMPORTANCE

The very nature of Acts gives it great doctrinal significance for Christianity. Doctrinal truths are presented in various ways throughout the story, but especially in the recorded speeches setting forth the apostolic preaching. "All the notes of the Christian Gospel," says Scroggie, "are here sounded, and they peal forth in rapturous harmony. The Message, though presented by many, and in varying terms, is always the same, Jesus was the promised Messiah, the Son of God, and the Redeemer of the world."[63] Today it is generally accepted that Luke had strong doctrinal interests in presenting his story; but there is no evidence that he deliberately shaded historical facts in the interest of doctrine. The theological presentation is true to the primitive doctrine of the early church. "The importance of the book of Acts is in its preservation of the main doctrinal themes presented in apostolic preaching, even if there is no evidence of an at-

60. A. N. Sherwin-White, *Roman Society and Roman Law in the New Testament*, p. 189.
61. Proposed dates for the appointment of Festus vary from A.D. 55 to 60. For a table of varied dates, and their advocates, for this and other events in Acts see C. S. C. Williams, *A Commentary on the Acts of the Apostles*, pp. 33-34.
62. W. P. Armstrong, "Chronology of the New Testament," in *International Standard Bible Encyclopaedia*, 1:647-50; Jack Finegan, *Handbook of Biblical Chronology*, pp. 315-25; George Ogg, *The Chronology of the Life of Paul*; R. B. Rackham, *The Acts of the Apostles: A Commentary*, pp. 60-71; Haenchen, p. 60-71.
63. Scroggie, 2:72-73.

tempt to develop a systematized theology."[64] Creedal formulations belong to a later date.

8. LANGUAGE AND STYLE

Luke's Greek is recognized as being among the best in the New Testament. He reveals himself to be an accomplished literary artist, to whom only the writer of Hebrews can be favorably compared. Luke had the ability to adapt his language to the atmosphere of the situation being described. Thus Moulton remarks, "He steeps his style in Biblical phraseology, drawn from the Greek Old Testament, so long as his narrative moves in Palestinian circles, where the speakers use Greek that obviously represents a foreign idiom," but he "instinctively departs from that style when his subject takes him away from the Biblical land and people."[65] This stylistic versatility heightens the impact of his story. The variations indicate that "Luke had an extraordinary talent for all types of writing and an excellent command of language, such as characterize the true writer."[66] He was a writer of natural ability and training. But Luke did not write in the style of the classical masters. He wrote in the Koine Greek, which was used by the ordinary people of that day. Occasionally he used expressions no longer current in common speech. Like the other New Testament writers, Luke was familiar with the Septuagint and it influenced and colored his style.

Luke's two volumes reveal that he had a large vocabulary; only Paul's was comparable. Hawkins calculates that Luke used 732 words not found elsewhere in the New Testament, 413 in Acts and 58 common to the gospel and the Acts.[67] Approximately nine-tenths of these words peculiar to Luke are also found in the Septuagint. Haenchen points out that in his vocabulary Luke compares favorably with the noted Greek writer, Xenophon.[68]

THE TEXT OF ACTS

Acts is unique among the books of the New Testament in that two

64. Guthrie, p. 338.
65. James Hope Moulton, *A Grammar of New Testament Greek*, 2:7-8.
66. L. Cerfaux, in *Introduction to the New Testament*, A. Robert and A. Feuillet, eds., p. 365.
67. John C. Hawkins, *Horae Synopticae: Contributions to the Study of the Synoptic Problem*, pp. 201-7.
68. Haenchen, p. 72.

versions of it, which differ from each other, have come down to us.[69] They are currently designated as the Alexandrian and the Western texts. The former, which has traditionally been accepted as the authentic text and lies behind our common English versions, is represented by the earliest Uncial manuscripts: B, Aleph, A, C, Psi, and Papyri 45 and 74; important minuscle manuscripts: 33, 81, 104, 326, 1175; and the Alexandrian Church Fathers. The Western text is chiefly represented by Codex D, the fragmentary papyri 29, 38, 48, the marginal readings in the Harclean Syrian version, one Old Latin manuscript (*h*), and citations of Acts by Cyprian and Augustine.

The Western text, as represented by Codex D, is nearly ten percent longer than the common Alexandrian text.[70] Metzger points out that it is also characterized by a number of readings which are "generally more picturesque and circumstantial" than the Alexandrian text.[71] The origin and relationship of the two forms of the text have been much discussed, and several explanations have been advanced.

It has been suggested that both forms of the text come from Luke himself. The German philologist, Friedrich Blass, in 1894 propounded the theory that the Western text was a rough draft and that the Alexandrian text represents Luke's revision, incorporating stylistic improvements. This theory gained some support but most scholars found it difficult to understand why Luke would omit vivid details found in the original text from the revision. They also noted that the Western text exhibits characteristic marks of embodying later additions.

J. H. Ropes, in his scholarly study of the text of Acts, advocates the theory that the Alexandrian text preserves the original work of Luke and the Western text reflects the work of a reviser.[72] This view has commanded wide scholarly acceptance.

Albert C. Clark champions the view that the Western text is the original and the Alexandrian is a scholarly, methodical abbreviation of it.[73] It has not won any strong following, since some of the omis-

69. See the discussion in Bruce M. Metzger, *A Textual Commentary on the Greek New Testament*, pp. 259-72 and the evidence for the variant reading throughout Acts, pp. 272-503. See further Haenchen, pp. 50-60 and the bibliography.
70. For Codex Vaticanus (B) and Codex Bezae (D) on parallel pages, with critical notes, see James Hardy Ropes, *The Beginnings of Christianity*, vol. 3, *The Text of Acts*.
71. Metzger, p. 260.
72. Ropes, *Beginnings of Christianity*, vol. 3, *The Text of Acts*.
73. A. C. Clark, *The Acts of the Apostles*, pp. 374-76.

sions which, according to this theory, were made in the Alexandrian show a singular lack of good judgment, as even Clark has to admit.

Views have been advanced which appeal to the influence of the Latin version or presume an Aramaic version which influenced the Western text. After surveying the various theories, Metzger is "impressed by the wide diversity of hypotheses and the lack of any generally accepted explanation."[74]

The prevailing attitude of the textual critics today is to reject neither form of the text arbitrarily but to endeavor to establish an eclectic text by weighing each variant on its own merits. On this basis some of the Western readings leave the impression that they are based on good authority and may well be authentic. But on the whole, modern eclectic textual criticism concludes that the Alexandrian text is probably the original.

The longer Western readings seem most easily explained as being an expansion of the original text. The reviser who produced the D text was evidently a careful and well-informed scholar, who eliminated seams in the original and added historical, biographical, and geographical details.

An Outline of Acts

Acts may be divided into two parts: chapters 1-12, in which Peter is the central figure, and chapters 13-28, in which Paul is central. This division is not exact, since Peter also appears as a leader in the second part and Paul is prominently brought into the picture in the first part. Neither does it seem to do justice to the progression in Luke's account implied in Acts 1:8. It seems best to take this verse as providing the intended structural outline for Luke's account.

On the basis of Acts 1:8, the theme of Acts may be stated as "The Expanding Witness of the Spirit-Empowered Church."

I. Introduction, 1:1-11
   A. Summary preface by Luke, vv. 1-5
   B. Parting instructions of Jesus, vv. 6-11

74. Metzger, p. 270.

II. The Church Witnessing in Jerusalem, 1:12—8:3
   A. Birth of the Church, 1:12—2:47
      1. Days of preparation, 1:12-28
         a) Waiting disciples, vv. 12-14
         b) Filling up of the apostolic witness, vv. 15-26
      2. Day of Pentecost, 2:1-41
         a) Manifestations of the Spirit, vv. 1-4
         b) Reactions of the multitude, vv. 5-13
         c) Preaching of Peter, vv. 14-36
            (1) Explanation of the scene, vv. 14-21
            (2) Exhortation to the hearers, vv. 22-36
         d) Results of the message, vv. 37-41
      3. Summary: Life of the Christian community, 2:42-47
   B. Experience of official opposition, 3:1—4:35 (attack from without)
      1. Occasion of the opposition, 3:1-26
         a) Healing of the lame man, vv. 1-10
         b) Peter's sermon to the people, vv. 11-26
      2. Expression of opposition, 4:1-22
         a) Arrest of Peter and John, vv. 1-4
         b) Trial before the Sanhedrin, vv. 5-12
         c) Outcome of the trial, vv. 13-22
      3. Effect of the opposition, 4:23-31
         a) United prayer of the church, vv. 23-30
         b) Spirit-empowered witness, v. 31
      4. Summary: Communal spirit of the believers, 4:32-35
   C. Problem of church purity, 4:36—5:16 (attack from within)
      1. Noble deed of Barnabas, 4:36-37
      2. Spirit's judgment on hypocrisy, 5:1-11
         a) Judgment upon Ananias, vv. 1-6
         b) Judgment upon his wife, vv. 7-11
      3. Summary: Activity of the purified church, 5:12-16
   D. Renewed hostility of Judaism, 5:17-42 (attack from without)
      1. Imprisonment and release of the apostles, vv. 17-25
      2. Arraignment before the Sanhedrin, vv. 26-32
      3. Deliberations of the Sanhedrin, vv. 33-40
      4. Attitude of the apostles toward suffering, v. 41
      5. Summary: Continued apostolic preaching, v. 42

E. Problem of disharmony in the church, 6:1-7 (attack from within)
   1. Apostolic solution to the problem, vv. 1-6
   2. Summary: Great growth in Jerusalem, v. 7
F. Witness of Stephen, the first martyr, 6:8—8:1*a* (attack from without)
   1. Stephen's powerful ministry, 6:8-10
   2. Arraignment before the Sanhedrin, 6:11—7:1
   3. Address to the Sanhedrin, 7:2-53
      a) God's grace to Abraham and the patriarchal disobedience, vv. 2-16
      b) God's grace through Moses and Israel's disobedience, vv. 17-43
      c) God's grace manifested in a dwelling place, vv. 44-50
      d) Conclusion: The present disobedience, vv. 51-53
   4. Stephen's testimony in the face of death, vv. 54-60
   5. Approval of Saul, 8:1*a*
G. Jerusalem church scattered by persecution, 8:1*b*-3

III. Church Witnessing in Judea-Samaria and Beyond, 8:4—12:25
A. Ministry of Philip, 8:4-40
   1. Work of Philip in Samaria, vv. 4-25
      a) Triumph of the Gospel in Samaria, vv. 4-8
      b) Story of a notable convert, vv. 9-13
      c) Confirmation of the work through Peter and John, vv. 14-24
      d) Ministry of Peter and John in Samaria, v. 25
   2. Work of Philip with the Ethiopian eunuch, vv. 26-39
   3. Subsequent ministry of Philip, v. 40
B. Apprehension and Preparation of Saul, 9:1-31
   1. Apprehension of Saul by Christ, vv. 1-19*a*
      a) Vision on the road, vv. 1-9
      b) Commission through Ananias, vv. 10-19*a*
   2. Preparatory experiences of Saul, vv. 19*b*-30
      a) Witness in the Damascus synagogues, vv. 19*b*-22
      b) Escape from enemies in Damascus, vv. 23-25
      c) Reactions to Saul in Jerusalem, vv. 26-30
   3. Summary: Peace and growth of the church, v. 31

B. Conference about the gospel for the Gentiles, 15:1-35
  1. Occasion for the conference, vv. 1-3
  2. Sessions of the conference, vv. 4-29
    a) First public session, vv. 4-5
    b) Second public session, vv. 6-29
      (1) Protracted discussion, vv. 6-7*a*
      (2) Speech of Peter, vv. 7*b*-11
      (3) Testimonies of Barnabas and Paul, v. 12
      (4) Recommendation of James, vv. 13-21
      (5) Decision embodied in the conference letter, vv. 22-29
  3. Messengers sent to the Gentile churches, vv. 30-33
  4. Summary: Protracted ministry in Syrian Antioch, v. 35
C. Paul's Second Mission to Gentiles, 15:36—18:22
  1. Separation of Paul and Barnabas, 15:36-40
  2. Gentile churches revisited, 15:41—16:4
  3. Summary: Strengthening of the Gentile churches, 16:5
  4. Missionary call to Macedonia, 16:6-10
  5. Missionary work in Macedonia, 16:11—17:15
    a) Mission in Philippi, 16:11-40
      (1) Beginning of the work at Philippi, vv. 11-15
      (2) Exorcism of a demon, vv. 16-18
      (3) Imprisonment of the missionaries, vv. 19-24
      (4) Establishment of the work by God, vv. 25-40
        (*a*) Conversion of the jailor, vv. 25-34
        (*b*) Retraction by the magistrates, vv. 35-40
    b) Mission at Thessalonica, 17:1-9
    c) Mission at Beroea, 17:10-15
  6. Missionary work in Achaia, 17:16—18:17
    a) Work of Paul in Athens, 17:16-34
      (1) Work in the synagogue and the marketplace, vv. 16-18
      (2) Address to the Areopagus, vv. 19-31
      (3) Results of the work in Athens, vv. 32-34
    b) New center at Corinth, 18:1-17
      (1) Period of manual labor and synagogue preaching, vv. 1-4

(2) Full time ministry to Jews and Gentiles, vv. 5-11

(3) Refusal of Gallio to act against Paul, vv. 12-17

    7. Return to Antioch in Syria, 18:18-22

C. Third mission to Gentiles, with Ephesus as headquarters, 18:23–20:3

    1. Visit to the Galatian disciples, 18:23

    2. Ministry of Apollos at Ephesus, 18:24-28

    3. Work of Paul at Ephesus, 19:1-41

      a) Encounter with the disciples of John, vv. 1-7

      b) Triumph of the gospel at Ephesus, vv. 8-20

      c) Plans of Paul for the future, vv. 21-22

      d) Riot of the idol-makers at Ephesus, vv. 23-41

    4. Visit to Macedonia and Achaia, 20:1-3

D. Journey to Jerusalem in the face of warnings, 20:4–21:16

    1. Companions of Paul on the trip, 20:4-5

    2. Trip from Philippi to Troas, 20:6

    3. Meeting with the believers at Troas, 20:7-12

    4. Trip from Troas to Miletus, 20:13-16

    5. Farewell to the Ephesian Elders, 20:17-38

    6. Journey from Miletus to Tyre, 21:1-6

    7. Warning to Paul at Caesarea, 21:7-14

    8. Trip to Jerusalem as guest of Mnason, 21:15-16

E. Outcome of the visit to Jerusalem, 21:17–23:30

    1. Meeting of Paul and the Jerusalem leaders, 21:17-26

    2. Riot in the Temple and Paul's seizure, 21:27-40

      a) Riot against Paul led by Asian Jews, vv. 27-30

      b) Rescue of Paul by the Roman officer, vv. 31-36

      c) Permission given Paul to address the mob, vv. 37-40

    3. Defense by Paul from the fortress stairs, vv. 22:1-21

    4. Reactions to Paul's defense, 22:22-29

    5. Appearance of Paul before the Sanhedrin, 22:30–23:11

      a) Reason for the appearance, 22:30

      b) Events at the meeting, 23:1-9

      c) Outcome of the meeting, 23:10-11

    6. Failure of the conspiracy against Paul, 23:12-30

      a) Conspiracy exposed by Paul's nephew, vv. 12-22

      b) Conspiracy frustrated by Claudius Lysias, vv. 23-30

F. Imprisonment of Paul in Caesarea, 23:31–26:32
  1. Transfer to Caesarea under military guard, 23:31-35
  2. Imprisonment under Felix as governor, 24:1-27
    a) Trial before Felix, vv. 1-23
      (1) Charges against Paul, vv. 1-9
      (2) Paul's self-defense, vv. 10-21
      (3) Postponement of a decision by Felix, vv. 22-23
    b) Detention in Caesarea for two years, vv. 24-27

  3. Imprisonment under Festus as governor, 25:1–26:32
    a) Festus' visit to Jerusalem, 25:1-5
    b) Paul's appeal to Caesar before Festus, 25:6-12
    c) Visit of Agrippa II and Paul's defense, 25:13–26:32
      (1) Case of Paul discussed with Agrippa, 25:13-22
      (2) Appearance of Paul before Agrippa, 25:23–26:32
        (*a*) Presentation of Paul's case by Festus, 25:23-27
        (*b*) Address of Paul to Agrippa, 26:1-23
        (*c*) Reaction of the audience, 26:24-29
        (*d*) Result of the meeting, 26:30-32

G. Voyage to Rome, 27:1–28:15
  1. Voyage from Caesarea to Fair Havens, 27:1-8
  2. Departure from Fair Havens and two weeks of storm, 27:9-26
  3. Shipwreck on the Island of Malta, 27:27-44
  4. Winter on the Island of Malta, 28:1-10
    a) Experience with the viper, vv. 1-6
    b) Healing of Publius' father, vv. 7-10
  5. Voyage from Malta to Rome, 28:11-15

H. Imprisonment in Rome, 28:16-31
  1. Arrangements for Paul in Rome, v. 16
  2. Meeting with the Jews at Rome, vv. 17-28
    a) First meeting with the Jewish leaders, vv. 17-22
    b) Second interview and Paul's warning to the Jews, vv. 23-28
  3. Unhindered preaching in Rome for two years, vv. 30-31

A Book List on Acts

Alexander, J. A. *Commentary on the Acts of the Apostles.* 1875. Reprint. Grand Rapids: Zondervan, 1956.

An exhaustive (960 pages) exposition of Acts by a conservative Presbyterian scholar of the past century. Gives a precise interpretation of the text on the basis of the original. Omission of technical matters makes it suitable to the English reader.

Barclay, William. "The Acts of the Apostles." In *The Daily Study Bible.* Edinburgh: St. Andrew Press, 1953.

Divides Acts into brief paragraphs, with the author's translation of the portion printed at the beginning. The comments are generally devotional in character, containing various religious and literary quotations. The author is at his best in his discriminating discussion of Greek words. The interpretation is liberal in spots.

Blaiklock, E. M. "The Acts of the Apostles, An Historical Commentary." In *Tyndale New Testament Commentaries.* Grand Rapids: Eerdmans, 1959.

A brief, conservative commentary well adapted to the lay Bible reader. The exposition is developed by paragraph, followed by additional notes on selected points concerning the text. Combines thorough knowledge of the historical background with a concise unfolding of the central thrust of the biblical text.

Blunt, A. W. F. "The Acts of the Apostles in the Revised Version." In *The Clarendon Bible.* Oxford: Clarendon, 1922.

A liberal interpretation that opens with the assertion that verbal inspiration can no longer be accepted. Nearly half of the volume is given to the introduction and the printed text of Acts. Contains numerous illustrations and photographs pertinent to Acts.

Bruce, F. F. *The Acts of the Apostles.* London: Tyndale, 1951.

Greek text. The work of a noted British conservative scholar, devoted primarily to a critical study of linguistic, textual, and historical aspects of Acts. The sixty-page introduction deals with various problems of introduction. Bruce argues for an early date of Acts. Significant for the Greek student.

———. "Commentary on the Book of the Acts." In *The New International Commentary on the New Testament.* Grand Rapids: Eerdmans, 1954.

A full, up-to-date exposition by an accomplished conservative scholar. The stress is upon exposition. The comments are comprehensive, clear, and carry a devotional overtone. The footnotes provide much technical material on the text. One of the best volumes on Acts for the serious English student.

Carter, Charles W., Earle, Ralph. *The Acts of the Apostles.* 1959. Reprint. Grand Rapids: Zondervan, 1973.

A full commentary by two evangelical scholars in the Wesleyan tradition. The exegesis by Earle is technical, seeking to clarify the text on the basis of the Greek. Carter's exposition is well outlined and provides rich material on the meaning of the text verse by verse. Has a fine bibliography.

Erdman, Charles R. *The Acts: An Exposition.* Philadelphia: Westminster, 1919.

A devotional and practical commentary by a conservative Presbyterian professor. The exposition, given by paragraphs, is adapted to lay readers.

Fieldhouse, Marvin L. "The Book of the Acts." In *The Missionary's Bible Commentary.* Nagano Ken, Japan: Oriental Bible Study Fellowship, n.d.

A staunchly conservative interpretation of Acts by a missionary in Japan. The volume, intended as a guide for group study of Acts, divides Acts into 61 lessons, with introduction, expository notes, and closing thought for each lesson. The aim is to make the truth of Acts clear and relevant to the Bible believer. Does not deal with critical problems.

Foakes-Jackson, F. J. "The Acts of the Apostles." In *The Moffatt New Testament Commentary.* New York: Harper, 1931.

Prints and uses the Moffatt translation as the starting point for the commentary. Supplies valuable background information. Written in a non-technical manner. The approach is liberal, in keeping with the character of the series to which it belongs.

Gaebelein, A. C. *The Acts of the Apostles.* Glasgow: Pickering & Inglis, n.d.

A forceful, conservative unfolding of the message of Acts by a noted premillennial, dispensational Bible teacher active during the first half of this century. Emphasizes the transition from Judaism to Christianity as portrayed in Acts.

Hackett, Horatio B. "A Commentary on the Acts of the Apostles." In *An American Commentary.* Revised and enlarged by the author, with added notes by Alvah Hovey. Reprint. Philadelphia: Amer. Bapt. Pub. Soc., 1882, n.d.

A full verse-by-verse commentary by a conservative Baptist professor of the past century. Still valuable for a clear unfolding of the text of Acts.

Haenchen, Ernst. *The Acts of the Apostles: A Commentary.* Trans. 14th German ed., 1965. Philadelphia: Westminster, 1971.

A massive (730 pages), scholarly treatment of the narrative of Acts and its problems. The 132-page introduction provides a masterly survey of modern Acts studies. The volume is a treasury of bibliographical, philological, and exegetical details. The author applies the principles of redaction criticism to Acts and concludes with an almost total rejection of its historicity. Indispensable for the advanced student as a thorough work of modern radical scholarship.

Hanson, R. P. C. "The Acts in the Revised Standard Version." In *The New Clarendon Bible.* Oxford: Clarendon, 1967.

Contains a perceptive fifty-page introduction. The full RSV text is printed at the top of the page with brief notes below. A concise interpretation by a liberal British university professor.

Kelly, William. *An Exposition of the Acts of the Apostles.* Reprint. London: Hammond, 1952.

Prints the author's own translation. An able devotional exposition by a noted Plymouth Brethren scholar of the past century. The viewpoint is premillennial; the volume reflects something of the author's ecclesiastical views. Contains much rich material on the meaning of Acts.

Kent, Homer A., Jr. *Jerusalem to Rome: Studies in the Book of Acts.* Grand Rapids: Baker *or* Winona Lake: BMH Books, 1972.

A conservative unfolding of the story of Acts, well adapted to the collegiate classroom or individual study. Questions for discussion appear at the end of each section. Contains numerous photographs and illustrations, as well as a good bibliography. Kent seeks to trace the story of Acts against the historical background with attention to its crucial moments.

Knowling, R. K. "The Acts of the Apostles." In *The Expositor's Greek Testament,* vol. 2. Reprint. Grand Rapids: Eerdmans, n.d.

Greek text. Still one of the most thorough commentaries on the Greek text. Signicant for the Greek student.

Lake, Kirsopp, and Cadbury, Henry J. "The Acts of the Apostles." In *The Beginnings of Christianity,* vols. 4-5. 1932. Reprint. Grand Rapids: Baker, 1965.

Volume 4 contains the translation by the authors and a technical commentary that provides a wealth of material for the advanced student. Has thorough indexes. Volume 5 is supplemental, providing a mass of learned, technical information on various subjects related to Acts. An erudite work of critical scholarship, important for the advanced student.

Lenski, R. C. H. *The Interpretation of the Acts of the Apostles.* Columbus, Ohio: Wartburg, 1934.

Prints the author's own literal translation. A massive (1134-page) interpretation by a conservative Lutheran scholar. Amillennial in viewpoint. Of abiding value for an exegetical unfolding of Acts.

Macgregor, G. H. C., and Ferris, Theodore P. "The Acts of the Apostles." In *The Interpreter's Bible*, vol. 9. New York: Abingdon-Cokesbury, 1954.

Introduction and exegesis by Macgregor, the exposition by Ferris. A liberal commentary by two modern scholars. Does not accept Luke's complete historical accuracy. Gives cautious acceptance to Lucan authorship.

Meyer, Heinrich August Wilhelm. *Critical and Exegetical Handbook to the Acts of the Apostles.* Translated by Paton J. Gloag. New York: Funk & Wagnalls, 1889.

Greek text. An exhaustive exegetical study of Acts by a well-known German scholar of the past century. Still contains much of value, although unaware of later developments in the understanding of the Koine Greek.

Morgan, G. Campbell. *The Acts of the Apostles.* New York: Revell, 1924.

Expository messages on Acts by a noted Bible teacher-preacher. His exposition aims at setting forth the spiritual force and method of early Christianity. Stress is placed on the variety of ways in which the Spirit is seen at work in Acts. Offers many illuminating insights.

Munch, Johannes. *The Acts of the Apostles.* The Anchor Bible. Vol. 31. Garden City, N. Y.: Doubleday, 1967.

Prints the author's translation of Acts, and offers notes on the original text, and brief comments. The notes and comments are disappointingly brief, and do not cover all verses of Acts. Some critical views.

Rackham, Richard Belward. *The Acts of the Apostles: An Exposition.* Westminster Commentaries. 9th ed. London: Methuen, 1922.

A thorough (513-page), informative exposition by a conservative Anglican scholar. Full treatment of introductory problems. Has a full index. One of the standard older commentaries on Acts.

Stagg, Frank. *The Book of Acts: The Early Struggle for an Unhindered Gospel.* Nashville, Tenn.: Broadman, 1955.

A neo-evangelical exposition that seeks to focus attention on the major message of Acts. Stagg finds the central theme in the concluding word of Acts—"unhindered." The running exposition does not offer a verse-by-verse exegesis and avoids lengthy technical discussions.

Walker, Thomas. *The Acts of the Apostles.* Introduction and biographical sketch by Wilbur M. Smith. 1910. Reprint. Chicago: Moody, 1965.

This warm evangelical commentary, written by an English missionary in India, reveals the author's strong missionary interest. A thorough verse-by-verse exposition. Has been called "the greatest commentary on the Book of Acts from a missionary standpoint that has been written in our language."

Williams, C. S. C. *A Commentary on the Acts of the Apostles.* Harper's New Testament Commentary. New York: Harper, 1957.

Prints author's own translation. A perceptive commentary by an accomplished British scholar. The introduction and commentary provide a good summary of the results of modern scholarship on Acts.

Williams, R. R. *The Acts of the Apostles.* Torch Bible Paperbacks. London: SCM, 1953; paperback ed., 1965.

A brief liberal interpretation. Acts is divided into twelve sections, each of which is viewed as a stage in the unfolding of Luke's purpose. Holds that the overall theme of Acts is "nothing can stop the Gospel."

Winn, Albert C. *The Layman's Bible Commentary*, vol. 20 *Acts.* Richmond, Va.: Knox, 1960.

The exposition, based on the RSV text, is presented by paragraphs and is intended as a non-technical guide for the layman. The treatment is stimulating and generally conservative in viewpoint. It stresses the relevance of Acts for the modern world.

BIBLIOGRAPHY

NOTE: The commentaries listed in the various book lists are not included here, except as they are quoted or referred to in the body of the text.

BIBLICAL TEXT

GREEK

Aland, Kurt; Black, Matthew; Metzger, Bruce M.; and Wikgren, Allen. *The Greek New Testament.* London: United Bible Soc., 1966.

Aland, Kurt, ed. *Synopsis of the Four Gospels: Greek-English Edition of the Synopsis Quattuor Evangeliorum with the Text of the Revised Standard Version.* New York: United Bible Soc., 1972.

Aland, Kurt. *Synopsis Quattuor Evangeliorum.* 5th ed. Stuttgart: Württembergische Bibelanstalt, 1968.

Lindsey, Robert Lisle. *A Hebrew Translation of the Gospel of Mark, Greek-Hebrew Diglot with English Introduction.* Jerusalem: Dugith, n.d.

Metzger, Bruce M. *A Textual Commentary on the Greek New Testament: A Companion Volume to the United Societies' Greek New Testament.* 3d ed. London: United Bible Soc., 1971.

Nestle, Erwin, and Aland, Kurt. *Novum Testamentum Graece.* 24th ed. New York: Amer. Bible Soc., 1966.

Westcott, Brooke Foss, and Hort, Fenton John Anthony. *The New Testament in the Original Greek.* Reprint. New York: Macmillan, 1935.

———. *The New Testament in the Original Greek: Introduction, Appendix.* Vol. 2. London: Macmillan, 1907.

ENGLISH

Allen, Charles L. *The Life of Christ.* Westwood, N.J.: Revell, 1962.

American Standard Version. New York: Nelson, 1901.

Burton, Ernest DeWitt, and Goodspeed, Edgar Johnson. *A Harmony of the Synoptic Gospels for Historical and Critical Study.* 1917. Reprint. New York: Scribner, 1929.

Carey, Edward F. *The Life of Jesus in the Words of the Four Gospels: Arranged and Translated from the Greek Text of Westcott and Hort.* Poughkeepsie, N.Y.: Edward F. Carey, 1951.

Carter, John Franklin. *A Layman's Harmony of the Gospels.* Nashville, Tenn.: Broadman, 1961.

Cheney, Johnston M. *The Life of Christ in Stereo: The Four Gospels Combined As One.* Edited by Stanley A. Ellisen. Portland, Ore.: Western Baptist Seminary, 1969.

Darby, J. N. *The 'Holy Scriptures': A New Translation from the Original Languages.* Reprint. Kingston-on-Thames: Stow Hill Bible and Tract Depot, 1949.

Ebersol, Charles E. *The Four Gospels in One Made Plain.* New York: Revell, 1937.

Huck, Albert. *Synopsis of the First Three Gospels.* 9th ed. rev. Oxford: Basil Blackwell, 1968.

Lamsa, George M. *The Four Gospels According to the Eastern Version: Translated from the Aramaic.* Philadelphia: A. J. Holman, 1933.

Modern Language Bible: The New Berkeley Version. Grand Rapids: Zondervan, 1969.

Moffatt, James. *The Historical New Testament: Being the Literature of the New Testament Arranged in the Order of Its Literary Growth and According to the Dates of the Documents. A New Translation.* New York: Scribner, 1901.

———. *The New Testament: A New Translation.* Rev. ed. New York: George H. Doran, n.d.

Montgomery, Helen Barrett. *The New Testament in Modern English.* Reprint. Philadelphia: Judson, 1964.

New American Standard Bible. Reference Edition. Chicago: Moody, 1973.

New International Version: The New Testament. Grand Rapids: Zondervan Bible Publ., 1973.

Phillips, J. B. *The New Testament in Modern English.* New York: Macmillan, 1962.

Pierson, Arthur T. *The One Gospel: or, The Combination of the Narratives of the Four Evangelists in One Complete Record.* St. Paul, Minn.: Asher, 1889.

Revised Standard Version. Philadelphia: A. J. Holman, 1962.

Robertson, A. T. *A Harmony of the Gospels For Students of the Life of Christ: Based on the Broadus Harmony in the Revised Version.* 1922. Reprint. New York: Harper, 1950.

Sparks, H. F. D. *A Synopsis of the Gospels: The Synoptic Gospels with the Johannine Parallels.* Philadelphia: Fortress, 1964.

Stevens, Wm. Arnold, and Burton, Ernest DeWitt. *A Harmony of the Gospels For Historical Study: An Analytical Synopsis of the Four Gospels.* New York: Scribner, 1911.

Taylor, Kenneth N. *The Living Bible.* Wheaton, Ill.: Tyndale, 1971.

The New English Bible. Oxford University Press, Cambridge University Press, 1970.

Throckmorton, Burton H., Jr., ed. *Gospel Parallels: A Synopsis of the First Three Gospels.* 9th ed. Camden, N.J.: Nelson, 1967. The arrangement follows the Huck-Lietzmann synopsis.

Weymouth, Richard Francis. *The New Testament in Modern Speech.* Revised by James Alexander Robertson. New York: Harper, 1929.

Wieand, Albert C. *New Harmony of the Gospels.* Grand Rapids: Eerdmans, 1947.

Williams, Charles B. *The New Testament: A Private Translation in the Language of the People.* 1937. Reprint. Chicago: Moody, 1949.

NEW TESTAMENT INTRODUCTION

Cartledge, Samuel A. *A Conservative Introduction to the New Testament.* Grand Rapids: Zondervan, 1938.

Clogg, Frank Bertram. *An Introduction to the New Testament.* 3d ed. 1937. Reprint. London: U. of London, 1949.

Dods, Marcus. *An Introduction to the New Testament.* London: Hodder & Stoughton, 1905.

Goodspeed, Edgar J. *An Introduction to the New Testament.* Chicago: U. of Chicago, 1937.

Gundry, Robert H. *A Survey of the New Testament.* Grand Rapids: Zondervan, 1970.

Guthrie, Donald. *New Testament Introduction.* 3d ed., rev. Downers Grove, Ill.: Inter-Varsity, 1970.

Hadjiantoniou, George A. *New Testament Introduction.* Chicago: Moody, 1957.

Harrison, Everett F. *Introduction to the New Testament.* Rev. ed. Grand Rapids: Eerdmans, 1971.

Heard, Richard. *An Introduction to the New Testament.* New York: Harper & Row, 1950.

Hendriksen, William. *Bible Survey: A Treasury of Bible Information.* 3d ed. Grand Rapids: Baker, 1949.

Hiebert, D. Edmond. *An Introduction to the Non-Pauline Epistles.* Chicago: Moody, 1962.

———. *An Introduction to the Pauline Epistles.* Chicago: Moody, 1954.

Hunter, A. M. *Introducing the New Testament*. Philadelphia: Westminster, 1946.

Jackson, F. J. Foakes, and Lake, Kirsopp, eds. *The Beginnings of Christianity*. Vol. 2. London: Macmillan, 1922.

Kendall, Guy. *A Modern Introduction to the New Testament*. London: Methuen, 1938.

Klijn, A. F. *An Introduction to the New Testament*. Leiden: E. J. Brill, 1967.

Kümmel, Werner Georg. *Introduction to the New Testament*. Translated by A. J. Mattill, Jr. Nashville: Abingdon, 1966.

Lake, Kirsopp, and Lake, Silva. *An Introduction to the New Testament*. London: Christophers, 1938.

M'Clymont, J. A. *The New Testament and Its Writers*. New York: Revell, n.d.

Marxsen, W. *Introduction to the New Testament: An Approach to Its Problems*. Translated by G. Buswell. Philadelphia: Fortress, 1968.

Metzger, Bruce M. *The New Testament: Its Background, Growth, and Content*. New York: Abingdon, 1965.

Miller, Adam W. *An Introduction to the New Testament*. 2d ed. Anderson, Ind.: Warner, 1946.

Moffatt, James. *An Introduction to the Literature of the New Testament*. 3d ed. Edinburgh: T. & T. Clark, 1949.

Neill, Stephen. *The Interpretation of the New Testament: 1861-1961*. London: Oxford U., 1966.

Robert, A., and Feuillet, A. *Introduction to the New Testament*. Translated by Patrick W. Skehan [and others]. New York: Desclee, 1965.

Salmon, George. *An Historical Introduction to the Study of the Books of the New Testament*. London: Murray, 1904.

Scott, Ernest Findlay. *The Literature of the New Testament*. 1932. Reprint. New York: Columbia U., 1948.

Scroggie, W. Graham. *A Guide to the Gospels*. Reprint. Westwood, N.J.: Revell, 1965.

———. *Know Your Bible: A Brief Introduction to the Scriptures*. Vol. 2. *The New Testament*. London: Pickering & Inglis, n.d.

Selby, Donald J. *Introduction to the New Testament: "The Word Became Flesh."* New York: Macmillan, 1971.

Sloan, W. W. *A Survey of the New Testament*. New York: Philosophical Library, 1961.

Taylor, Vincent. *The Gospels: A Short Introduction*. 2d ed. London: Epworth, 1933.

Tenney, Merrill C. *The New Testament: An Historical and Analytic Survey.* Grand Rapids: Eerdmans, 1953.

Thiessen, Henry Clarence. *Introduction to the New Testament.* Grand Rapids: Eerdmans, 1943.

Westcott, Brooke Foss. *An Introduction to the Study of the Gospels.* 8th ed. London: Macmillan, 1895.

Wikenhauser, Alfred. *New Testament Introduction.* 1958. Reprint. New York: Herder & Herder, 1963.

Williams, Charles B. *An Introduction to New Testament Literature.* Kansas City, Mo.: Western Baptist, 1929.

Zahn, Theodor. *Introduction to the New Testament.* 3 vols. Translated by John Moore Trout et al. Grand Rapids: Kregel, 1953.

Bible Commentaries

Albright, W. F., and Mann, C. S. *Matthew.* The Anchor Bible. Garden City, N.Y.: Doubleday, 1971.

Allen, Willoughby C. "A Critical and Exegetical Commentary on the Gospel According to St. Matthew." In *The International Critical Commentary.* Reprint. Edinburgh: T. & T. Clark, 1957.

Arndt, William F. *The Gospel According to St. Luke.* St. Louis: Concordia, 1956.

Barrett, C. K. *The Gospel According to St. John: An Introduction with Commentary and Notes on the Greek Text.* London: S. P. C. K., 1960.

Bernard, J. H. "A Critical and Exegetical Commentary on the Gospel According to St. John." In *The International Critical Commentary.* 2 vols. 1928. Reprint. Edinburgh: T. & T. Clark, 1958.

Bickersteth, E. "The Gospel According to St. Mark." In *The Pulpit Commentary,* vol. 1. Reprint. Chicago: Wilcox & Follett, n.d.

Bigg, Charles. "A Critical and Exegetical Commentary on the Epistles of St. Peter and St. Jude." In *The International Critical Commentary.* 2d ed. Edinburgh: T. & T. Clark, 1910.

Blaiklock, E. M. "The Acts of the Apostles: An Historical Commentary." In *Tyndale New Testament Commentaries.* Grand Rapids: Eerdmans, 1959.

Branscomb, B. Harvie. "The Gospel of Mark." In *The Moffatt New Testament Commentary.* London: Hodder & Stoughton, 1937.

Brown, Raymond E. *The Gospel According to John.* The Anchor Bible. Garden City, N.Y.: Doubleday, 1966.

Bruce, Alexander Balmain. "The Synoptic Gospels." In *The Expositor's Greek Testament.* Vol. 1. Reprint. Grand Rapids: Eerdmans, n.d.

Bruce, F. F. *The Acts of the Apostles: The Greek Text with Introduction and Commentary*. London: Tyndale, 1951.

Bultmann, Rudolf. *Das Evangelium des Johannes*. Göttingen: Vandenhoech & Ruprecht, 1941.

Carver, William Owen. *The Acts of the Apostles*. Nashville, Tenn.: Broadman, 1916.

Clark, A. C. *The Acts of the Apostles*. Oxford: Clarendon Press, 1933.

Cole, R. A. "The Gospel According to St. Mark." In *The Tyndale New Testament Commentaries*. Grand Rapids: Eerdmans, 1961.

Cranfield, C. E. B. "The Gospel According to Saint Mark." In *Cambridge Greek Testament Commentary*. Cambridge: Cambridge U., 1966.

Creed, John Martin. *The Gospel According to St. Luke*. Reprint. London: Macmillan, 1942.

Ellis, E. Earle. *The Gospel of Luke*. The Century Bible: New Edition. London: Nelson, 1966.

Evans, William. *The Gospels and the Acts of the Apostles*. New York: Revell, 1917.

Filson, Floyd V. *A Commentary on the Gospel According to St. Matthew*. Harper's New Testament Commentaries. New York: Harper, 1960.

Geldenhuys, Norval. "Commentary on the Gospel of Luke." In *The New International Commentary on the New Testament*. Grand Rapids: Eerdmans, 1950.

Gilmour, S. MacLean; Bowie, Walter Russel; Knox, John; Buttrick, George Arthur; and Scherer, Paul. "The Gospel According to St. Luke." In *The Interpreter's Bible*, vol. 8. New York: Abingdon-Cokesbury, 1952.

Godet, F. *A Commentary on the Gospel of St. Luke*. 2 vols. Edinburgh: T. & T. Clark, 1881.

Haenchen, Ernst. *The Acts of the Apostles: A Commentary*. Translated by Bernard Noble and Gerald Shinn. Philadelphia: Westminster, 1971.

Hanson, R. P. C. "The Acts in the Revised Standard Version." In *The New Clarendon Bible*. Oxford: Clarendon, 1967.

Hendriksen, William. "Exposition of the Gospel According to John." In *New Testament Commentary*. Grand Rapids: Baker, 1953, 1954.

———. "Exposition of the Gospel According to Matthew." In *New Testament Commentary*. Grand Rapids: Baker, 1973.

Hiebert, D. Edmond. *Mark: A Portrait of the Servant*. Chicago: Moody, 1974.

Hort, A. F. *The Gospel According to St. Mark*. 1902. Reprint. Cambridge: Cambridge U., 1928.

Howard, Wilbert F., and Gossip, Arthur John. "The Gospel According to St. John." In *The Interpreter's Bible*, vol. 8. New York: Abingdon-Cokesbury, 1952.

Hughes, Philip Edgcumbe. "Paul's Second Epistle to the Corinthians." In *The New International Commentary on the New Testament*. Grand Rapids: Eerdmans, 1962.

Johnson, Sherman E., and Buttrick, George A. "The Gospel According to St. Matthew." In *The Interpreter's Bible*, vol. 7. New York: Abingdon-Cokesbury, 1951.

Kelly, J. N. D. *A Commentary on the Epistles of Peter and of Jude*. Harper's New Testament Commentaries. New York: Harper & Row, 1969.

Kelly, William. *Notes on the Second Epistle of Paul to the Corinthians*. Reprint. London: G. Morish, n.d.

Lane, William L. "The Gospel According to Mark." In *The New International Commentary on the New Testament*. Grand Rapids: Eerdmans, 1974.

Lange, John Peter. "The Gospel According to Mark." In Lange's *Commentary on the Holy Scriptures: Critical, Doctrinal and Homiletical*. Translated and edited by Philip Schaff. Reprint. Grand Rapids: Zondervan, n.d.

Leaney, A. R. *A Commentary on the Gospel According to St. Luke*. Harper's New Testament Commentaries. New York: Harper & Brothers, 1958.

Lenski, R. C. H. *The Interpretation of St. John's Gospel*. Columbus, Ohio: Lutheran Book Concern, 1942.

———. *The Interpretation of St. Mark's and St. Luke's Gospels*. Columbus, Ohio: Lutheran Book Concern, 1934.

———. *The Interpretation of St. Matthew's Gospel*. Columbus, Ohio: Lutheran Book Concern, 1943.

Lightfoot, R. H. *St. John's Gospel: A Commentary*. Oxford: Clarendon, 1956.

Macgregor, G. H. C., and Ferris, Theodore P. "The Acts of the Apostles." In *The Interpreter's Bible*, vol. 9. New York: Abingdon-Cokesbury, 1954.

Macgregor, G. H. C. "The Gospel of John." In *The Moffatt New Testament Commentary*. New York: Harper, n.d. [apparently 1929].

Martindale, C. C. *The Gospel According to Saint Mark*. Stonyhurst Scripture Manuals. London: Longmans, Green, 1955.

Moody, Dale. *The Letters of John*. Waco, Tex.: Word, 1970.

Morgan, G. Campbell. *The Gospel According to John.* New York: Revell, n.d.

Morison, James. *A Practical Commentary on the Gospel According to St. Mark.* 8th ed. London: Hodder & Stoughton, 1896.

Morris, Leon. "The Gospel According to John." In *The New International Commentary on the New Testament.* Grand Rapids: Eerdmans, 1971.

Nineham, D. E. *The Gospel of St. Mark.* The Pelican Gospel Commentaries. 1963. Reprint. Baltimore, Md.: Penguin, 1967.

Plummer, Alfred. *An Exegetical Commentary on the Gospel According to St. Matthew.* Reprint. Grand Rapids: Eerdmans, 1953.

———. "A Critical and Exegetical Commentary on the Gospel According to St. Luke." In *The International Critical Commentary.* Edinburgh: T. & T. Clark, 1901.

———. "The Gospel According to St. John." In *Cambridge Greek Testament for Schools and Colleges.* 1882. Reprint. Cambridge: Cambridge U., 1905.

———. "The Gospel According to St. Mark." In *Cambridge Greek Testament for Schools and Colleges.* 1914. Reprint. Cambridge: Cambridge U., 1938.

Rackham, Richard Belward. *The Acts of the Apostles.* Westminster Commentaries. Reprint. London: Methuen, 1922.

Ramsay, W. M. *St. Paul the Traveller and the Roman Citizen.* New York: Putnam, 1896.

Reike, Bo. *The Gospel of Luke.* Translated by Ross Mackenzie. Richmond, Va.: Knox, 1964.

Richardson, Alan. *The Gospel According to Saint John: A Commentary.* Torch Bible Commentaries. New York: Collier, 1962.

Robertson, A. T. *Studies in Mark's Gospel.* Edited and revised by Heber F. Peacock. Nashville, Tenn.: Broadman, 1958.

Sloyan, Gerard S. "The Gospel of St. Mark." In *New Testament Reading Guide.* Collegeville, Minn.: Liturgical Press, 1960.

Stagg, Frank. *The Book of Acts: The Early Struggle for an Unhindered Gospel.* Nashville, Tenn.: Broadman, 1955.

Swete, Henry Barclay. *The Gospel According to St. Mark.* 2d ed. London: Macmillan, 1905.

Tasker, R. V. G. "The Gospel According to St. John." In *Tyndale New Testament Commentaries.* Grand Rapids: Eerdmans, 1960.

———. "The Gospel According to St. Matthew." In *Tyndale New Testament Commentaries.* Grand Rapids: Eerdmans, 1961.

Taylor, Vincent. *The Gospel According to St. Mark.* New York: St. Martin's, 1966.

Temple, William. *Readings in St. John's Gospel.* London: Macmillan, 1945.

Turner, George Allen, and Mantey, Julius R. "The Gospel According to John." In *The Evangelical Commentary.* Grand Rapids: Eerdmans, 1964.

Westcott, B. F. "St. John." In *The Speaker's Commentary: New Testament.* Edited by F. C. Cook. Vol. 2. London: Murray, 1880. Republished in 1881 as *The Gospel According to St. John.* Reprint. Grand Rapids: Eerdmans, 1950.

Williams, C. S. C. *A Commentary on the Acts of the Apostles.* Harper's New Testament Commentaries. New York: Harper, 1957.

Williams, R. R. *The Acts of the Apostles.* Torch Bible Commentaries. London: SCM, 1953.

Books About the Gospels and Acts

Aland, Kurt; Cross, F. L.; Danielou, Jean; Riesenfeld, Harald; and Van Unnik, W. C. *Studia Evangelica.* Papers presented to the International Congress on "The Four Gospels in 1957" held at Christ Church, Oxford, 1957. Berlin, Akademie-Verlag, 1959.

Black, Matthew. *An Aramaic Approach to the Gospels and Acts.* 2d ed. Oxford: Clarendon, 1954.

Boice, James Montgomery. *Witness and Revelation in the Gospel of John.* Grand Rapids: Zondervan, 1970.

Briggs, R. C. *Interpreting the Gospels: An Introduction to Methods and Issues in the Study of the Synoptic Gospels.* Nashville: Abingdon, 1969.

Brownlee, William H. "When the Gospel According to John?" In *John and Qumran.* Edited by James H. Charlesworth. London: Geoffrey Chapman, 1972.

Burgon, John W. *The Last Twelve Verses of the Gospel According to St. Mark.* 1871. Reprint. Ann Arbor, Mich.: Sovereign Grace Book Club, 1959.

Butler, B. C. *The Originality of St. Matthew: A Critique of the Two-Document Hypothesis.* Cambridge: Cambridge U., 1951.

Cadbury, H. J. *The Style and Literary Method of Luke.* Cambridge: Cambridge U., 1920.

Charlesworth, James H., ed. *John and Qumran.* London: Geoffrey Chapman, 1972.

Dodd, C. H. *The Interpretation of the Fourth Gospel.* Reprint. Cambridge: Cambridge U., 1965.

Farmer, William R. *The Synoptic Problem: A Critical Analysis.* New York: Macmillan, 1964.

Filson, Floyd V. "The Gospel of Life." In *Current Issues in New Testament Interpretation.* Edited by William Klassen and Graydon F. Snyder. New York: Harper & Row, 1962.

———. *Origins of the Gospels.* New York: Abingdon, 1938.

Goodspeed, Edgar J. *Matthew: Apostle and Evangelist.* Philadelphia: John C. Winston, 1959.

Gardner-Smith, Percy. *Saint John and the Synoptic Gospels.* Cambridge: Cambridge U., 1938.

Gregory, D. S. *Why Four Gospels? or, The Gospel for All the World.* Cincinnati: Hitchcock & Walden, 1880.

Hawkins, Sir John C. *Horae Synopticae: Contributions to the Study of the Synoptic Problem.* Reprint. Grand Rapids: Baker, 1968.

Hayes, Doremus Almy. *The Synoptic Problem.* New York: Eaton & Mains, 1912.

Hoare, F. R. *The Original Order and Chapters of St. John's Gospel.* London: Burns, Oates & Washbourne, 1944.

Jukes, Andrew. *The Differences of the Four Gospels.* Reprint. London: Pickering & Inglis, n.d. Original title: *The Characteristic Differences of the Four Gospels.*

Kistemaker, Simon. *The Gospels in Current Study.* Grand Rapids: Baker, 1972.

McIntyre, D. M. *Some Notes on the Gospels.* Edited by F. F. Bruce. London: Inter-Varsity, 1943.

McKnight, Edgar V. *What Is Form Criticism?* Philadelphia: Fortress, 1969.

Marshall, I. Howard. *Luke: Historian and Theologian.* Grand Rapids: Zondervan, 1971.

Martin, Ralph P. *Mark: Evangelist and Theologian.* Exeter: Paternoster, 1973.

Marxsen, Willi. *Mark the Evangelist: Studies on the Redaction History of the Gospel.* Translated by James Boyce, Donald Juel, William Poehlmann, with Roy A. Harrisville. Nashville: Abingdon, 1969.

Perrin, Norman. *What Is Redaction Criticism?* Philadelphia: Fortress, 1969.

Pink, Arthur W. *Why Four Gospels?* Swengel, Pa.: Bible Truth Depot, 1921.

Ridout, S. *The Four Gospels.* New York: Loizeaux, n.d.

Rohde, Joachim. *Rediscovering the Teaching of the Evangelists.* Philadelphia: Westminster, 1968.

Rollins, Wayne G. *The Gospels: Portraits of Christ.* Philadelphia: Westminster, 1963.

Ropes, J. H. *The Synoptic Gospels.* Cambridge: Harvard U., 1934.

Sanders, J. N. *The Fourth Gospel in the Early Church.* New York: Macmillan, 1943.

Smith, H. Framer. *Why Four Gospel Accounts?* Philadelphia: Westbrook, 1941.

Stonehouse, Ned B. *Origins of the Synoptic Gospels.* Grand Rapids: Eerdmans, 1963.

———. *The Witness of Matthew and Mark to Christ.* 2d ed. Grand Rapids: Eerdmans, 1958.

Streeter, Burnett Hillman. *The Four Gospels: A Study of Origins.* 1924. Reprint. London: Macmillan, 1951.

Talbot, Louis. *Why Four Gospels? The Four-Fold Portrait of Christ in Matthew, Mark, Luke, and John.* Los Angeles: Louis Talbot, 1944.

Taylor, Vincent. *The Formation of the Gospel Tradition.* Reprint. London: Macmillan, 1968.

Tenney, Merrill C. *The Genius of the Gospels.* Grand Rapids: Eerdmans, 1951.

Torrey, C. C. *The Four Gospels.* New York: Harper, 1933.

Van Unnik, W. C. "The Purpose of St. John's Gospel." In *Studia Evangelica.* Edited by Aland, Cross, Danielou, Risenfeld, and van Unnik. Berlin: Academie-Verlag, 1959.

Wrede, William. *The Messianic Secret.* Translated by J. C. G. Grieg. Cambridge: James Clark, 1971.

Wright, Arthur. *The Composition of the Four Gospels.* London: Macmillan, 1890.

OTHER BOOKS

Albright, W. F. *History, Archaeology and Christian Humanism.* New York: McGraw-Hill, 1964.

Barclay, William. *The Master's Men.* New York: Abingdon, 1959.

Baxter, J. Sidlow. *Explore the Book: A Basic and Broadly Interpretative Course of Bible Study from Genesis to Revelation.* Vol. 5. London: Marshall, Morgan & Scott, 1955.

Bell, H. Idris, and Skeat, T. C. *Fragments of an Unknown Gospel and Other Early Christian Papyri.* London: British Museum, 1935.

Bruce, F. F. *New Testament Development of Old Testament Themes.* Grand Rapids: Eerdmans, 1968.

Clapton, Ernest. *Our Lord's Quotations from the Old Testament.* London: Skeffington, 1922.

Cross, F. L., ed. *The Oxford Dictionary of the Christian Church.* London: Oxford U., 1958.

Dillenberger, John, ed. *Martin Luther: Selections from His Writings.* Garden City, N.Y.: Anchor, 1961.

Dodd, C. H. *New Testament Studies.* New York: Scribner, n.d. [apparently 1953].

Farrar, F. W. *The Early Days of Christianity.* Author's ed. New York: Cassell, n.d.

Finegan, Jack. *Handbook of Biblical Chronology: Principles of Time Reckoning in the Ancient World and Problems of Chronology in the Bible.* Princeton: Princeton U., 1964.

France, R. T. *Jesus and the Old Testament.* Downers Grove, Ill.: Inter-Varsity, 1971.

Fuller, Reginald H. *The New Testament in Current Study.* New York: Scribner, 1962.

Goodwin, Frank J. *A Harmony of the Life of St. Paul According to the Acts of the Apostles and the Pauline Epistles.* 3d ed. Grand Rapids: Baker, 1953.

Harnack, Adolf. *Luke the Physician.* Translated by Rev. J. R. Wilkinson. New York: Putnam, 1908.

Hayes, D. A. *John and His Writings.* New York: Methodist Book Concern, 1917.

Hills, Edward F. *The King James Version Defended!* Des Moines, Iowa: Christian Research, 1956.

Hobart, William Kirk. *The Medical Language of St. Luke.* Reprint. Grand Rapids: Baker, 1954.

Klassen, William, and Snyder, Graydon F. *Current Issues in New Testament Interpretation.* New York: Harper & Row, 1962.

Knox, John. *Marcion and the New Testament: An Essay in the Early History of the Canon.* Chicago: U. of Chicago, 1942.

Lees, Harrington C. *St. Paul's Friends.* London: Religious Tract Society, 1918.

Lightfoot, J. B. *Biblical Essays.* London: Macmillan, 1893.

Lightner, Robert P. *The Saviour and the Scriptures.* Philadelphia: Presbyterian and Reformed, 1966.

McBirnie, William Stewart. *The Search for the Twelve Apostles.* Wheaton, Ill.: Tyndale, 1973.

Manson, T. W. *Studies in the Gospels and Epistles.* Edited by Matthew Black. Philadelphia: Westminster, 1962.

Moulton, James Hope. *A Grammar of New Testament Greek.* Vol. 1. *Prolegomena.* Edinburgh: T. & T. Clark, 1908.

———. *A Grammar of New Testament Greek.* Vol. 2. *Accidence & Word Formation.* Edinburgh: T. & T. Clark, 1929.

Ogg, George. *The Chronology of the Life of Paul.* London: Epworth, 1968.

Ramsay, W. M. *The Bearing of Recent Discovery on the Trustworthiness of the New Testament.* Reprint. London: Hodder & Stoughton, 1920.

Robertson, A. T. *Luke the Historian in the Light of Research.* New York: Scribner, 1934.

Ropes, James Hardy. *The Beginnings of Christianity.* Vol. 3. *The Text of Acts.* London: Macmillan, 1926.

Schaff, Philip. *History of the Christian Church.* Vol. 1. *Apostolic Christianity.* Reprint. Grand Rapids: Eerdmans, 1955.

Sherwin-White, A. N. *Roman Society and Roman Law in the New Testament.* Oxford: Clarendon, 1963.

Surburg, Raymond F. *How Dependable Is the Bible?* Philadelphia: Lippincott, 1972.

Tasker, R. V. G. *The Old Testament in the New Testament.* Grand Rapids: Eerdmans, 1963.

Thayer, Joseph Henry. *A Greek-English Lexicon of the New Testament.* 1889. Reprint. New York: American Book Co., n.d.

Willett, Herbert L., and Campbell, James M. *The Teachings of the Books.* New York: Revell, 1899.

Zwemer, Samuel M. *"Into All the World."* Grand Rapids: Zondervan, 1943.

BIBLE DICTIONARY AND ENCYCLOPEDIA ARTICLES

Armstrong, W. P. "Chronology of the New Testament." In *The International Standard Bible Encyclopaedia.* Edited by James Orr. Grand Rapids: Eerdmans, 1939.

Blair, E. P. "Luke (Evangelist)." In *The Interpreter's Dictionary of the Bible.* Edited by George Arthur Butrick. Vol. 3. New York: Abingdon, 1962.

Bruce, F. F. "Form Criticism." In *Baker's Dictionary of Theology.* Edited by Everett F. Harrison. Grand Rapids: Baker, 1960.

———. "Gospel." In *The New Bible Dictionary,* Edited by J. D. Douglas. Grand Rapids: Eerdmans, 1962.

Friedrich, Gerhard. "Euanggelion." In *Theological Dictionary of the New Testament.* Edited by Gerhard Kittel. Vol. 2. Grand Rapids: Eerdmans, 1964.

Grosheide, F. W. "Acts of the Apostles, The." In *The Encyclopedia of Christianity.* Edited by Edwin H. Palmer. Vol. 1. Wilmington, Del.: National Foundation for Christian Education, 1964.

Hutchison, J. "Apocryphal Gospels." In *The International Standard Bible Encyclopaedia*. Edited by James Orr. Grand Rapids: Eerdmans, 1939.

Iverach, James. "John, Gospel of." In *The International Standard Bible Encyclopaedia*. Edited by James Orr. Grand Rapids: Eerdmans, 1939.

Kittel, Gerhard. "Logion." In *Theological Dictionary of the New Testament*. Edited by Gerhard Kittel. Grand Rapids: Eerdmans, 1964.

Lane, William L. "Apocrypha." In *The Encyclopedia of Christianity*. Edited by Edwin H. Palmer. Wilmington, Del.: The National Foundation for Christian Education, 1964.

Marshall, I. H. "John, Gospel of." In *The New Bible Dictionary*. Edited by J. D. Douglas. Grand Rapids: Eerdmans, 1962.

Pfeiffer, Charles F. "Aramaic Language." In *The Encyclopedia of Christianity*. Edited by Edwin H. Palmer. Wilmington, Del.: The National Foundation for Christian Education, 1964.

Pratt, Dwight M. "Epistle." In *The International Standard Bible Encyclopaedia*. Edited by James Orr. Grand Rapids: Eerdmans, 1939.

Robertson, A. T. "Acts of the Apostles." In *The International Standard Bible Encyclopaedia*. Edited by James Orr. Grand Rapids: Eerdmans, 1939.

Sanders, J. N. "John, Gospel of." In *The Interpreter's Dictionary of the Bible*. Edited by George Arthur Buttrick. New York: Abingdon, 1962.

Schodde, G. H. "Matthew, Gospel of." In *The International Standard Bible Encyclopaedia*. Edited by James Orr. Grand Rapids: Eerdmans, 1939.

Souter, A. "Luke." In *A Dictionary of Christ and the Gospels*. Edited by Hastings. Edinburgh: T. & T. Clark, 1909.

Zahn, T. "John the Apostle." In *The New Schaff-Herzog Encyclopedia of Religious Knowledge*. Edited by Samuel Macauley Jackson. Reprint. Grand Rapids: Baker, 1950.

MAGAZINE ARTICLES

Filson, Floyd V. "Who Was the Beloved Disciple?" *Journal of Biblical Literature* 68 (June 1949): 83-88.

Foster, Lewis A. "The 'Q' Myth in Synoptic Studies." *Bulletin of the Evangelical Theological Society* 7 (Fall 1964): 111-19.

Gasque, W. W. "The Historical Value of the Book of Acts: An Essay in the History of New Testament Criticism." *The Evangelical Quarterly* 41 (April-June 1969): 68-88.

Grant, Robert H. "The Origin of the Fourth Gospel." *Journal of Biblical Literature* 69 (December 1950): 305-22.

Gundry, Robert H. "The Language Milieu of First-Century Palestine." *Journal of Biblical Literature* 83 (1964): 404-8.

Ladd, George Eldon. "More Light on the Synoptics." *Christianity Today,* March 1959, pp. 12-16.

Ludlum, John H., Jr. "Are We Sure of Mark's Priority?" *Christianity Today,* September 14, 1959, pp. 11-14; and September 28, 1959, pp. 9-10.

———. "More Light on the Synoptic Problem." *Christianity Today,* November 10, 1958, pp. 6-9; and November 4, 1958, pp. 10-14.

Mare, W. Harold. "The Role of the Note-Taking Historian and His Emphasis on the Person and Work of Christ." *Journal of the Evangelical Theological Society* 15 (Spring 1972): 107-21.

Parker, Pierson. "John and John Mark." *Journal of Biblical Literature* 70 (June 1960): 97-110.

Petrie, Stewart. " 'Q' Is Only What You Make It." *Novum Testamentum* 3 (1959): 28-33.

Riddle, D. W. "The Logic of the Theory of Translation Greek." *Journal of Biblical Literature* 51 (March 1932): 18-19.

Smith, D. Moody, Jr. "A Major New Commentary on John" [a book review]. *Interpretation* 21 (October 1967): 469-75.

Stein, Robert H. "What Is Redaktionsgeschichte?" *Journal of Biblical Literature* 88 (March 1969): 45-50.

Teeple, Howard M. "Methodology in Source Analysis of the Fourth Gospel." *Journal of Biblical Literature* 81 (September 1962): 279-86.

Vo, Thien An N. "Interpretation of Mark's Gospel in the Last Two Decades." *Studia Biblica Et Theologica* 2 (March 1972): 37-62.

Wiens, Devon. "Biblical Criticism: Historical and Personal Reflections." *Directions* 1 (October 1972): 107-11.

GENERAL INDEX

NOTE: The contents of the Gospels and the Acts have not been entered in this index. See the outlines.